THE EXODUS CHRONICLES

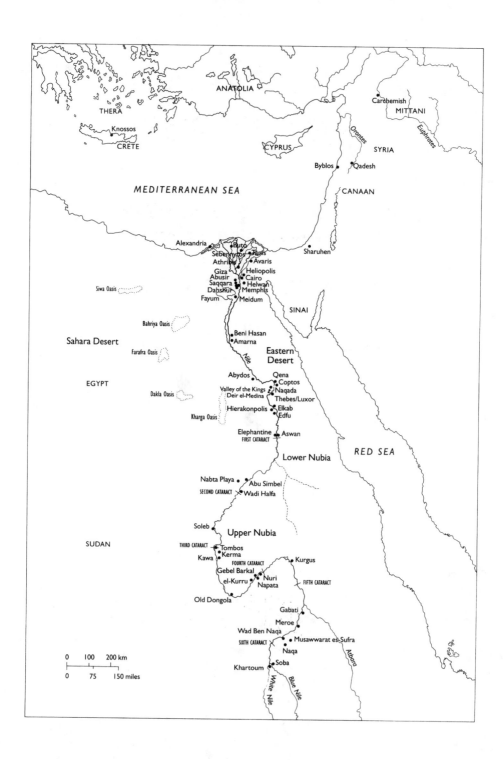

ANATOLIA

THERA

Knossos
CRETE

CYPRUS

Carchemish
MITTANI

Orontes

Euphrates

SYRIA

Byblos   Qadesh

CANAAN

MEDITERRANEAN SEA

Alexandria
Buto
Sebennytos   Tanis
Athribis   Avaris
Giza   Heliopolis
Abusir   Cairo
Saqqara   Helwan
Dahshur   Memphis
Fayum   Meidum

Sharuhen

SINAI

Siwa Oasis

Bahriya Oasis

Sahara Desert

Farafra Oasis

EGYPT

Beni Hasan
Amarna

Eastern
Desert

Nile

Dakla Oasis

Abydos   Qena
Coptos
Valley of the Kings   Naqada
Deir el-Medina   Thebes/Luxor
Hierakonpolis   Elkab
Edfu

Kharga Oasis

Elephantine   Aswan
FIRST CATARACT

Lower Nubia

RED SEA

Nabta Playa
Abu Simbel
SECOND CATARACT   Wadi Halfa

Soleb

Upper Nubia

SUDAN

THIRD CATARACT   Tombos
Kerma
Kawa   FOURTH CATARACT   Kurgus
Gebel Barkal
el-Kurru   Nuri
Napata   FIFTH CATARACT

Old Dongola

Gabati

Meroe
Wad Ben Naqa
SIXTH CATARACT   Musawwarat es-Sufra
Naqa

Khartoum   Soba

Atbara

White Nile

Blue Nile

0   100   200 km

0   75   150 miles

ii

THE EXODUS CHRONICLES

Beliefs, Legends & Rumors from
Antiquity Regarding the Exodus
of the Jews from Egypt

Marianne Luban

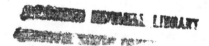

Pacific Moon Publications

Cover design: Myra Rochelle Jensen

Map: (c) 1992 The Trustees of the British Museum. *Thebes in Egypt*, by Nigel and Helen Strudwick. British Museum Press, London

Copyright © 2003 by Marianne Luban

Library of Congress Control Number: 2003103872

Luban, Marianne, 1946-
The Exodus Chronicles: Beliefs, Legends & Rumors from Antiquity Regarding the Exodus of the Jews from Egypt/Marianne Luban

ISBN: 0-9729524-0-3

Printed in the United States

Pacific Moon Publications
P.O. Box 17138
Encino, CA 91416-7138

To My Beloved Daughters
Myra, Melissa, Raine, Madeleine

Also By Marianne Luban:

The Samaritan Treasure

Chapter One

Jews may say that the Exodus celebrated at Passover is a matter of fact. Certain Egyptologists, Biblical archaeologists and minimalists may take the viewpoint that the event is a matter of faith based upon nothing concrete. As someone who has been studying Egyptian history for a lifetime, I can safely relate that those who say that the Biblical Exodus is nothing more than a myth are ignoring a pattern that repeated itself over the millennia.

Without a doubt, there was more than one exodus of Semitic peoples from Egypt, both before the Common Era and afterward, the most recent taking place during the Nasser regime. Most of these adhered to the model of a Golden Age, followed by edicts, murder and flight of the survivors. For example, it is not commonly known that there was once a temple on the island of Elephantine, on the southernmost boundary of Egypt, founded by the Jewish refugee colony there while the great Temple at Jerusalem, destroyed by the Babylonians in 587 BCE, had not yet been rebuilt. This colony eventually disappeared when its Persian protectors[1] were somehow superceded by a new native king of Egypt, Amyrtaeus[2]. Nor do most people know that the personal physician of Saladin, the Sultan of Egypt, was a

---

[1] The Persians, led by Cambyses II, conquered Egypt in 525 BCE.

[2] Probably "Amenerdit" of Sais, the sole representative of the 28th Dynasty, who rebelled against the Persian occupation, declared himself king and evidently exerted power as far south as Elephantine. After a brief reign, Amyrtaeus was displaced by Nepherites and it is during his time, after 399 BCE, that the Elephantine Jewish colony leaves no further traces of its existence. The legend has persisted that, since Elephantine temporarily replaced Jerusalem, the Ark of the Covenant was housed there and then later taken to Aksum, Ethiopia, where it purportedly rests to this day.

Jew called Moses Maimonides[3], who enjoyed a period of prosperity along the Nile with his co-religionists that lasted until 1200 CE.

A Talmudic sage, Rabbi Simeon ben Yohai, said of what he considered the "post-Exodus" sojourns:

> *"Thrice has Israel been warned not to return to Egypt and thrice has Israel disobeyed."*

On the last of those occasions, the Jews of Alexandria were massacred by the Romans around 117 CE. What Rabbi Simeon meant was that the Jews, perhaps because of geographical considerations, had always been attracted to Egypt and had not learned the lesson of the time of Moses. Flavius Josephus[4] wrote:

> *"Alexander's (high) opinion of the Jews of Alexandria[5] was shared by Ptolemy, son of Lagus. He entrusted the fortresses of Egypt to their keeping, confident of their loyalty and bravery as guards; and when he was desirous of strengthening his hold upon Cyrene and the other cities of Lybia, he dispatched a party of Jews to settle there."*

Josephus goes on to relate that the successor of Lagus, Ptolemy Philadelphus *"had a keen desire to know our laws*

---

[3] Moses ben Maimon (1135-1204 CE), Jewish philosopher and famed physician, born in Córdoba, Spain, emigrated to Cairo where he became the Chief Rabbi of the Jewish community. His greatest accomplishment in the field of Jewish law is the *Mishnah Torah*, an ongoing project that he continued to revise until he died. Maimonides, also known as Rambam, was considered the outstanding Jewish philosopher of the Middle Ages. The saying went "From Moses to Moses, there was nobody like Moses", meaning that many considered Maimonides the reincarnation of the Moses of the Torah.

[4] A Jewish historian under the Roman Empire, circa 80 CE.

[5] The conqueror, himself, gave them permission to settle there.

and to read the books of our sacred scriptures".[6] Indeed, most of the Ptolemies were philo-Judaic. *"Ptolemy Philometer and his consort, Cleopatra, entrusted the whole of their realm to Jews and placed their entire army under the command of Jewish generals, Onias and Dositheus."* However, the heir of Philometer, Ptolemy Physcon, was of a different disposition and "...*arrested all the Jews in the city with their wives and children, and exposed them, naked and in chains, to be trampled to death by elephants."*

In order to enliven the spectacle, the pachyderms were made drunk but, as Josephus tells it, refused to harm any of the Jews and instead *"rushed at Physcon's friends, killing a large number of them."* This miraculous turnabout had considerable effect:

> *"Afterwards, Ptolemy saw a terrible apparition, which forbade him to injure these people. His favorite concubine (some call her Ithaca, others Irene) adding her plea to him not to continue such misdeeds, he gave way and repented of his past actions and further plans. That is the origin of the well-known feast which the Jews of Alexandria keep[7], with good reason, on this day, because of the miraculous deliverance afforded them by God."*

This is the Jewish way; eternal gratitude on a large or even more personal scale. Moses Maimonides wrote in his memoirs that in the year 1165 CE

> *"I put to sea on Sunday, the fourth day of the second month, and on the following Sabbath we encountered very rough weather. The storm was so fierce that I vowed to observe these two days as strict fast days*

---

[6] The legend is that the *Septuagint*, the ancient Greek translation of the Hebrew Bible, was commissioned by Ptolemy II and accomplished by 70 (hence the name "Septuagint") or 72 Jewish scholars.

[7] Rather reminiscent of the Feast of Purim.

together with my people and the entire household each year. I also ordered my children always to keep these fasts in our home, and laid upon them the duty of making charitable donations as generously as their means permitted. As for myself, I vowed solemnly that as on this occasion I was alone with God on the tempestuous sea and aided by Him alone, so every year on this day I will cease all work, withdraw from the society of others, and devote myself completely to study and prayer in His presence.

On Sunday night, the 3rd of Sivan, I landed safe and happy in Acco and thereby escaped enforced apostasy. So at last we arrived in the Land of Israel, and I vowed to set aside this day of our arrival as an annual family holiday to be celebrated lavishly with a banquet and the distribution of alms to the poor. We left Acco on Wednesday, the 4th of Marheshvan, and reached Jerusalem after a perilous journey. I spent the entire day, as well as the following two days, praying at the remains (the Wailing Wall) of the ancient Temple. On Sunday, the 9th of Marheshvan, I left Jerusalem for Hebron where I prayed at the graves of the Patriarchs in the Cave of Machpelah. These two days, the 6th and 9th of Marheshvan, I appointed as festivals for me and mine, which should be passed in prayer and feasting. May God help me and bring to fulfillment in me the words of the Psalmist, 'My vows will I pay unto the Lord.'"

Currently, Egyptologists do not want to discuss the Exodus—with the exception of a few. This, I think, is primarily because they feel they cannot securely place it within a certain dynasty or a chronological timeframe. They cannot positively identify the pharaoh who presided over this Biblical event. However, given the long history of Semitic-speaking people in Egypt, there is no possibility even the most skeptical minimalist can state with any authority "The Exodus never occurred". There had to be an Exodus because there eventually was always an exodus. Nothing could be simpler.   It is those who have, for thousands of years, insisted that there was only one great migration of the Jewish people who have complicated everything.

I think it best, at the very outset, to provide both the good and the bad news about the Biblical Book of Exodus. The positive aspect is, of course, that the Jews really did leave Egypt in pharaonic times, just as our forefathers have always maintained. The second book of the Torah did not engender a lie that has been perpetuated over the millennia. The Hebrews were, indeed, slaves in Egypt and, contrary to current belief, they did build pyramids—only not the famous ones that are seen on the Giza Plateau in the company of the Great Sphinx. These are far older than the history of the Israelites in the land of the pharaohs.

The "bad news", at least in the eyes of those who believe in the absolute veracity of the Bible, is that the Exodus did not occur quite as written in the Pentateuch or as has been popularly imagined in films and books—that is to say in any single year in the long history of ancient Egypt.   That is my conclusion, in light of what my research has shown me.

I assert that the Book of Exodus is a story, containing elements of both truth and fiction. It is a composition that incorporates bits of reality from perhaps **four** separate exodoi of the Children of Israel —the first taking place at the start of the 18th Dynasty and the last at the beginning of the 20th. At Passover, Jews commemorate all the episodes, as is quite fitting.[8] Yet these experiences were protracted over a span of 400 years and the particular circumstances of each migration, although no doubt spectacular, are now difficult to isolate. Even so, all have left some trace within either recorded history or folk-memory. If all the rumors of these four exodoi really do have a basis in fact, then the first took place under conditions where it seemed the world was coming to an end; the second occurred when a sleeping lion awoke with a terrible roar; the third became the by-product of a religious

---

[8] Either by coincidence or design, the Temple of Jerusalem was destroyed twice on the 9th day of the month of Av. The Jews commemorate these occurrences on one day, the holiday being known as Tisha B'Av.

reformation, led by a fanatic; and the fourth was the denouement of a great drama, surpassing Shakespeare's *Richard the Third*, complete with a power-seeking manipulator, helpless young prince, and a queen as a pawn.

Unfortunately, this amalgam of several incidents to create one dramatic account has been the downfall of those who have attempted to correlate the events of the Book of Exodus to the era of a single Egyptian monarch. Historians have, by turns, lamented and derided the fact that the author of the story failed to specify the name of the king, merely referring to him as "Pharaoh"—hardly suspecting that this was neither a lapse of memory (the Bible contains attempts to name other kings of Egypt) nor proof of the narrative being pure invention, but a deliberate avoidance of identification. Going further, one might ask why the writer did not relate the sequence of expulsions and returns, rendering a fuller and richer saga of his people.

For one thing, the author may never have aspired to pen an actual history, at all, but what we nowadays call a "novelization", complete with imaginary dialogue and various elements of dubious veracity added for greater effect. Secondly, as happens in many histories prepared for popular consumption, including autobiographies, factual but unflattering components are omitted on purpose. There is no reason to believe the scribe of the Book of Exodus was above doing this and there may, indeed, have been reasons why he thought it best to leave out many details altogether.

And thirdly, while this may offend some readers, the author never suspected that what he wrote would be taken, at some future date, for God's own truth. He may not even have imagined that anyone would accept his work as accurate history in the simplest and soberest definition of the term. However, this proved to be the case for a very long time. As Flavius Josephus wrote:

> "We have given practical proof of our reverence for our own Scriptures. For although such long ages have now passed, no one has ventured either to add, or to remove, or to alter a syllable; and it is an instinct with every Jew, from the

day of his birth, to regard them as the decrees of God, to abide by them, and, if need be, cheerfully to die for them. Time and again ere now the sight has been witnessed of prisoners enduring tortures and death in every form in the theatres, rather than utter a single word against the laws and the allied documents."

Poignant words, indeed. Yet, in our own time, we have made a clear distinction between "questioning", in a scholarly fashion, these "allied documents" and "refutation", in a scoffing sense, of matters both sensitive and dear. In the first spirit of inquiry I have begun and will continue and even have hopes of balancing that which I may render less plausible with an ability to vindicate other factors as being quite accurate.

Moreover, I think the pharaohs who were a part of the mass migrations can be named, if one were to re-evaluate the evidence at hand. That is what I will attempt to do in this book. I will also describe the conditions that gradually led up to the expulsions of a people, many of whose ancestors had been forcibly brought to the Two Lands[9] in the first place. My goal is to do this, not so much in my own words, but by quoting those of the ancients, themselves.

Much of the information we have about Moses and the kings who oppressed the Hebrews is from extra-Biblical sources. The difficulty lies in discerning whether any of this so-called "knowledge" is reliable tradition or simply frivolous fiction—or a bewildering combination of both. Even though the Book of Exodus fails to supply any pharaonic names[10], the fact that Jewish legend amazingly purports to identify virtually the entire royal family is scarcely more enlightening. While ones interest is piqued at the description of Pharaoh in the folklore of the Jews as being an Egyptian

---

[9] Upper and Lower Egypt, also known in the plural as "Mizraim" in Hebrew.

[10] It does mention the city, "Raamses" or "Per-Ramesses-Meryamun", which a pharaoh called after himself.

11

Rumpelstiltskin, practically a dwarf with a beard down to his ankles, anyone familiar with ancient Egyptian customs will know that no king of that country ever sported anything other than a tuft of hair on his chin at best.[11]

Nevertheless, the rabbinic tradition has it that the tyrant who sought to slay the newborn children of the Hebrew slaves was called "Malol", the son of "Magron," and his wife was "Alfar'anit". The pharaoh had three sons and two daughters with "Alfar'anit" and additional children by concubines. The eldest son was "'Atro", an idiot, the clever middle one "Adikam", and the third went by the name of "Moryon". "Bithiah" and "'Akuzit" were the royal princesses.[12] When the old king of Egypt became mortally wounded in a mishap with his chariot, he had to choose among his sons for a successor. "Adikam" was deemed the most likely candidate, even though he appeared "*fleshy and short of stature*", measuring no more than "*a cubit and a space*".[13] King "Malol" lingered for a time and then died, his body growing putrid while he lived, emitting such a stench that he could not be embalmed in the usual Egyptian manner. According to legend, the pharaoh had contracted a loathsome disease, leprosy, which afflicted him for ten years and then turned into "boils". Other members of his family had it, as well, including the princess who adopted Moses.

---

[11] Not counting the braided ceremonial beard, which was tied on. When the pharaoh was in mourning, he left off shaving for a time.

[12] These are, in the main, not names at all but surely pejoratives in the ancient Egyptian language. "Magron" , for example, appears to be "mkr aA" or "Big Liar". (The Egyptian grapheme, transcribed /A/, was very likely an agent that facilitated the vocalization of the syllables "al, ar, ra, la" and even was heard, at times, as an "n", especially in ultimate place.) "Adikam" could be "iti kmt" (Sovereign of Egypt) or even "Black Prince" or "Black Eyes". Egypt was then called "kmt", the Black Land, after its fertile soil.

[13] Louis Ginzberg, *Legends of the Jews*, (Johns Hopkins University Press, 1998).

The heir was twenty years old[14] when he began his reign, although he had been married since the age of ten to a woman named *"Gedidah, the daughter of Abilat"*.[15]   This couple engendered four sons and later Adikam sired eight sons and three daughters by three other wives.   The new pharaoh's ministers referred to him as "Akuz" behind his back, a word supposedly meaning "short" in the Egyptian language.[16]   Adikam *"surpassed his father Malol and all the former kings in wickedness."* Even though something about all this seems vaguely familiar, one cannot actually recognize any of the people from this family with certainty. "Bithiah", as it turns out, was the king's daughter who became the foster-mother of Moses. [17]

When the two old men, Moses and Aaron, approached King Adikam about allowing the Children of Israel to end their long servitude and depart from Egypt, the pharaoh evidently proved that he not only recalled Joseph but Jacob, as well, for his waggish response was *"Had I Jacob-Israel here before me, I should put a trowel and bucket on his shoulder."* Such is the lore.

---

[14] Even though his father ruled for 94 years, Adikam managed only four years on the throne. Only one pharaoh was thought by the ancients to have reigned for nearly a century—King Pepi II (2278-2184 BCE) of the 6th Dynasty, who *"succeeding when six years old, reigned until his hundreth year"* (Manetho). After two brief subsequent reigns, the last possibly being a woman, Nitocris, the 6th Dynasty died out. While some elements fit the rabbinic legend, this period is surely too early to postdate Abraham and Jacob/Joseph.

[15] Undoubtedly Semitic names.

[16] More than likely the Egyptian term *XAzi*, which means "wretched" or "puny". One of Adikam's sisters seems to have borne the feminine equivalent of this designation.

[17] Bithiah was supposedly the first-born of her own mother. Her name is a Semitic one, meaning "Daughter of Yahweh".

A papyrus in the Brooklyn Museum[18], circa 1745 BCE, the 13th Dynasty, confirms that there were "Hebrews"[19] in Egypt that early. It contains a list of household servants, a group of slaves on an estate in Upper Egypt, more than fifty per cent of which have Asiatic or Semitic names, including Menachem, Issachar, Asher and Shifra. During the last years of the 13th Dynasty, some obscure rulers established a 14th Dynasty in the central part of the Delta.[20] During this same period, a group from outside Egypt called the Hyksos, by the classic writers, or the "Shepherd Kings", settled in the eastern Delta. They are the 15th Dynasty, as Egyptology dubs it.[21] Manetho, an Egyptian scholar, priest and astrologer, who lived in the Delta in the 3rd Century before the Common

---

[18] Catalogue #35.1446, dated to the reign of Sobekhotep III. The Egyptian names given to the slaves are also listed. In the papyrus they are termed the "Apiru-Reshep", after a Canaanite god.

[19] The term "Hebrew" has, off and on, been associated with the Egyptian word "apiru". Judging by a number of personal names , which consisted of "Aper + a deity", the first element seems to have had the connotation of "servant of" (such as Aper-El who was a vizier of the court during the 18th Dynasty) and was interchangeable with the Semitic "abed". It was also during the 18th Dynasty that the masters of the Egyptian Empire had difficulties with certain Levantine types, called "Apiru", clearly a group of rebels who remained unintimidated by the army of occupation and who led a semi-nomadic existence. At any rate, the name "Apiru" would have been an imperialist appellation and not what these people called themselves. A Biblical reference to "Hebrews" would also be from an Egyptian point of view—as opposed to the "Children of Israel" (i.e. Sons of Jacob) of the opposite perspective. Hebrew is the North-West Semitic dialect that was the language of Canaan or its evolution.

[20] Manetho calls them "seventy-six kings of Xois". From Strabo we learn that Xois was in the interior of Lower Egypt and was both an island and a city in the marshes.

[21] Because of conflicting information in the various preservations of Manetho's history, Egyptologists have striven to reconstruct the dynasties of the Second Intermediate Period of ancient Egyptian history from archaeological evidence, instead. 1666-70 is the period of the founding of Hyksos rule in Egypt—although these people had been in Egypt since ca 1720 BCE, when Memphis was sacked by them.

Era and wrote a history of Egypt in three books, attests in his powerful prose:

"*Tutimaeos.*[22] *In his reign, for what reason I cannot say, a blast of God smote us and, without warning, from the regions of the East, invaders of obscure race marched in confidence of victory against our land. By force of their sheer numbers they easily seized it without striking a blow; and having cowed the rulers of the land, they then burned our cities ruthlessly, razed to the ground the temples of the gods, and behaved cruelly and aggressively toward the people, massacring some and leading into slavery the wives and children of others.*"

Finally, they set up one of their own as king whose name was Salitis. He had his seat at Memphis, levying tribute from Upper and Lower Egypt, and always leaving garrisons behind in the most advantageous positions. Above all, he fortified the district to the east, anticipating that the Assyrians, as they grew ever mightier, would one day covet and attack his kingdom. In the Saite nome he established a city very conveniently situated on the east of the Bubastite branch of the Nile and called it Avaris[23], after an ancient religious tradition. This place he renovated and fortified with massive walls, creating there a garrison of as many as 240,000 heavily-armed men to guard his frontier. Here he would come in summertime, partly to supply the rations and pay his troops, partly to instruct them carefully in his plans to instill fear of him into every foreign tribe. After reigning for 19 years, Salitis died....[Here Manetho lists the names of successors of Salitis]....These six kings,

---

[22] At this juncture Egypt seems to have been ruled by a considerable number of petty kings, Dudimose being one of them, perhaps the most significant of the lot, as Manetho appears to single him out.

[23] The Greek name for Haware, thought to be at modern Tell el Daba (Mound of the Hyena), the site of an ongoing excavation headed by Dr. Manfred Bietak. At this same location was later built the city of Pi-Ramesses, the "Raamses" of the Book of Exodus.

their first rulers, were ever more and more desirous of wiping out the Egyptian nation. Their race as a whole was called Hyksos, that is "shepherd-kings": for hyk in the sacred language means 'king' and sos in vulgar speech is 'shepherd' or 'shepherds'. Some say they were Arabs."[24]

Many centuries before Manetho, an Old Kingdom sage called Neferti evidently made a prophesy that foretold much the same situation:

"A strange bird will breed in the Delta marsh,
Having made its nest beside the people,
The people having let it approach by default....
Desert flocks will drink at the river of Egypt,
Take their ease for lack of one to fear...."

The 16th Dynasty was also "shepherd kings", of Semitic background, who lived in "the Land of Goshen"[25] according to the Bible, and the Book of Genesis tells us they were invited to remain there by the pharaoh who knew Joseph, one of their tribe who had become a great man in Egypt. Although the 16th Dynasty had no pharaohs among their number, they had chieftains who were regarded as "kings" by their own people, Jacob probably being one of these. Evidently, they lived in peace with the 15th Dynasty. In fact, exactly how long this 16th Dynasty had been in Egypt is not well-understood and whether or not they were the same people who had become slaves to the Egyptians of the south is also open to question. The matter cannot be sorted out with any great certainty, but it is possible that, while the Hyksos of the 15th Dynasty worshipped a god named Sutekh,

---

[24] They may, in fact, have been the Amalekites, as Arab historians have asserted. The Hyksos have also been rumored to have been Phoenicians or Minoans.

[25] The Wadi Tumilat in the eastern Delta. Manetho refers to them as "thirty-two shepherds".

the 16th Dynasty shepherds had their own deity, who came to be called "El".

Lastly, the 17th Dynasty consisted of some princes of Thebes who ruled concurrently with their adversaries in the north. This dynasty arose after the last 13th Dynasty king died.

> "*Now it befell that Egypt was in dire affliction, and there was no sovereign as king of the time*[26]. *And it happened that King Seqenenre was Ruler of the Southern City...while the chieftain Apophis was in Avaris and the entire land paid tribute to him in full, as well as all the good things of Tamera.*[27] *Then King Apophis took Sutekh*[28] *to himself as lord, and served not any god which was in the entire land except Sutekh.*"[29]

As far as we know, the rule of the 15th Dynasty Hyksos lasted about 108 years, during which time their kings adopted Egyptian throne names and much of Egyptian culture, as well.

> Manetho: "*Thereafter came a revolt of the princes of the South, the Thebans, and a fierce and prolonged war broke out between them and the Shepherds.*"

The reason for the conflict, the story has it, was the roaring of the hippopotami of Thebes. Apophis, the king of the Hyksos, complained he was unable to get a good night's rest due to his claim that these beasts could be heard even at Avaris, a considerable distance.[30] Apophis wrote a

---

26 Meaning Egypt was not unified, with one ruler over the Two Lands.

27 Another name for Egypt, meaning "the beloved land".

28 The Semitic equivalent of the Egyptian deity, Seth, a demonic god.

29 From an Egyptian story, of which only the beginning has survived.

30 800 kilometers or 400 miles.

demanding letter to the Theban prince and so hostilities began in earnest.

Apophis to (the Prince of the Southern City, which is Thebes), Seqenenre:

> "*Have the hippopotamus pool, which is in the vicinity of the city, done away with! For they (the hippos) do not let sleep come to me by day or by night.*"

Seqenenre assembled his counselors and they pondered what answer they should give. At last, it could not be avoided that the message had been a challenge, and the answer was war. Seqenenre lost his life battling the Hyksos. His son, Kamose, continued the fight.

King Kamose (addressing the council of nobles on the situation of the Theban King):

> "*Let me understand what this power of mine is all about! One prince is in Avaris, another is in Ethiopia—and here I sit, a partner with an Asiatic and a Black! Each man has his slice of this Egypt, dividing up the land with me.*"

We know that Kamose perceived Apepi (Apophis) as a "man of Retenu", that is someone associated with the Levant. The Hyksos had forged an alliance with the Nubians and the King of Thebes found himself between the hammer and the anvil.

> "*I am going to come to grips with him and break his body. My desire is to save Egypt which the Asiatics have smitten.*"

The young Theban began the civil war with an attack on Teti son of Pepi, an Egyptian vassal of the Hyksos who lived at Nefrusi, just north of Hermopolis. On the eve of the battle, Kamose was wakeful, remembering the horrific mortal wounds on the head of his father from the mace and the battle-axe and knowing that a dutiful son could never rest until vengeance was exacted. If one was killed in the pursuit of retribution, then honor was satisfied, but it was better to be victorious and be able to go forward, at last, with ones life.

> "*I spent the night in my boat, with my heart rejoicing. When day broke, I was on him (Teti) as though I were a falcon. I attacked him while he was eating his breakfast. I broke down his walls; I killed his people and I made his wife come down to the riverbank. My soldiers were as lions with their spoil...*"

Kamose claimed, in his stela of victory, that there was a kind of eerie silence when the Egyptian forces first approached Avaris. They came by ships as the target city was on the river.

> "*My valiant army was in front of me like a blast of fire. The troops of the Medjai[31] were on the upper part of our cabins, to seek out the Asiatics and to ascertain their positions...I caught sight of his women on the roof of his palace looking out of their lattices at the river bank, their bodies not stirring when they saw me—as they peeped through the holes in their walls like the young of lizards from within their holes.*"[32]

---

[31] Desert-dwellers of Nubia, a hardy people who made up a goodly portion of the pharaoh's army for centuries and also his police force.

[32] One is reminded that Sir Thomas Roe, the English Ambassador to the Great Mogul at Delhi in India, wrote of attending a durbar there in 1616. At one point he recalled getting a glimpse of the king's women: "*....At one side in a window were his two principall Wives, whose curiositie made them breake little holes in a grate of Reed that hung before it, to gaze on me. I saw first their fingers, and after laying their faces close, now one eye now another; sometime I could discern the full proportion, they were indifferently white, blacke hair smooth up, but if I had no other light, their Diamonds and Pearles had sufficed to shew them.*"

Evidently, however, King Kamose was not able to "root out" the Hyksos entirely, although he swore Avaris was deserted when he was finished with it.

> *"Does your heart fail, O miserable Asiatic? I am drinking the wine of your vineyards, which the Asiatics whom I captured trod out for me...All the good products of Syria, I seized them all. I left nothing belonging to Avaris, so that it is empty, and the Asiatic perished. Does your heart fail, O miserable Asiatic, you who used to say 'I am lord without rival from Hermopolis as far as Pi-Hathor on the banks of Avaris, in the two streams'?* "[33]

Kamose's reign appears to have been very short, no more than three years, and his brother (?), Ahmose I, inherited the task of dealing with this northern enemy. Indeed, scholars have generally assumed it was always the same foe— although quite another may have suddenly appeared, a people so different from both Egyptian and Canaanite that they might have fallen to earth from a distant planet. Like birds of rare and exotic plumage, they also made a nest in the eastern Delta, remaining for an indefinite span of time. Their art shows the wasp-waisted men with tendrils of hair hanging down their shoulders, leaping over the backs of bulls. The women, incredibly chic, wear long, flounced skirts with cinched waists and their little jackets are tailored to reveal bared, provocative bosoms.

A crew commander named Ahmose son of Ebana recorded, in a biography in his tomb at El Kab, how he accompanied Kamose's kinsman for the purpose of subsequent attacks on Avaris. Even though Kamose claimed that Avaris was empty when he was done with the city,

---

[33] Kamose further says that he "found 300 ships of Retenu moored in the harbor (of Avaris), filled with 'lapis lazuli, silver, turquoise, bronze axes, *ben*-oil, incense, fat, honey' and various types of timber." Amelie Kuhrt, *The Ancient Near East*, Volume I, page 180 (London and New York, 1995)

Ahmose son of Ebana indicates that the place was still inhabited.

> **Ahmose son of Ebana**: *"Then Avaris was despoiled. Then I carried off spoil from there: one man, three women, a total of four persons. Then his majesty gave them to me to be slaves. Then Sharuhen[34] was besieged for three years. Then his majesty despoiled it. Thereupon I carried off spoil from there: two women and a (severed) hand. Gold of Valor was given to me, and my spoil was given to me to be slaves. Now after his majesty had killed the Asiatics, then he sailed southward to Khenty-hen-nefer to destroy the Nubian nomads."*

However, Manetho appears to assert that the Hyksos were not actually all driven out of Egypt until the reign of a certain "Tethmosis". Ahmose son of Ebana, having fought for King Amenhotep I, in the interim, described his service under Aakheperkare Thutmose I, but failed to mention anything further about Avaris. Still, the old soldier indicates that nothing or no one stood in the way of the first Thutmose on his march to the east:

> *"After this he went forth to Retenu to assuage his heart throughout the foreign countries. His majesty reached Naharin[35] and his majesty—life, prosperity, health— found that enemy while he was marshaling the battle array. Then his majesty made a great slaughter among them. There was no number to the living prisoners whom his majesty carried off by his victory. Now I was in the*

---

[34] The place in Canaan, just south of Gaza, where the last 15th Dynasty Hyksos king had decided to fortify himself after leaving Egypt. It is possible that, while the Egyptians were busy in the Levant or in Nubia, the Aegean refugees managed to ensconce themselves in the desolated Avaris.

[35] Considered by the Egyptians to be practically the end of the earth. Probably Mesopotamia.

van of our army, and his majesty saw how valiant I was. I carried off a chariot, its horse, and him who was in it as a living prisoner. They were presented to his majesty. Then I was awarded gold another time."[36]

For some reason, it was concluded in antiquity by certain chroniclers that Ahmose was succeeded by a man named "Chebron or "Chebros" and then by a King Amenhotep. As far as we know, Amenhotep I was the son of Ahmose and his immediate successor. Josephus wrote: *"After the departure of the tribe of Shepherds from Egypt to Jerusalem, Tethmosis, the king who drove them out of Egypt, reigned for 25 years 4 months until his death, when he was succeeded by his son Chebron, who ruled 13 years."*

Before this book is finished, the reader will understand precisely why King Ahmose and a **certain pharaoh** named Thutmose were often confused, or actually fused into one. It was because each drove a **different** set of Hyksos from their land, a distinction later repressed. The **pseudo**-Manetho *Book of Sothis* actually states: *"Amosis, also called Tethmosis, 26 years."* An author named Theophilus wrote:

"Moses was the leader of the Jews, as I have already said, when they had been expelled from Egypt by King Pharaoh whose name was Tethmosis. After the expulsion of the people, this king, it is said, reigned for 25 years 4 months, according to Manetho's reckoning."

As it happened, the first two rulers named Thutmose never reigned as long as twenty years and the third was king of Egypt for more than fifty years. That Manetho, himself, had nothing to do with such a faulty attribution of

---

[36] The "gold" was either in the form of a necklace(s), consisting of closely-strung round discs, or three golden flies hung on a chain. The fly, being a creature that persists despite efforts to drive it off, was evidently a symbol of valor and determination. Queen Ah-hotep, the mother of Ahmose I, was herself awarded the "Order of the Fly", probably for service to her nation at a time when the men of her family were either too young or absent.

regnal years, will become clear later, too. Sextus Julius Africanus noted (according to the monk Syncellus):

> *"The Eighteenth Dynasty consisted of 16 kings of Diospolis (Thebes). The first of these was Amos, in whose reign Moses went forth from Egypt, as I here declare; but according to the convincing evidence of the present calculation (i.e. by Syncellus) it follows that in this reign Moses was still young."*

Although we are blessed with textual evidence from this time of strife, the expulsion of the Hyksos, there is, nevertheless, some difficulty in knowing how to interpret it. Manetho says that the "shepherds" were never so much slaughtered as besieged to a point where they simply gave in and agreed to go, something that appears to be contradicted by the testimony of Ahmose son of Ebana. This is curious, as one can think of no reason why Manetho, a presumably patriotic native Egyptian, would invent such a tale instead of reveling in the victories of the pharaohs of yore—so we are left to conclude that he was not referring to the exodus of the time of Ahmose, prince of Thebes.

> *"....Under a king, whose name was Misphragmuthosis[37], the shepherds were defeated and were indeed driven out of other parts of Egypt, but were shut up in a place called Avaris that contained ten thousand arourae.[38] According to Manetho, the shepherds encircled the whole of this place with a great, thick wall, in order to keep all their possessions and their spoils, but that Thummosis, the son of Misphragmuthosis,[39] attempted to take them by force and by siege, with four hundred and eighty*

---

[37] Josephus wrote "Mispragmuthosis" but intended Ahmose. More later on that curious name.

[38] An aroura is equal to a half acre.

[39] The ancient Egyptians did not often differentiate between "son", "grandson" or even "successor" and used the same term for all.

*thousand men. Despairing of the success of the siege,
they came to an agreement with them, that they should
leave Egypt, and go, without any harm to be done to
them, whatsoever; and that, after this treaty was formed,
they went away with their whole families and chattels,
not fewer in number than two hundred and forty
thousand, and took their journey from Egypt, through the
wilderness, for Syria; but being they were in fear of the
Assyrians, who had current control over Asia, they built
a city in that country which is now called Judea, large
enough to contain this great number of men, and called it
Jerusalem."*

Flavius Josephus, *Against Apion,*   Book 1:14

Where does the truth lie? The veteran, Ahmose son of
Ebana, says that, after Avaris was attacked, a siege was
made upon Sharuhen that lasted three years, implying that,
after the fall of the first fortification, the Hyksos were
pursued to the second one in Canaan. Yet why should
Avaris, with its legendary walls, have succumbed so easily on
several occasions when Sharuhen required so long to be
defeated?

Chapter Two

Curiously, Tacitus[40] mentions, among other rumors regarding the origin of the Jews, that they were perhaps refugees from Crete who fled to Africa. This was no doubt due to a conviction of some of the classic writers that the Biblical Exodus was to be equated with the Hyksos quitting Egypt.[41] Of course, this belief was quite correct; the proto-Jews, or "Children of Israel", were doubtless among the group that Ahmose I expelled from the eastern Delta.

A successor of Ahmose named Akhenaten, lord of the Egyptian empire, received correspondence from his vassal princes in Canaan referring to a dissident group called the "Apiru". These were likely the very same people as the "slaves" or "workers", named in the Brooklyn Papyrus, who had come to Egypt at the of time Abraham or Joseph and Jacob and still retained their old appellation, as far as the Egyptians and their allies were concerned—even though the "Apiru" now looked upon Canaan as their permanent home and were trying to acquire more territory for themselves. These "Hebrews" had not become settled but were still a semi-nomadic tribe or tribes in Akhenaten's day, being mentioned by his predecessors, Thutmose III and Amenhotep

---

[40] Cornelius Tacitus (55?-after 117 CE), Roman historian and author of *The Historiae*. "*Some say that the Jews were fugitives from the island of Crete, who settled on the nearest coast of Africa about the time when Saturn was driven from his throne by the power of Jupiter.*" The reference to the planets is possibly from the folklore that said Saturn was once larger and more prominent in the heavens but it approached Jupiter rather closely at one point, the result being violent tidal effects in each other's atmospheres and a stellar explosion, or nova. Hebrew legends claim that Saturn was especially brilliant just prior to the deluge of Noah. (see *Legends of the Jews*, supra.)

[41] This information was not disseminated by Manetho, who wrote of them "*Some say they were Arabs*".

II, as well.[42] From the Egyptian sources, one gathers that the Hebrews were no longer simply a pastoral people who fed small cattle, but were rather wild and even brigand-like, similar to the Shasu, another clan who had formerly been part of the generic "Hyksos. The Hebrews were certainly capable of organizing themselves into fighting groups and, by the reign of Akhenaten, they could be compared to the Scots rebelling against the English king, Edward Longshanks.

The information of Tacitus that the Jews may have been descended from the people of the island of Crete is not as strange as it may seem—if by "Jews" he actually was referring to people who were refugees from Egypt under similar circumstances and who had lived in the same area in the Delta. Some ancient historians evidently confused the Cretans with the earlier "shepherds"—all of which eventually resettled in the Levant, each in their time.

Dr. Manfred Bietak's excavation at the site he believes to be Avaris saw a Canaanite settlement in the 13th Dynasty with expansion during the Second Intermediate Period.[43] He further has concluded that a reoccupation of the Hyksos citadel took place in the early 18th Dynasty that may have been a royal habitation of the time of Ahmose I. Minoan-style paintings[44] are seen in that stratum, which resemble the artwork at Thera, a volcanic island in the Aegean,[45] and are perhaps contemporary with them. The Santorini (Thera) explosion is dated about 1628 BCE, based on radiocarbon and dendrochronology. Pumice found in the New Kingdom stratum certainly must have originated from the volcanic

---

[42] *"In those days there was no king in Israel and every man did that which was right in his own eyes."* Judges 21:24.

[43] With Avaris becoming one of the largest cities in Egypt.

[44] Probably from the Late Minoan IA Period.

[45] Now named "Santorini".

eruption[46] and all this combined seems to point to a chronological problem.

How does one account for Minoan wall paintings in the 18th Dynasty palace? Manfred Bietak suggests this was due to a foreign marriage, an alliance of the Hyksos with the Minoan thalassocracy, the most potent seapower of the time. This is certainly a possible result but, while there may have been a sudden Aegean presence in Avaris during the 18th Dynasty, the objective of matrimony was not necessarily the driving force.[47]

There is an inscription from the time of King Ahmose I[48] that seems to indicate that some disaster occurred within his reign, one that obliterated the sun. It is known as the "Tempest Stela" of Karnak.

> " ... now then ... the gods declared their discontent. The gods [caused] the sky to come in a tempest of r[ain], with darkness in the western region and the sky being unleashed without [cessation, louder than] the cries of the masses, more powerful than [...], [while the rain raged] on the mountains louder than the noise of the cataract which is at Elephantine."

---

[46] Pumice from Thera was discovered all the way to the Black Sea.

[47] The Thera explosion, twice that of Krakatoa and 40 times that of Mount St. Helens, destroyed the island's civilization. It caused tidal waves and earthquakes, which toppled Minoan cities on surrounding shores, especially on Crete.

[48]The stela, found at the third pylon of the Karnak temple, attests that Ahmose rebuilt structures in Egypt damaged by "a storm sent to Upper Egypt by the power of Amen". The inscription mentions flooding. Southern, or Upper Egypt, has virtually a desert climate, and while the occasional thunderstorm will create a flash flood every decade or so, these were not thought remarkable. Ahmose's account has been connected to the eruption of Thera. See Foster, Karen Polinger and Robert K. Ritner, *Texts, Storms, and the Thera Eruption*, JNES 55 (1996), 1-14.

This is suspiciously a reference to the Thera catastrophy and its effects and so, in view of the evidence found at Tell el Daba, we probably ought to conclude that the dating of the reign of Ahmose, which has been fixed from 1570 to 1546 BCE, should be set back by at very least half a century—or that the scientific results do not yield a narrow enough margin for arriving at a precise date for the eruption. It strikes me as rather obvious that the Egypt of Ahmose experienced an invasion of a whole new set of alien people, displaced by the great blast of the volcano and its aftermath, who duplicated their culture in the eastern Delta.[49]

There is an island in the Aegean, now called "Santorini", but once known as "Thera". The island was dominated by a volcano, whose ultimate eruption was one of the worst catastrophes in the history of the world. However, somehow, the inhabitants of Thera, who had a civilization evidently not unlike that of Crete, experienced a warning of volcanic activity in advance of the great final explosion and so were spared the fate of other peoples who lived in the shadow of similar smoldering peaks.

Excavations at Akrotiri, a site on Santorini, have revealed the sequence of events. The lowest stratum of the volcanic debris there is made up of a layer of pumice about 3 centimeters thick, the top of which was crusted as though water had fallen on it while it was still hot. Due to some slight oxidation being observed on this layer, it is estimated that it lay as it was for anywhere from a couple of months to two years prior to being covered by yet another layer of pumice. Following the final, devastating explosion, the island of Thera was not inhabited for the next 200 years.

Where did the islanders go? My contention is they probably ended up in northern Egypt, as Tacitus maintained, making their way to the abandoned fortified city of Avaris. At some future point they were joined by fugitives from

---

[49] An alabaster jar lid was found in the palace at Knossos, Crete, inscribed with the cartouche of Khyan, a king of the Hyksos. He was doubtless the "Iannas" of Manetho.

Crete.[50] The tuna population of the Aegean, a major source of food for those of the islands, had been decimated by the ash and lava from the cataclysmic blast. Agriculture had also been adversely affected. Egypt had long been considered the "bread-basket" of ancient nations who were experiencing drought and famine and the Egyptians were known to have silos in which grain was stored. In time, other people may have taken up residence at Avaris, as well. The new king of the renovated citadel was of unknown ethnicity, but his palace was decorated in unmistakable Aegean style.

The Rhind Papyrus is a mathematical text that dates from Year 33 of the Hyksos king, Apophis I.[51] The papyrus was discovered in Thebes in the ruins of a small building near the Ramesseum, the mortuary temple of Ramesses II, but, despite its Theban provenance,[52] it is a document belonging to the Delta. It is a copy made by the scribe, Ahmose, of a mathematical papyrus from the time of Amenemhat III. The Rhind Papyrus, written in hieratic, the cursive form of hieroglyphs, is a single roll which was orginally about 5.4 metres long by 32 centimetres wide. It dates from ca. 1650 BCE and contains a table of fractions and 84 mathematical problems that still have modern math experts wondering "How were they computed?"

---

[50] Crete is 70 miles to the south of Santorini.

[51] A piece of pseudo-Manetho, probably from the 3rd Century CE, known as *The Book of Sothis*, says of Apophis: "*Some say that this king was at first called Pharaoh, and that it was in the 4th year of his kingship that Joseph came as a slave into Egypt. He appointed Joseph lord of Egypt and all his kingdom in the 17th year of his rule, having learned from him the interpretation of dreams and having thus proved his divine wisdom. The Holy Scriptures, however, give the name of Pharaoh also to the king of Egypt in the time of Abraham.*"

[52] The papyrus was purchased by Alexander Henry Rhind in 1858.

The name of the scribe, Ahmose, compels one to comment on its apparent popularity during the relevant period of Egyptian history and one must give some consideration as to whether this was not the actual Egyptian name of Moses. It means "the moon is born"[53] and has to do with the god, Thoth, and his lunar connection. If Moses was really a contemporary of King Ahmose I, then it stands to reason that, not only would the prophet's name have been shortened to avoid any inference of a religious connotation, but the name of the pharaoh can have been entirely omitted to expunge any memory of the fact that these men, on opposite sides of a situation, had once shared the same appellation.

The verso of the pRhind was used by someone, at a later date, to record a momentous happening:

> "*Regnal year 11, second month of Shomu: Heliopolis was entered. First month of Akhet, day 23: this southern prince broke into Tjaru.*[54] *Day 25: It was heard tell that Tjaru had been entered. Regnal year 11, first month of Akhet, the birthday of Seth—a roar was emitted by the majesty of this god. The birthday of Isis—the sky poured rain.*"

This occurred in the 11th year of an unidentified Delta ruler, and was the same event that King Ahmose[55], in time, inscribed at Karnak.[56]   It appears that, in the season of

---

[53] Vocalized "Iookhmayes".

[54] The frontier fort on the edge of the Sinai. This means that Ahmose, at war with the Hyksos, was attempting to pen them in, but events transpired so that they ultimately fled across the desert and holed up at Sharuhen on the Mediterranean coast, a place south of Gaza. According to an old soldier's account, Ahmose remained there for three years, conducting a siege.

[55] Called "pn rsy" or "the one of the South" on the pRhind.

[56] The mummy of King Ahmose I, if it is truly he, seems to be that of a man who died rather young to have ruled for the 25 or so years ascribed to him.

Shomu, Ahmose took Heliopolis ("On" in Egyptian), which was a city near the apex of the Delta and just south of Tell el Yahudiyah, a Hyksos settlement. Following that, he would have gone in a north-easterly direction through the oasis and entered Tjaru (Sile), a fortress on the edge of the Sinai desert, flanked by two bodies of water. This could mean that the Theban devised the strategy of trapping the Hyksos and preventing them from escaping to Canaan by way of the area that the fort guarded—or allowing any allies they may have had in the Levant from entering Egypt. Oddly, after recording the breach of Djaru, the writer of the pRhind inscription mentions something that should have occurred just before Day One of the first month of Akhet, during the intercalary days—that is prior to the attack on the fortress.

The "birthdays of the gods" were the five epagomenal days at the end of the Egyptian civil calendar, following the last month of the season of Shomu. [57] The problem is that from about 2,500 BCE Egypt had three ways of reckoning time running concurrently. This is a complex subject, but suffice it to say that, since the Egyptians did not take leap years into account, their lunar calendar got further and further away from the three naturally occurring seasons of Egypt. This meant that at one point, the summer months actually fell in winter. Only every 1,460 years did their astronomical or "Sothic" year of 365 and one-quarter days synchronize with the old "civil" year of 365 days, the one that included the "birthdays of the gods".

Because the inundation never occurred at a fixed date, the brief annual appearance of the dog-star, Sirius,[58] at dawn along a certain latitude was used to mark the start of the natural flood season, but not the season of

---

Either Ahmose was a mere child when he took his brother's place—or he appropriated the regnal years of the Hyksos king whom he vanquished.

[57] These were called "the five days over the year" and were known as the "birthdays" of the gods, Osiris, Horus, Seth, Isis and Nepthys.

[58] *spdt*, pronounced "Sothi" by the Egyptians

31

Inundation/Akhet of the civil calendar. That, of course, could occur at any time in relation to the natural seasons. When every millennium and a half or so this astronomical event coincided with I Akhet day 1 of the civil calendar, or New Year's Day, this would have been seen as a great occasion and would have happened about July 19th by the Julian calendar. It would have been called a "Perfect Year".

Below, a ceremonial ax of King Ahmose, the griffon displaying Minoan influence.

These are the three seasons and their months:

Season	Month
Akhet (Inundation)	Thaout
1st Day of of Akhet	Phaophi
season would be July 19	Athor
_____	Khoiak
Peret (Winter)	Tobi
1st day of Peret season would	Mechir
be Nov. 16	Phamenoth
_____	Pharmuthi
Shômû (Summer)	Pakhons
1st day of Shomu season would	Paoni
be Mar. 17	Epipi
	Mesori

In four years following such an alignment or new "Sothic Cycle", the rising of Sirius would have taken place a day later in the civil calendar and the tardy appearance increased by a day every four years after that until the next synchronization 1,460 years later.

Month	Season
Epip	Normally Akhet, now
Mesori	"Shomu"--1st Day of
Thaout	Epip would be July 19
Paophi	
Athor	Normally Peret now
Khoiak	"Akhet"--1st day of
Tobi	Athor would be Nov. 16
Mechir	
Phamenoth	Normally Shomu now
Pharmuthi	"Peret"--1st day of
Pakhons	Phamenoth is Mar. 17
Paoni	

The above is how the civil seasons had shifted at the time of Ahmose I. There was also another year running alongside the civil and astronomical calendars by which the priests calculated the occurrence of the annual festivals—a rather confusing state of affairs, but that is how it was.

It is of some interest to relate that the pEbers, a medical papyrus, is thought to state that in Year 9 of Amenhotep I, the rising of Sirius took place on the 9th day of the 3rd month of the season of Shomu instead of on the 1st day of the premier month of Akhet—as it would have done in a "perfect year". This was a rare indication of the astronomical year in the context of the civil year.[59]

---

[59] There are other such concordances, one being from Year 7 of Sesostris III (12th Dynasty), which indicated that the rising of Sirius should take place on the 16th day of the 4th month of Peret (winter season). In an unspecified year of king Thutmose III, the event happened on the 29th day of the 3rd month of Shomu (probably very early in his long reign).

34

This means that the sighting of Sothis/Sirius was, at this period, occurring at the time of the Nile flooding, as it always did—but that the civil calendar had shifted so that it was the summer season for the purposes of dating a document—such as the pRhind! As another papyrus laments:

"Winter is come in summer, the months are reversed, the hours in confusion."

The same was true in the time of Ahmose, the father of Amenhotep I. Then the rising of the " dog star", Sirius, would have been observed on the first or second day of the 3rd month of Shomu.[60] Regardless, it was really the natural season of Inundation, the time we refer to as the "dog days" before the advent of autumn.

I propose that the Rhind Papyrus indicates that, in what we call the fall months, the volcano erupted on Thera, the explosion being heard all the way to Egypt's Delta and interpreted as Seth's mighty voice roaring like thunder on his natal day. During the night, the deluge or "tempest", described by Ahmose at Karnak, commenced.

It seems to me that both the pRhind and the Book of Exodus reflect what vulcanologists and archaeologists have noticed on Santorini. After the sound of the initial explosion, there was little else of consequence for the Delta scribe to record until the sky opened up on the birthday of Isis.

For some days, warfare would have been impossible due to the torrential rains but, since Ahmose had taken the trouble to mobilize all of the south of Egypt, there was no turning back. The north was going to be his, come hell or high water. Sure enough, 25 days after Thera had begun its spewing, Tjaru was entered and doubtless the assault on the

---

[60] The exact date of the rising would depend upon whether King Ahmose really did reign for the entire 25 years assigned to him—or whether he appropriated the 11 regnal years of the Hyksos king whom he vanquished.

major Hyksos strongholds took place at nearly the same time. [61]

The Book of Exodus says that the Hebrews left Egypt in the spring, or March/April, specifically on the 15th of Nisan, according to the Jewish calendar. In Exodus 12:2, God says to Moses and his brother Aaron, "*This month (Nisan) shall be the beginning of the months for you; it shall be the first of the months of the year for you*".[62]

After the Exodus has occurred, Moses commands the newly freed people to remember this day that happened at the time of "Aviv" (Exodus 13:4), another word for the month of Nisan. Aviv is to be roughly equated with the Vernal Equinox, the time when certain Egyptian crops ripened. Moreover, Moses tells the Hebrews, "*You shall therefore keep this statute* (commemorating the Exodus) *in its season from year to year*" (Exodus 13:10). As it happens, the solution was to observe Passover around the time of the equinox and to devise a new calendar, the Hebrew one, in which festivals could always fall at the same time.

It is Flavius Josephus, himself, who indicates the corresponding Egyptian month of the departure. In his *Antiquities of the Jews*, he writes

> "*But when God had indicated that with one plague he would compel the Egyptians to let Hebrews go, he commanded Moses to tell the people that they should prepare a sacrifice, and hold themselves ready on the tenth day of the month Xanthicus, in order to depart on the fourteenth, (which month is called by the Egyptians Pharmuth, Nisan by the Hebrews; but the Macedonians call it Xanthicus,)...*"

---

[61] I do not know precisely whether or not Egyptologist Hans Goedicke was the first to suggest that the Exodus and the eruption of Thera were connected, but his assertions with regard to this caused a stir some years ago. Some of his ideas are contained in *Egyptological Studies in Honor of Richard Parker* (1986) .

[62] That is, the first of the months of the religious or holiday calendar. Jewish New Year or Rosh Hashana is observed in the Fall.

At the time of Ahmose, "Pharmuth" or "Pharmouti" would have, indeed, fallen in April—whereas in a "perfect year" it would have fallen in February.[63] However, Josephus was, no doubt, not going by the ancient Egyptian calendar but the one revised at Alexandria in 30 BCE when new dates for the beginnings of the months were fixed, and when Pharmouti would begin on March 27 and end on April 26, the first day of the season of Shomu.

But the fact remains that, according to the pRhind, the "signs and wonders" couldn't have occurred until after the time of Inundation. If the 3rd month of Shomu, which is Epip, saw the rising of Sirius in the day of Ahmose, that means that the "Akhet" of the pRhind did not occur at this time until September[64], with the epagomenal or "days over the year", when the first explosion was heard, also being in that month by the Julian calendar. If the mass migration happened in the spring, that would mean it would have to have been at least six more months before the greatest explosion took place—probably in the middle of the siege of Avaris by Ahmose, the Southern Prince, and his men. Or perhaps the interval between the initial blast and the final one can have been much longer...

In fact, archaeologist Spyridon Marinatos favored the latter scenario, judging by what he saw at Akrotiri on Santorini. By his reckoning, a series of eruptions of the Thera volcano lasted for approximately five years.[65] In the

---

[63] As it happens, the names of the months of the Egyptian calendar would have been an anachronism in King Ahmose's day, as they did not come into usage until a much later date—but I refer to them for clarity's sake, as it is even more confusing just to call the months by their numbers.

[64] The rainfall must have been the result of the atmospheric disturbance caused by the eruption, as rain in September is practically unheard of in Egypt. Vulcanologists use the term "plinian" to refer to sustained explosive eruptions that form high-altitude columns and cover large areas with ash.

[65] This may have accounted for the fact that some men of the "Hau-nebu", the people of the "islands of the Great Green", actually seem to have served

initial year, there was a warning that prompted the islanders to evacuate. Within the same 12-month period, some of them returned and weeds had grown up. In the next year, there was evidently an eruption that put down a "*2 inch layer of rice-sized pumice stones hardened into cement by rain.*" Within a one to two-year time-span, the volcano resumed its belching, leaving a "*2 foot layer of pumice stones 2 inches in diameter*" and a "*6 foot layer of larger stones cut by streams of water.*" Within one more year, perhaps, allowing time for some reconstruction of habitation visible on the island, the final phase occurred with the volcano actually blowing itself up, depositing a "*12 foot layer of pumice and a 100 foot layer of fine hot ash*"! [66]

Christos Doumas, on the other hand, believes the events occurred within the space of a few months, just as had been the case with the volcano of Krakatoa.

During the 1883 eruption of Krakatoa,

"*the first phase was very mild and of short duration, commenced on 28 May and can be compared with that phase of the Thera eruption which warned the inhabitants of Akrotiri to leave their homes and which ended with the ejection and fall of pellety pumice over the whole island. The second phase of the Krakatoa eruption, much more intense, lasted seventy-one days, from 19 June to 29 August, and coincides with the phase on Thera when enormous quantities of pumice and ash were ejected, covering the entire island with a voluminous mantle. Within this phase, in both instances, is included the final explosion which produced fine dust and terminated in the total collapse of the volcano.*"[67]

---

as mercenaries for Ahmose and doubtless fought the 15th Dynasty Hyksos. However, it is difficult to identify these people with any certainty.

[66] *Excavations at Thera I-VII* (1968-1976)

[67] Christos G. Doumas, *Thera - Pompeii of the Ancient Aegean*, p. 141

Regardless of the time that had passed, it was probably due to the cataclysmic events connected to the ultimate eruption of the Thera volcano that concluded the siege of Avaris and caused the Egyptians to lose their hold over the strategic Djaru—allowing the Hyksos to make their escape to Canaan. This time the effects of the blast would have certainly been felt in the Delta with a vengeance and chaos would have been the result. The author of the Book of Exodus seemingly knew a great deal about the phenomena generated by the eruption. His word for them was, of course, "miracles". They were well-remembered, at that time being surely viewed as a wondrous reprieve, sent by the power of Seth or El, from the Egyptian onslaught.

There can be little doubt that the Book of Exodus takes "the exciting parts" from this expulsion and incorporates them into the narrative. If one intended to write a fictionalized account of how the Children of Israel left Egypt, one might as well make it as dramatic as possible. What could possibly appear more like heavenly intervention than the phenomena that occurred when Ahmose chased the "shepherds" into Canaan? The plethora of frogs, swarms of gnats and flies, cattle disease and a deadly pestilence that were a part of the story were bad enough, but not really unheard-of. Nobody could really call these "miracles" that no living man had ever experienced.

But a soot-like dust that caused people problems when it came into contact with their skin was another matter. The sky does not normally rain soot and this was clearly not the same as the sandstorms that were the result of the *Khamsin*[68] winds. Obviously, the black substance was the ash from the volcano of Thera, a great deal of it having been blown eastward, as scientists have determined. *"Thunder and hail and fire ran down unto the earth"*.[69] This was

---

[68] A hot wind from the south that that blows in Egypt from late in March until early May.

[69] Exodus 9:23

doubtless the pumice rocks that traveled from the blast as far as Egypt's Delta and remained for Dr. Bietak to see.

According to the Book of Exodus, the locusts, which had settled in with all the other pests sent to plague the Egyptians, suddenly felt the great whoosh of a wind out of the west, whisking them straight into the Red Sea. Then there was darkness for three days. The final eruption of Thera did probably occur at harvest time—but the Egyptian harvest time is not in the fall. It is in the spring. According to another modern writer, Charles Pellegrino:

> "The death cloud deposited a dense ash layer hundreds of miles east of Thera, but penetrated west only sixty miles, stopping at the island of Melos. To halt the cloud at Melos, the headwinds from the west must have been very strong, and from the meteorologists came word that Westerly squalls were almost exclusively a September through November phenomenon on the Aegean."[70]

This suggests, of course, that the final eruption occurred in autumn, not spring, no matter how close or distant it was in relation to the initial warning turbulence—so, once again, we are faced with a problem of time and the timing implied in the Book of Exodus. Conclusion? I believe this signifies another conflict between different dates of departure in separate exodoi.

The death of the first-born, the ultimate plague, cannot be blamed on the eruption of the volcano and surely must signify the pestilence that is described in the Egyptian version of the Exodus as the "disfiguring disease" that was prevalent in the land and that haunts all the renditions of the story. But the cataclysmic blast and its aftermath are recognizable once again in the "pillar of cloud" by day and the "pillar of fire" by night that are interpreted by the Israelites as the watchful presence of God. In fact, the Hebrews tended to think of the Almighty as manifesting

---

[70] Charles Pellegrino, *Unearthing Atlantis* (1991) p. 233

himself in the form of a cloud for a long time afterward. Land that was, at one moment, dry and passable suddenly being engulfed with water is attributable to the Thera phenomenon, also, as by then the Egyptians were certainly near the sea-coast, giving chase on the way to Sharuhen.

That the Egyptian forces were already in the eastern Delta is crucial to the story, in my opinion. Since one cannot muster an army in an instant, all parties concerned would have had to be in the same area when the Thera eruption happened and, as we now know, Ahmose would not normally have been found in the Delta at all. He would only have gone there to wage war. How the Hyksos of days gone by and their Egyptian foes retrospectively viewed tidal waves, seismic shocks and the other amazing signs that intruded upon their conflict is exemplified in the passage:

> *"Thou sendest forth Thy wrath, it consumeth them as stubble. And with the blast of thy nostrils the waters were piled up— The floods stood upright as a heap; The deeps were congealed in the heart of the sea. The enemy said: 'I will pursue, I will overtake, I will divide the spoil; My lust shall be satisfied upon them; I will draw my sword, my hand shall destroy them.' Thou didst blow with Thy wind, The sea covered them; They sank as lead in the mighty waters."*
> **Exodus** 15: 1-10

As for earthquakes: *"He did unto Dathan and Abiram, the sons of Eliab, the son of Reuben; how the earth opened her mouth, and swallowed them up, and their households, and their tents, and every living substance that followed them, in the midst of Israel."* [71]   **Deuteronomy** 11:6

---

[71] The context of this passage is significant. It follows directly upon *"....the Lord your God, His greatness, His mighty hand, and his outstretched arm, and his His signs and His works....what he did unto the army of Egypt, unto their horses, unto their chariots; how he made the water of the Red Sea to overflow them as they pursued after you, and how the Lord hath destroyed them unto this day...."* In other words, the earthquakes caused both the waters to behave strangely and opened chasms in the earth.

Josephus, too, describes the event in his most dramatic prose:

> " When Moses had made this declaration to God, he smote the sea with his rod, which parted at the stroke, the waters rolling back, leaving the ground dry, as a road and a place of flight for the Hebrews. Now when Moses saw this appearance of God, and that the sea receded and left dry land, he ventured first into it, and bid the Hebrews to follow him along that divine road, and to rejoice at the danger their enemies that followed them were in; and gave thanks to God for this so surprising a deliverance which appeared from him. Now, while these Hebrews did not tarry, but advanced steadfastly, as led by the presence of God, the Egyptians supposed at first that they were rashly headed for destruction. But when they saw that they were continuing a distance without any harm, and that no obstacle or difficulty fell in their journey, they made haste to pursue them, hoping that the sea would be calm for them also. They urged their horses forward, and went down themselves into the sea.
>
> Now the Hebrews, while these were still putting on their armor, and otherwise wasting time, escaped them, and got first over to the land on the other side without any mishap. Whereupon the others were encouraged, and pursued them with even greater energy, hoping no harm would come to them neither. However, the Egyptians were not aware that they went into a road made for the Hebrews, and not for others; that this road was created for the deliverance of those in danger, but not for those intent upon the destruction of others. As soon, therefore, as the whole Egyptian army was within it, the sea rushed back to its own place, and came down with a

---

Since Dathan and Abiram were the grandsons of Reuben, the brother of Joseph, this also serves as a chronological marker, very appropriate for the reign of Ahmose.

torrent raised by gales of wind, and engulfed the Egyptians. Showers of rain also came down from the sky, and terrible thunder and lightning, with flashes of fire. Thunderbolts also were darted upon them. Nor was there anything that God could show to men, as indications of his wrath, which did not happen at this time, for a dark and dismal night oppressed them. Under these circumstances did all these men perish, so that there was not one man left to be a messenger of the disaster to the rest of the Egyptians."

If at one moment, a large group of people was able to pass over some stretch of land and that, shortly afterward, earthquakes had caused it to become awash is perfectly credible, under the circumstances, but to identify the exact location is a problem.

At this point it is appropriate to address the situation of Djaru/Sile, the fortification, and its proximity to the Red Sea. The reason Djaru was so important is that it was difficult to enter or exit Egypt without passing it. It cannot have been more than a few miles wide and could be well-monitored from a watchtower. On its one side was an inlet of the Mediterranean Sea at the Pelusiac arm of the Nile, forming a sort of reed-infested lake[72], and on the opposite side were other lakes that were lined up before the northernmost tip of the Red Sea. This was a caravan route utilized for many centuries and also the starting point for the armies of the pharaohs whenever they sallied forth on their Asiatic campaigns.

Another "gateway" to or from Egypt lay to the south, at the "Kam Ur", the area of the Bitter Lakes, near modern Ismailiyah. This was a far less pleasant route, which had been frequented by Bedu from the Negev and Sinai deserts over the centuries.

---

[72] Today known as Lake Manzala, but anciently as the Shi-Hor or "Sea of Horus".

Sinuhe, an Egyptian fugitive, who was attached to the court of King Amenemhat I, takes this way out in a story dated to the 12th Dynasty:

"I halted at the Isle-of-Kam-Ur. Thirst came over me. I was parched and my throat was dusty. I said 'This is the taste of death!' But then I lifted up my heart and collected myself, for I had heard the sound of the lowing of cattle, and I spied Asiatics. The sheik among them, who had been in Egypt, recognized me.[73] *Then he gave me water while he boiled milk for me. I went with him to his tribe. What they did for me was good."*

In the Book of Exodus, it is stressed that the Hebrews avoided "the Way of the Philistines", which was the northern passage, due to fighting that was going on there, but...

Another incident included in the flight from Egypt is reflected in a passage from Diodorus Siculus. The Bible says: *"And it came to pass that at even the quails came up and covered the camp..."* Ex. 16: 13

Diodorus wrote that a certain Ethiopian king of Egypt, Actisanes, set up a penal colony on the edge of the desert dubbed "Rhinocolura" because of the inhabitants having had

---

[73] This passage has always interested me because it suggests an Abraham-like chieftain who recognized Sinuhe because he had actually been to the royal palace. Abraham, as we know, had dealings with the pharaoh because of the extreme beauty of his wife, Sarah, who was taken into the king's household. Sinuhe was *"a servant of the royal harem, waiting on the Princess, the highly praised royal wife of King Senusret"* (I), who was the daughter of King Amenemhat the First. The Egyptian lived happily with the Asiatics and virtually became one of them until, not wishing to be buried outside of Egypt, he finally returned to his native land. The tale of Sinuhe also is reminiscent of what happened to Moses when he fled Egypt and even contains a contest between the Egyptian and an Asiatic champion that resembles the showdown between David and Goliath in the Bible. Sinuhe left Egypt due to overhearing a plot to assassinate King Amenemhat and fearing he would be implicated. Much later in Egyptian history, a "harem plot" of the 20th Dynasty caused the downfall of many a servant of the pharaoh's women.

their noses cut off, a well-known form of punishment in Egypt.

> "This city, which lies on the border between Egypt and Syria,[74] not far from the seacoast, is devoid of practically everything which is necessary for a man's existence; for it is surrounded by land which is full of brine, while within the walls there is but a small supply of well water, and that is tainted and very bitter to the taste. But he settled them in this country in order that, in case they continued to practice their well-known ways, they might not prey upon innocent people....and yet, despite the fact that they had been cast out into a desert country which lacked practically every useful thing, they contrived a way of living in keeping with the austerity around them, since nature forced them to be creative in their need. For instance, by cutting down reeds in the neighborhood and splitting them, they made long nets, which they set up along the beach for a distance of many stades for catching quails; for these arrive in large coveys from the open sea, and in hunting them they caught a sufficient number to provide themselves with food."[75]

This appears to prove that the Israelites-cum-Hyksos were, at some point, encamped near the "sea of reeds", the Shi-Hor, prior to entering Canaan, and not just the "Red Sea", further to the south. Which route did the Hyksos take

---

[74] The name by which the entire Levant was often known. Of interest to note is that Diodorus also wrote in Book I. 33. 3-9 that *"From the Pelusiac mouth (of the Nile) there is an artificial canal to the Arabian Gulf and the Red Sea. The first to undertake the construction of this was Necho the son of Psammetichus and after him Darius the Persian made progress with the work for a time but finally left it unfinished."* But Darius makes claim to the contrary on a stela which states *"So was this canal built, as I had commanded, and ships passed from Egypt through this canal to Persia, as was my purpose."*

[75] The great migration of these birds takes place in autumn.

in actuality?   Probably the coastal route, the road to Sharuhen.

So here I believe we have some more contradictions resulting from separate exodoi being incorporated into one tale.

After "Marah", the site of the bitter water, the company went to a spot called "Elim" where *were twelve springs of water and three score and ten palm trees; and they encamped there by the waters.*[76]

Thereafter followed a series of water-holes which led to the land of Canaan. As for the southern route, as Sinuhe discovered and as Herodotus pointed out in his account of the Persian, Cambyses, and his plans to march on Egypt via the desert, there was no water. At least, there was precious little and one had to know where to find it.   One could not simply wander into the wasteland unprepared.   Cambyses got the King of Arabia to supply his army with skins filled with water, enough for 12 days, and Sinuhe, as we know, encountered sympathetic Bedouins, who doubtless carried their own water-supply, as well.

That the phenomena mentioned in connection with the Exodus do, indeed, resemble what happens when a volcano explodes, can be better illustrated by comparing them with the eye-witness account of Pliny the Younger. The following is taken from the experience of this writer and his family upon the eruption of Mount Vesuvius in 79 CE:

"....The cloud was rising...it's general appearance can best be expressed as being like an umbrella pine, for it rose to a great height on a sort of trunk and then split off into branches, I imagine because it was thrust upwards by the first blast and then left unsupported as the pressure subsided, or else it was borne down by its own weight so that it spread out and gradually dispersed....Ashes were already falling, hotter and thicker as the ships drew near, followed by bits of pumice and blackened stones, charred and cracked by the

---

[76] Exodus 15:27

46

flames....Meanwhile, on Mount Vesuvius, broad sheets of fire and leaping flames blazed at several points, their bright glare emphasized by the darkness of night....Elsewhere there was daylight by this time, but they were still in darkness, blacker and denser than any ordinary night, which they relieved by lighting torches and various kinds of lamp. My uncle decided to go down to the shore and investigate on the spot the possibility of any escape by sea, but he found the waves still wild and dangerous...[Pliny's uncle, known as Pliny the Elder, was, at that point, overcome by the choking fumes and died]....Meanwhile my mother and I were at Misenum....For several days there had been earth tremors which were not particularly alarming because they are frequent in Campania, but that night the shocks were so violent that everything felt as if it were not only shaken but overturned....The buildings were already tottering....This finally decided us to leave the town....We also saw the sea sucked away and apparently forced back by the earthquake: at any rate it receded from the shore so that quantities of sea creatures were left stranded on dry sand. On the landward side a fearful black cloud was rent by forked and quivering bursts of flame, and parted to reveal great tongues of fire, like flashes of lightening magnified in size....Soon afterward the cloud sank down to earth and covered the sea; it had already blotted out Capri and hidden the promontory of Misenum from sight....Ashes were already falling, not as yet very thickly....a dense black cloud was coming up behind us, spreading over the earth like a flood...We had scarcely sat down to rest when darkness fell, not the dark of a moonless or cloudy night, but as if the lamp had been put out in a closed room. You could hear the shrieks of the women, the wailing of infants, and the shouting of men....Many besought the aide of the gods, but still more imagined there were no gods left, and that the universe was plunged into eternal darkness forever more....ashes began to fall again, this time in heavy showers....At last the darkness thinned and dispersed like smoke or a cloud; then there was genuine daylight, and the sun actually shone out, but yellowish as it is during an eclipse. We were terrified to see everthing changed, buried deep in ashes like snowdrifts. We

47

returned to Misenum where we attended to our physical needs as best we could, and then spent an anxious night alternating between hope and fear. Fear predominated, for the earthquakes went on...."

One can imagine peoples of the Aegean fleeing from a like catastrophe to Africa, as mentioned by Tacitus. Because of the duration of the siege of Sharuhen, they had three years, at very least, to settle themselves at Tell el Daba before the pharaoh's army was at liberty to deal with them and, at the end of that time, Ahmose was perhaps too exhausted from his last campaign to bother. Besides, as the warrior, Ahmose son of Ebana, testified, the pharaoh's attention was called to problems in Nubia. It is even possible that the Egyptian king was able to live in peace with the Aegean people for the balance of his twenty-five-year reign, a situation that prevailed until the day of a certain Thutmose.

Although there is much uncertainty regarding these matters, it is scarcely a wonder that this age of chaos was still recalled by the Egyptians many centuries later. Not only was the time marked by warring, exodoi and influx of great numbers—all this was accompanied by phenomena which, as the Egyptians liked to put it, "had not been seen since the time of the gods", the very dawn of creation.

There is a Greek "myth" that refers to "the flood of Deucalion". A certain king of Thessaly, Deucalion, and his wife, Pyrrha, were the only survivors when the god Zeus caused the earth to be destroyed by flood. It poured rain for nine days and nights. The couple was saved because they were the only people who had led good lives—just as were Noah and his family in the Hebrew Bible. According to Manetho's text, Deucalion's flood occurred in Egypt in the time of the pharaoh, "Misphragmoutosis".[77]

---

[77] Arab legends say "Many perished during the migration in a sudden flood that swept the land of Arabia." Kitab-Alaghaniy (transl. Fresnel), p. 207.

A rumor, possibly begun by the Chaldeans, circulated in antiquity that the Egyptians had lost all their records in this disaster and therefore were forced to rely on Chaldean knowledge:

> "The Nile once flooded (sic!) the country of the Egyptians and destroyed, besides their other possessons, all the astronomical data which they had collected in books. Then, because they needed to know the eclipses and conjunctions, they collected the basic data about these from the Chaldeans."[78]

However...

> "There are also syringes, subterranean and winding passages, which, it is said, those acquainted with the most ancient rites dug in the earth in many places with great labor, since they had foreknowledge that a deluge was coming and feared that the memory of the ceremonies might be destroyed. And on the walls of these caverns they carved many kinds of birds and beasts and countless forms of animals which they called hierographic writing."[79]

Regardless of a rivalry over wisdom between two ancient nations and the common notion that the ancient Egyptians could predict every sort of natural disaster by the heavens, a legend of nine terrible days of tempest seems to have persisted in Egypt and was even incorporated into the mythology of that country.

---

[78] Michaelis Pselli scripta minora I, Milano, from *Chaeremon, Egyptian Priest and Stoic Philosopher* by Pieter Willem van der Horst (Leiden, 1987). See also ff 31.

[79] Ammianus Marcellinus, XXII, 15, 30. Probably not a description of a legendary "Hall of Records" but merely referring to the tombs of the Egyptian kings, some of which had very lengthy passageways, indeed, the walls of which were gloriously painted and carved.

A shrine of Ptolemaic times, carved from stone, was found at El 'Arish[80], a place in the seacoast corridor between Egypt and the Levant, overturned and used as a cattle-trough. The inscription had suffered somewhat, but some 74 interesting lines had remained. That nine days of terrible weather was visited upon the land at some point seems not to have been forgotten, as is witnessed by the El 'Arish naos.

The naos would have received scant notice if Immanuel Velikovsky[81] had not theorized that it was a documentation of the Biblical Exodus. His ideas regarding the artifact have been discussed rather acrimoniously by others, who could see little in the shrine's text that would merit the effort expended by Velikovsky to establish such a connection. But Velikovsky's intuition about the shrine was not nearly as misguided as has been claimed, as the inscription does seem to indicate some sort of dealings of a god/pharaoh with Asiatics—a not uncommon situation for kings of Egypt. And, yes, it does mention the same natural phenomenon that occurred at the same time as an exodus from Egypt and which was interpreted as the Lord having *"brought us forth from Egypt with great terribleness and with signs and wonders"*.[82]

If there is any actual history connected with the El 'Arish naos, it is far from clear what episode would be involved. Regardless, Velikovsky can still be basically correct in that the shrine possibly reflects an old conflict in this part of Egypt's north, one usually culminating in battles and an attempt at ethnic cleansing.

The text of the shrine is couched in language that makes it seem like a myth whose characters come straight out of the ancient Egyptian Ennead—Ra-Horakhti, Atum, Shu and Geb (also called Seb). Perhaps that was all it was ever intended to be. The enemies of Ra referred to in the El 'Arish

---

[80] It should be noted that the word "Arish" is Arabic for "booth".

[81] Author of *Worlds in Collision* (1950) and *Ages in Chaos* (1952) and others
.
[82] Deuteronomy 26:8

naos text are "the Children of Apophis". Apophis was, of course, the monstrous snake that tried to prevent Ra from making his nightly journey through the perilous Duat, the course the sun followed from dusk until dawn. In all the recorded myths that center around the sun-god, Ra, he is placed in the role of an all-powerful king, rather like the Zeus of the Greeks.

The inscription tells of a heroic king, Atum[83], and Shu, his son, who is also admirable. However, at some point, Shu either takes a bad turn or is beset by evil forces because there is an insurrection in his household. The implication is that Shu's son, Geb, the Crown Prince, has something to do with his mother that offends propriety—what difficulty they have with one another is not clear at all in the text. The mother, called Tefnut, the goddess/sister-spouse of Shu, seems to be "enthroned at Memphis" because her husband, Shu, had flown to heaven, which is the Egyptian way of saying a king had died. Geb finds Tefnut at a place called Pi-Kharti or Pi-Kharoti and "takes her by force". This could either mean he raped her or captured her. Then comes the significant

" *there was no exit from the palace for the space of nine days. The land was in great affliction. Evil fell on this earth....It was a great upheaval in the residence....Nobody left the palace during nine days, and during these nine days of upheaval there was such a tempest that neither the men nor the gods could see the faces of their next.*"

Velikovsky seized upon this passage as confirming Exodus 10:21-22, "*Then the Lord said to Moses, 'Stretch out your hand toward the sky so that darkness will spread over Egypt—darkness that can be felt.' So Moses stretched out his hand toward the sky, and total darkness covered all Egypt for three days.*"

Yet three days are not the same as nine. We have seen that, in the series of explosions of the volcano on Thera,

---

[83] The name of Ra as the setting sun. Shu is the god of light and Tefnut, his spouse, is in charge of moisture. Geb, their son, is the "earth-god".

there was sufficient activity to account for at least two periods of darkness and a tempest as well.   Whatever else this El 'Arish inscription is all about, there is no doubt that it stresses the importance of the places in the Eastern Delta to the Egyptian pharaoh in relation to the "Asiatics" who had either lived there or attempted to make their way there. In fact, when Geb became king, his "*scepter was carried by the Degai*", the Asiatics. I do agree with Velikovsky insofar that the text of the shrine reflects the threatening position of these resident aliens during various periods in Egyptian history and that, periodically, a fierce "tempest" brewed up on account of this.

18th Dynasty

Ahmose 1	1570-1546
Amenhotep I	1551-1524
Thutmose I	1524-1518
Thutmose II	1518-1504
Hatshepsut	1498-1483
Thutmose III	1504-1450
Amenhotep II	1453-1419
Thutmose IV	1419-1386
Amenhotep III	1386-1349
Akhenaten	1350-1334
Smenkhkare	1336-1334?
Tutankhamen	1334-1325
Ay	1325-1321
Horemheb	1321-1293?

19th Dynasty

Ramesses I	1293-1291
Seti I	1291-1278
Ramesses II	1279-1212
Merneptah	1212-1202?
Amenmesse	1202-1199
Seti II	1199-1193?
Siptah	?

Chapter Three

Flavius Josephus "followed the Scriptures", he assures us, when he wrote of Moses and the Exodus in his book, *Antiquities of the Jews*. Nevertheless, the historian supplies some details that are not contained in the Old Testament:

"So the Hebrews went out of Egypt, while the Egyptians wept, and repented that they had treated them so harshly. They traveled by Letopolis,[84] a place at that time deserted, but where Babylon was built later on[85], when Cambyses plundered Egypt. Leaving hastily on the third day they came to a place called Beelzephon, on the Red Sea; and when they could find no food in the desert, they ate loaves kneaded of flour, only warmed by the climate. This food lasted them for thirty days; for what they brought with them out of Egypt was depleted, even though they had meted it out sparingly. That is why, in memory of the deprivation in that place, we keep a holiday for eight days, which is called the feast of unleavened bread. Now the entire multitude of those that went out, including the women and children, was not easily numbered, but those that were of an age fit for combat, were six hundred thousand. They left Egypt in the month Xanthicus, on the fifteenth day of the lunar month; four hundred and thirty years after our forefather

---

[84] Unfortunately, the location of Letopolis, probably ancient Zikhemu, a name which had to do with the shrine of a god, is not certain. The same can be said for Baal-Zephon. Sir Alan Gardiner, for one, believed Letopolis to be just 8 miles NW of Cairo on the west bank of the Nile—which means the Hebrews would have had to cross the river to get to the Red Sea!

[85] According to the nautical map of Battista Agnese, dating from 1554 CE, "Babylon" was the extreme eastern Delta.

Abraham came into Canaan, but two hundred and fifteen years only after Jacob removed into Egypt. It was the eightieth year of Moses, and of that of Aaron three more. They also carried out the bones of Joseph with them, as he had charged his sons to do."

I think that Abraham was, indeed, a great nomadic sheik of his time[86] and a contemporary of the murdered Amenemhat I, who began his reign in 1991 BCE.[87] Abba Eban, in his *Heritage: Civilization and the Jews*[88] provides the information:

> *"About a century after Ur-Nammu (a ruler of Ur of the Chaldees), Ur also fell. It is at this point, about 2,000 BCE, with the fall of Ur and the advent of Abraham, that the history of the Jewish people begins."*

Therefore, if we accept the arbitrary datum of 2000 BCE as the beginning of our chronicles, we ought to get, roughly speaking:

Abraham ....2000 BCE
Joseph..................1785 BCE
Departure............1570 BCE

---

[86] It was likely one such as he that the old prophet, Neferti, intended when he foretold *"Then a king will come from the South, Ameny, (Amenemhat I) the justified, by name...as the serpent on his brow subdues the rebels for him...One will build the Wall-of-the-Ruler to bar Asiatics from entering Egypt; they shall beg for water as supplicants so as to let their cattle drink. Then Order will return to its seat and Chaos is driven away."* Abraham, the Bible tells us, originally migrated from Ur of the Chaldees.

[87] These dates are taken from *Chronicle of the Pharaohs* by Peter Clayton (London, 1994). The start of the 12th Dynasty is astronomically fixed.

[88] New York, 1984, page 13. Ur-Nammu devised laws for living at least 300 years before the Babylonian king, Hammurabi, handed down his code.

Ginzberg's *The Legends of the Jews*[89] adds up the reason the patriarch—or any other Semite—journeyed to Egypt:

> *"Scarcely had Abraham established himself in Canaan when a devastating famine broke out—one of the ten God-appointed famines for the chastisement of men. The first of them came in the time of Adam, when God cursed the ground for his sake; the second was the one in the time of Abraham; the third compelled Isaac to take up his abode among the Philistines; the ravages of the fourth drove the sons of Jacob into Egypt to buy grain for food; the fifth came in the time of Judges, when Elimelech and his family had to seek refuge in the land of Moab; the sixth occurred during the reign of David, and it lasted three years; the seventh happened in the day of Elijah, who had sworn that neither rain nor dew shall fall upon the earth; the eighth was in the time of Elisha, when an ass's head was sold for fourscore pieces of silver; the ninth is the famine that comes upon men piecemeal from time to time; and the tenth will scourge men before the advent of the Messiah..."*

In the Levant, where the regions were arable, a good year for crops depended upon the initial rain, (called by the Arabs "el wasm el bedry" or "the early sign" and "yoreh" in Hebrew) to moisten the earth for the reception of seed and plentiful spring rains ("malkosh") to enable the wheat and barley to support the dry heat of the early summer—without which the harvest failed. Copious winter rains ("geshem") were needed to fill the cisterns and pools and replenish the springs. The winter was also the season of earthquakes, not infrequent in this part of the world. The wind, by itself, played a significant role in the health and comfort of the inhabitants of the area. The north wind was a cold one, the south warm. The east wind was dry and the one from the west was considered filled with moisture. The north wind was feared

---

[89] Volume One, pp. 220-221.

even in summer months because it was thought to produce sore throats, fevers and dysenteries. However, when there was little breeze in the summer, the result was a great heat. When the hot wind blew from the south-east, it was what is known as the "sirocco", which made people feel ill, bad tempered and generally listless. A sirocco could last from three to thirty days. This wind sometimes felt like the blast of a furnace and had the smell of a burning brick kiln. Clouds of sand flew about in powerful whirlwinds, sometimes so great as to knock people down. In winter, there was the "cold sirocco", which was known to come on suddenly and kill those without sufficient clothing who were exposed to it. Blizzards were not unknown to occur.

Life for the inhabitants of the Levant was not an easy one, whether in the malaria-ridden plains, the rocky hills of the north or the stark desert of the south. Even in modern times, about half of the people who went from the mountains to the plains for the harvest, were carried off by the malarial-typhoid fever. Circa 1890 of our own era, when a railway was built in Palestine across swampy ground the fellahin or farmers of the region, who worked on it, died of fever by the hundreds and so Egyptians, a people who had managed to become immune to all sorts of maladies over time, had to be employed. In antiquity, the soldiers of the Egyptian empire found it quite disagreeable to be stationed in Canaan. Naturally, the Canaanites had no sympathy for them, whatsoever.

If Ahmose I compelled an exodus in 1570 BCE[90], 430 years before that is 2000 BCE—not a bad match to the time of Amenemhat I. Adding 215 years to 1570 BCE, we obtain 1785 BCE, compatible with the 12th Dynasty, as well.

---

[90] We might as well use this date, even though it is probably not dead-on accurate. We have no way of knowing in which year of his reign Ahmose I undertook to besiege Avaris, even though the ancient authors seem to imply that he ruled a united Egypt for some 25 years after the expulsion of the Hyksos.

However, 215 years added to 1510 BCE, **the possible year of the Exodus in another tradition**, amounts to 1725 and the reign of Khaneferre Sobekhotep of Dynasty 13. Or, if we move things forward to Year 22 of Thutmose III, which could be 1482 BCE, then Joseph will have to have lived around 1697 BCE, in the nebulous time just after the Hyksos invaded Egypt. We will look at these dates again when we examine the etymology of the name of Joseph and the story of his rise to power and renown, **for they all represent times during which various ancient historians believed the patriarch had flourished.**

The Book of Exodus, on the one hand, indicates that the earthquake that swallowed the grandsons of Reuben, Joseph's elder brother, occurred only two generations after the great man, which could hardly have accounted for 215 years—unless everybody lived to be as superannuated as the patriarchs. In fact, in *Against Apion*, Josephus expressly states that Joseph died four generations, "*that is to say 170 years before Moses*" (was born). He said this is in order to refute the claim of an Egyptian historian that Joseph and Moses were leaders of the Hebrews—simultaneously![91]

The Bible asserts that the Children of Israel had sojourned in Egypt for 430 years, which Josephus interpreted as being from the time that Abraham came to Canaan—not Egypt—which seems a bit evasive. While Abraham visited Egypt, he did not remain there. Did the author of Exodus know that there had been Asiatic slaves in Egypt as far back as the early 12th Dynasty? That, of course, was the case[92], and 430 years is a very plausible duration of the

---

[91] If what is written in the *Book of Sothis* about Apophis being the pharaoh of the time of Joseph really had Manetho as its source, one can readily see why some Egyptian chroniclers might have thought that Joseph, who lived so long, would have known Moses, who was already an old man in the heyday of Ahmose I.

[92] The co-regents, Amenemhat I and Senusret I, fought the "sand-dwellers" or Asiatics and no doubt enslaved some of these. On the other hand, Abraham had an Egyptian female slave, Hagar. There can be no doubt that Asiatics had a hand in erecting the pyramids, made of brick, of the father and son pharaohs at Lisht, including the 9 small pyramids of their

Hebrews until the **first exodus**, considering all the factors presented so far.

Some preservers of Manetho's *Aegyptiaca*, his history of Egypt, explicitly state that Joseph rose to prominence in the era of the shepherd kings. If we assume that this was not something interposed into Manetho's text at a later time, then it appears that Manetho considered Joseph's nation was under the thrall of the puissant 15th Dynasty. A kinglist of pharaonic times, the Turin Canon, **allows all the Hyksos rulers no more than 108 years**, from start to finish, before the advent of the New Kingdom, which began with Ahmose I.

The Book of Genesis says that Joseph, himself, lived 110 years and saw his sons' grandchildren. In order to have died 170 years before Moses was born and if Moses was 80 in 1570 BCE, Joseph would have needed to die in 1820 BCE— a hundred years before the Hyksos arrived! (In the *Chronicle* of P. Clayton, the 15th Dynasty starts in 1663 BCE, although he asserts the Hyksos plundered Memphis ca. 1720 BCE. Sir Alan Gardiner wrote in his *Egypt of the Pharaohs*: "...*the Hyksos might have held Avaris for more than fifty years before one of their number felt strong enough to pose as the legitimate Pharaoh*.")

The problem with the figures is readily apparent, and it is difficult to comprehend how a long-deceased Joseph can have been carried out of Egypt as a mummy at the start of the 18th Dynasty if he had actually served a 15th Dynasty Hyksos king. To solve the difficulty, either Joseph would have had to have lived earlier than the period of 1663 to 1570 BCE –or Moses would have had to have lived later.

If Manetho believed that Joseph was the vizier of a pharaoh of the 15th Dynasty, it was because he also thought that Moses led the Hebrews at the time of Thutmose III.

---

ladies. Successors Amenemhat II and Senusret II also built brick pyramids at Dahshur and Lahun.

Yet Clement of Alexandria,[93] following an Egyptian called "Ptolemy of Mendes", definitely places Moses in the time of the pharaoh, Ahmose:

> "Apion[94], then, the grammarian, surnamed Pleistonices, in the fourth book of The Egyptian Histories, although of so hostile a disposition towards the Hebrews, being by race an Egyptian, as to compose a work against the Jews, when referring to Amosis king of the Egyptians, and his exploits, adduces, as a witness, Ptolemy of Mendes. And his remarks are to the following effect: Amosis, who lived in the time of the Argive Inachus, overthrew Athyria[95], as Ptolemy of Mendes relates in his Chronology. Now this Ptolemy was a priest; and setting forth the deeds of the Egyptian kings in three entire books, he says, that the exodus of the Jews from Egypt, under the conduct of Moses, took place while Amosis was king of Egypt. Whence it is seen that Moses flourished in the time of Inachus." Moreover: "And from the time of Inachus to the Trojan war twenty generations or more are reckoned; let us say, four hundred years and more. And if Ctesias says that the Assyrian power is many years older than the Greek, the exodus of Moses from Egypt will appear to have taken place in the forty-second year of the Assyrian empire, in the time of Amosis the Egyptian, and of Inachus the Argive."

Clement was correct in that it was, indeed, more than 400 years from the reign of Ahmose to the Trojan Wars, but less than 500. We now see how well –known this fact was to the ancient historians, even to the time of Clement, who wrote three centuries after the Common Era. We also observe how

---

[93] Full name Titus Flavius Clemens (150?-215?), early father of the Christian church and author of "The Miscellany".

[94] The same Egyptian author who is the subject of the *Against Apion* of Flavius Josephus.

[95] Pi-Hathor.

positively Moses was connected to Ahmose[96]and we can also at this point, comprehend how easy it would have been for Ahmose (or a king named Thutmose) to have been named as the pharaoh in the Book of Exodus if the author had wished to chronicle **only** the expulsion of the "foreign peoples" that took place in one reign.

Clement of Alexandria: *"It is worth our while, at this point, to examine the dates of the other prophets among the Hebrews who succeeded Moses."*

It certainly is instructive to take a look at the theologian's expanded chronological remarks, as they seem to answer the question "What were the Hebrews up to for the next four centuries?"

"After the end of Moses's life, Joshua assumed the leadership of the people, and he, after waging war for sixty-five years, rested in the good land other five-and-twenty. As the book of Joshua relates, the above-mentioned man was the successor of Moses twenty-seven years. Because the Hebrews sinned, they were delivered into the hand of Chusachar king of Mesopotamia[97] for eight years, as the book of Judges mentions. But having afterwards turned to the Lord, they received for a leader Gothniel, the younger brother of Caleb, of the tribe of Judah, who, having slain the king of Mesopotamia, ruled over the people forty years. And having again sinned, the people eighteen years. But on their repentance, Aod, an

---

[96] According to the 7th century *Chronicle* of John of Nikiu, an Ethiopic text, *"Pharaoh Petissonius, who is Amosis, King of Egypt, reigned with the help of the book of the magicians Jannes and Jambres."* These last were legendary opponents of Moses.

[97] Cushan-rishathaim of Aram-naharaim, Judges 3: 8-10. Aram-naharaim is translated "highland of the two rivers" and is the high part of Syria to the North East of Palestine.

ambidextrous man of the tribe of Ephraim, was their leader for eighty years. It was he that killed Æglom.

On the death of Aod, due to their sinning again, the [Hebrews] were delivered into the hand of Jabim king of Canaan for twenty years. After him Deborah the wife of Lapidoth, of the tribe of Ephraim, prophesied; and Ozias the son of Rhiesu was high priest. Barak the son of Bener, of the tribe of Naphtali, commanded the army and, having joined battle with Sisera, Jabim's commander-in-chief, conquered him. After that Deborah ruled, judging the people forty years. On her death, the people having again strayed, were delivered into the hands of the Midianites seven years. Then the time came when Gideon, of the tribe of Manasseh, the son of Joas, fought with his three hundred men, and killed a hundred and twenty thousand, ruling forty years after. He was succeeded by the son of Ahimelech for three years and then by Boleas, the son of Bedan, the son of Charran, of the tribe of Ephraim, who ruled twenty-three years. After him, the people having sinned again, were delivered to the Ammonites eighteen years; and when at last they repented, were commanded by Jephtha the Gileadite, of the tribe of Manasseh. He ruled six years. After whom, Abatthan of Bethlehem, of the tribe of Judah, ruled seven years. Then Ebron the Zebulonite, eight years. Then Eglom of Ephraim, eight years. Some add to the seven years of Abatthan the eight of Ebrom.

The people having again transgressed, it happened they came under the power of the foreigners, the Philistines, for forty years. But on their returning [to God], they found a leader in Samson, of the tribe of Dan, who conquered the strangers in battle. He ruled twenty years. And after him, there being no one to govern, Eli the priest judged the people for forty years. He was succeeded by Samuel the prophet; in whose time Saul reigned, holding sway for twenty-seven years. He anointed David. Samuel died two years before Saul, while Abimelech was high priest. He *anointed Saul as king, who was the first ruled over Israel after the judges; the whole duration of whom, down to Saul, was four hundred and sixty-three years and seven months.*"[96]

As fascinating as it is—a glaring problem with the encapsulation of the books of Joshua and Judges by Clement of Alexandria is that it makes no mention of the Egyptian presence in Canaan, the empire having been established not so terribly long after the death of King Ahmose. In other words, much of what Clement describes was supposedly transpiring under the noses of the Egyptians, who were the masters of the Levant!

It is not at all clear how, lacking a real monarchy and an administration with clerks and annals, anybody really knew the detailed fate or chronological history of the scattered tribes of the Hebrews or Children of Israel until the advent of Saul and David, but some of it was probably recorded in a document known as *The Book of Jashar*.[97] Apparently the folk memory could not bear to acknowledge that the Egyptian yoke had only followed the Israelites to the Promised Land, even though we have testimony from Egyptian records of the "Apiru" making a stand against the pharaoh and his vassal princes in Canaan and capturing certain areas for themselves.

There are two ways to look at all this. The camp that says the struggles recorded in Joshua and Judges could not have occurred until the Late Bronze Age, the 19th Dynasty of

---

[96] By the present calculation, that means Saul was anointed king of Israel ca. 1106 BCE, presumably during the reign of Khepermaare Ramesses X (1108-1098 BCE). According to P. Clayton, *Chronicle of the Pharaohs*, "*...the great influence and possessions of Egypt to the north-west, into Palestine and Syria, were now things of the past.*" (page 170).

[97] A lost Hebrew text, mentioned in the books of Joshua and Second Samuel. Perhaps it was the same as "*The Book of the Wars of the Lord*", Numbers 21:14. It is likely the work on which the books of Joshua and Judges is based, presumably, judging by excerpts, being a transcription of a bardic tradition, much like the Homeric one.

Egypt, might argue that the lack of acknowledgement of Egyptians in Canaan implies that the Egyptian hold on the Levant was so tenuous 40 years after the Exodus that it was not even worthy of comment. On the other hand, those who maintain the Exodus took place much earlier, could point to an Egyptian monument from the late 19th Dynasty that seems to bear witness that by then the Hebrews had already been in Canaan for so long that even the King of Egypt was now prepared to refer to these people as "Israel".

Circa 1207 BCE, a pharaoh named Merneptah proclaimed in stone that he had destroyed a nation called "Israel"[98] at about the time, by the math of Clement of Alexandria, that they were ruled by one *"Boleas of the tribe of Ephraim"*— circa 1210 BCE—yet there is no whisper of such a devastating encounter with the Egyptians in the Hebrew Bible.[99] Did the king of Egypt lie? Well, he certainly exaggerated the demise of the Israelites.

The problem of the Philistines is handled in the story of Samson in the Book of Judges, with the champion making a spectacular but unlikely single-handed slaughter among them. Then the Biblical narrative abruptly shifts to the hill-country in the north, far from the Gaza of the Philistines. After that, there is only fighting among the tribes, themselves, until the Book of Samuel, when we see that it becomes necessary once again to battle the Philistines, who, not very surprisingly, had not been entirely killed off by

---

[98] Ancient Egyptian words and names were written with "determinatives", which, ideally, give clues as to their precise meanings. On this particular stela, the designation "Israel" is written with the *people* determinative instead of the one that indicated *foreign land*. This is a rather convincing sign that Merneptah was dealing with a "tribe" instead of, say, a kingdom or city whose people tended to remain within certain boundaries.

[99] Unless, by some chance, the "children of Ammon", mentioned in Judges 10:7, included the Egyptians this time. *"And the anger of the Lord was kindled against Israel and he gave them over into the hand of the Philistines, and into the hand of the children of Ammon. And they oppressed and crushed the children of Israel that year."*

Samson—or by a powerful successor of Merneptah, Ramesses III, who fought them, as well. In fact, in this skirmish, Israel lost 30,000 men and the Ark of the Covenant was captured. Yet it was returned, we are told, because of a plague that broke out among the Philistines, who arrived at the conclusion that it was a punishment from the God of Israel for having seized this holy object from His people.[100]

So, yes, if we follow the chronology conveniently laid out by Clement of Alexandria, we can get from the reign of Ahmose, whom he and others considered the Pharaoh of the Exodus, to the sway of Merneptah—where we need to be in order to discuss the final phase of our Exodus Chronicles. However, Biblical archaeology does not by and large support such an early timeframe for the period of the books of Joshua and Judges as the beginning of the 18th Dynasty—if it can be said to corroborate these texts at all.

To make a long and heated controversy short, the earliest evidence for a conquest of Canaan has been suggested at around 1400 BCE, far too late for the reign of Ahmose, who died in 1546 BCE by the orthodox chronology.[101] Others, like William F. Albright, the leading American Biblical archaeologist, proposed a much later dating scheme, which placed the Exodus at ca. 1290 BCE and the conquest of Canaan at 1250 to1200 BCE, marking the transition from the Late Bronze Age to the Iron Age. Arguments for this paradigm, combined with the mention of the cities Pithom and Raamses in the Book of Exodus, prevailed and scarcely anyone suggests any longer that the Exodus took place in the time of Ahmose, even though it is quite clear that it did, to a considerable extent[102].

---

[100] Even the King of Egypt, Ramesses V (reigned ca. 1145-1141 BCE), evidently succumbed to this plague—which may have been smallpox. At any rate, his mummy evidences the characteristic eruptions.

[101] But well-suited to the reign of Thutmose III, who certainly did conquer much of Canaan.

[102] However, when Kathleen Kenyon re-excavated Jericho in the 1950's, she found that the 13th Century destruction layer, estimated by an earlier

Other models have been proposed, in addition, one of which argues for a peaceful settlement, a kind of infiltration by the earliest Israelites into Canaan, where they co-existed with the inhabitants, taking part only in minor clashes with various peoples and amongst themselves.

As far as Egyptians are concerned, Benaiah, the son of Jehoida, a henchman of David, slew a "goodly" representative of this people with his own spear in II Samuel 23: 21. But this period is the first we read in the Bible of Israelites fighting Egyptians in Canaan. Just who was this handsome man of Egypt and why he attracted the ill-will of Benaiah one longs to know. In order to go about with a spear, the Egyptian could have been a soldier—but of which pharaoh?

Many scholars believe there is little point in wondering. They maintain that the Book of Judges is an artificial construction, peppered with anachronisms. These historians tend to see the text as being based upon half-remembered historical figures and conclude it is no more reliable than medieval "Grail" legends, or the Alexander Romance.

However, most of these scholars, if they give any credit to the Book of Exodus at all, believe the event took place in the 19th Dynasty, assigning merely 200 years to the period preceding the United Monarchy,[103] more than 250 years short of the chronology of Clement of Alexandria, who was convinced it was Ahmose who was the pharaoh hot on the heels of Moses and his people. Therefore, if the books of Joshua and Judges actually require a time span of 450 years for their narratives, one can see why modern interpreters may encounter problems attempting to squeeze it all into less than half the time.

As to the authenticity of the people involved, one of the individuals mentioned in the Book of Numbers has possibly

---

digger, John Garstang, was actually a Middle Bronze destruction dating to ca. 1560 BCE! Kenyon concluded that Jericho lay abandoned through much of the Late Bronze Age, with only a small occupation existing from around 1400-1300 BCE, most probably an unwalled settlement, the Middle Bronze Age walls having become useless.

[103] Beginning with Saul and David.

been dug up by archaeology—at least there is an ancient text mentioning his name. Over 100 fragments of plaster inscribed with black and red ink were found among the rubble of a building destroyed in an earthquake at Deir Alla, Jordan, in 1967. In the first four lines of the assembled text there are three references to a "Balaam son of Beor," exactly the name of the man who was called upon by Balak, king of Moab, to curse the Israelites. Reference to the "Book of Balaam" indicates that the writing was part of an earlier document that pre-dates the plaster text itself, which had been on the wall for some time prior to the earthquake. The Deir Alla text is evidence that Balaam was an actual person who was known as a "cursing prophet"[104] on the east side of the Jordan river, revered hundreds of years after his death, like the sages of ancient Egypt. If the Balaam of Numbers 22-24 was a living person, the chances of Balak, Moses, Joshua and all of the other persons named in the Biblical narrative being authentic are not exactly nil, either.

Let us view Clement's chronology of the Books of Joshua and Judges vis a vis the accepted chronology of ancient Egypt and see what happens:

We start with the exodus under Ahmose, ca. 1570 BCE , after which comes the passage of 65 years during which most of the adults who had left Egypt had died. This includes the 25-27 year era of Joshua, who purportedly lived to the age of 110. Before advancing upon Jericho, Joshua was visited, it is written, by an extra-terrestrial being (Joshua 5:13-15), who seemed to suggest that the Lord was with the Israelites. The destruction of the city would be, at 1530 BCE, after 40 years of wandering[105], consistent with the Middle Bronze Age estimate of archaeologist, Kathleen Kenyon. Amenhotep I, king of Egypt, would have been in the

---

[104] "Witch-doctor" is also not an inappropriate description. The Egyptians cursed people, as well, by writing their names with maledictions on pottery, which was then smashed. In the time of Ramesses III, we know that a kind of voodoo was practiced, utilizing wax figurines. The Egyptians of all periods were great believers in magic.

[105] Joshua 5:6.

middle of his reign. This pharaoh, unfortunately, left few records.

During a conflict with the Amorites, a celestial phenomenon occurred that is described in Joshua 10:12. The great leader reportedly said:

> *"Sun, stand thou still upon Gibeon; and thou Moon, in the valley of Aijalon."*

And it happened that

> *"the sun stood still, and the moon stayed, until the nation had avenged themselves on their enemies. Is this not written in the book of Jashar? And the sun stayed in the midst of heaven, and hasted not to go down about a whole day. And there was no day like that before it or after it, that the Lord hearkened unto the voice of a man; for the Lord fought for Israel."* [106]

Yet another "other-worldly being", called an "Angel of the Lord" materialized in Judges 2: 1-5 and prophesied hard times ahead for the tribes with the inhabitants of the land they wished to conquer. This apparition, if that is what it was, was a "mass-sighting" and caused much the same emotional reaction as others have done since.

> *"And it came to pass, when the Angel of the Lord spoke these words unto all the Children of Israel, that the people lifted up their voices and wept. And they called the name of that place Bochim[107]; and they sacrificed there unto the Lord."* [108]

---

[106] Time stopped for Joshua, and it ran backwards for Hezekiah (2 Kings 20: 9-11). Since it is not possible that the earth could halt its progress in relation to the sun, perhaps what was observed in the heavens amounted to a USO (Unidentified Stationary Object), visible by day and night.

[107] Weepers.

The inescapable question would be—where were these Hebrews for the past 40 years prior to the "conquest"? **Numbers** 33: 1-50 gives the whole itinerary until Jericho.[109] Aaron had gone up to Mt. Hor "*in the edge of the land of Edom*" and died there at the ripe old age of 123—forty years from the time they had left Egypt. His brother, Moses, did not have much longer on earth, himself, dying on Mt. Nebo in Moab. Why the Almighty did not allow these two stalwart old Hebrews to hang on a bit longer in order to reach their goal, even though He had preserved them to a tremendously advanced age, is rather an odd thing and, unhappily, not very plausible.

Werner Keller takes pains to discuss the "stations" of the post-Exodus period and their possible modern counterparts, but even though he is another who assumes that the Exodus took place solely in the 19th Dynasty, he does make the sensible observation that:

> *"The Bible is right if we accept that the traditions concerning the occupation of the country mingle facts from the Bronze Age and the Iron Age.... an extremely complicated and lengthy process which lasted for several centuries, but which the Bible presents to us in compressed form concentrating it all on the person of*

---

[108] These Biblical sightings of phenomena and "angels" have always intrigued me. As a result, I wrote the novella, "The Samaritan Treasure", which is part of the short fiction collection *The Samaritan Treasure* (Coffee House Press, Minneapolis, 1990). In this tale "angels" visit Nablus, Jordan, in order to inquire of a Samaritan what happened to an object left there by one of their kind thousands of years previously. Mirabile dictu, a UFO was reported in Jordan on August 15, 1967—the summer that Israel fought and won its Six Day War.

[109] According to Werner Keller and Judges 3:13, Jericho was the site of an oasis, "the city of palm trees". Keller cites Kathleen Kenyon as declaring Jericho the "oldest city in the world". After its destruction in the Middle Bronze Age, Jericho was not rebuilt until the 9th Century BCE, in the day of King Ahab (I Kings 16:34) (Keller).

Joshua...Many scholars are of the opinion that the subsequent influx of Israelites occurred in several waves."[110]

To illustrate his point, Keller offers the example of Joshua assembling "all Israel" at Shechem, "*as well as the stranger, as he that was born among them.*"[111] Keller begs the rhetorical question "What strangers?" as the Israelites had presumably just entered the Promised Land.

A good explanation, in my opinion, would be that the original Hyksos-cum-Hebrews, who left during the assault on the Delta by Ahmose I, had by then already been joined by others, who had left in fear of the warrior pharaoh, Thutmose I, in Joshua's own time. And there were many more refugees to come in the not-too-distant future, if Manetho is correct.

Just when was this time of a pharaoh named Thutmose making a treaty with the current inhabitants of Avaris, allowing them to depart without bloodshed? Was this the occasion of yet another exodus—recorded nowhere by the king due to the fact that it was not a great military victory? Queen Hatshepsut, the female pharaoh, engraved a text on the façade of a little temple, known as the Speos Artemidos by the Greeks, in Middle Egypt. Among other things, it gave the information:

> "....*the Asiatics were in Avaris of the North Land, barbarians in the midst of them, overturning what had been made, and they ruled without Re, and he acted not with divine command down to the time of My Majesty.*"

---

[110] Pages 168-169 of *The Bible As History*.

[111] Joshua 8:33.

Certain scholars, like Sir Alan Gardiner, accused Hatshepsut of exaggeration and doing "*scant justice to the merits of her predecessors*", but what if the queen was telling the truth and the foreigners were a more immediate concern for her than has been suspected?

The fact is, there is one ancient tradition that holds that the Year 490 of the period starting with Abraham, which could be 1510 BCE, was the date of an exodus. This year, 60 years after the expulsion of the Hyksos, would have fallen within the 13-year reign of Thutmose II, half-brother and spouse of the amazing Hatshepsut. This king would seem an unlikely "Tethmosis", but when Hatshepsut wrote "*the time of My Majesty*", what she really may have meant was the time when she was a mere consort of her brother.

Thutmose II, whose prenomen was Akheperenre, seems an insignificant pharaoh as far as recorded history is concerned. Little is known about his rule by Egyptology, except that it saw successful campaigns both in Palestine and Nubia. Judging by his mummy, scholars have pronounced him a "sickly individual". Thutmose II was between 30 and 35 when he died. Professor G. Elliot Smith, the anatomist, wrote of him:

"*The skin of the thorax, shoulders and arms (excluding the hands), the whole of the back, the buttocks and legs (excluding the feet) is studded with raised macules varying in size from minute points to patches a centimeter in diameter. The skin of the head is not affected. A condition precisely similar to this is also found in the mummy of Amenothes II and in a less marked form in Thoutmosis III; and the question is raised as to whether these macules are due to some cutaneous eruption or are the result of the action of the preservative bath post mortem. On the whole I am inclined to to look upon them as the manifestation of some disease, the nature of which is not altogether clear.*"[112]

Smith's contemporary, Gaston Maspero, made the observations:

"He had scarcely reached the age of thirty when he fell a victim of some disease of which the process of embalming could not remove the traces. The skin is scabrous in patches and covered with scars, while the upper part of the [scalp] is bald; the body is thin and somewhat shrunken, and appears to have lacked vigour and muscular power."

Thutmose II was 1m 684 mm tall[113], and the extreme wrinkling of his face suggests he was, in life, rather a chubby individual. He had been born of a secondary wife of Thutmose I named Mutnofret. The pharaoh had two brothers, Wadjmose and Amenmose[114] and two sisters, Hatshepsut and Neferubity. Strange to say, there was even a certain

---

[112] *The Royal Mummies* (Cairo, 1912).

[113] About 5'7" or 5' 8" in life, a very normal height for an ancient Egyptian, the average male height being 5'6".

[114] Also possibly a third, Prince Ramose. (Joyce Tyldesley, *Hatchepsut* (London, 1996) page 75. Tyldesley cautions that we are " *in some danger*

Amenhotep, who styled himself "First King's Son (of Thutmose I) even though he supplies the names of his actual commoner parents! Thutmose II had a daughter, Neferure, by Hatshepsut and his son, the future Thutmose III, was born of a concubine named Isis. Thutmose II may also be the "Chebron" of Manetho. After his death, his sister/wife, Hatshepsut, preferred to ignore his existence in every way and always stressed her relationship to her late father, Thutmose I, who, according to her, had always meant his daughter to be his heir in the first place.

Was Thutmose II really capable of forming a great army, besieging Avaris once again and causing the inhabitants to flee? We cannot know, but it is known for certain that his son was more than equal to the task. Again, the 1510 year is calculated simply by assuming the convenient, millennial datum of 2000 BCE for Abraham—and could have been off by any number of years in relation to actual Egyptian historical dating.[115]

If we take the chronology of the Bible and that of Clement of Alexandria literally and Jericho was devastated in 1530 BCE with Joshua living 25 more years or so, the 8 years that follow the death of Joshua[116] make up the era of

---

of underestimating Thutmose II's military prowess, and indeed of underestimating his entire personality". However, she quotes H. E. Winlock, who wrote: *"The young king Thutmosis II was a youth of no more than twenty, physically frail and mentally far from energetic, who let the country run itself. Old officials who had started their careers in the day of his grandfather—and even of his great-grandfather—occupied their places throughout his reign, and it was his father's generals who suppressed a rebellion which broke out in Nubia."* (page 82).

[115] Amenemhat I, we will recall, did not take the throne until 1991 BCE and reigned for nearly 30 years. Perhaps it was not until his Year 20, (1971 BCE) when his son, Senusret, was associated with him as co-regent, that the Era of Abraham began. 490 years later would be 1481 BCE, fitting admirably to Year 22 of Thutmose III.

[116] Even though Joshua supposedly lived to be over a hundred, the Bible says that *the Lord remained on the side of the Israelites for as long as the elders who had been with him were still alive* (Joshua 24:31). That would

Cushan-rishathaim, which corresponds to ca. 1497. The four-decade era of peace under the leadership of Othniel the son of Kenaz, the "Gothniel" of Clement of Alexandria, ended ca. 1457.

Meanwhile, sometime previous to 1457 BCE, a young pharaoh called Menkheperre Thutmose III had come of age and Hatshepsut, his overbearing aunt and regent, was gone. This king, now sole ruler of Egypt, decided to march into Canaan, the combination of his internalized anger and military genius making him a lethal weapon. In the 22nd year of his long reign, when he may not have been much older than 22, himself, Thutmose III recorded that he and his army passed through the fortress of Djaru in order to extend the frontiers of his empire and to quell the rebellion that was taking place in Syria-Palestine. The time of departure was the Fourth Month of Peret (Winter), day 25.[117] In later times, the month would have been called "Pharmouti". This would indicate that, in reality, there cannot have been so much tranquility in Canaan until the Egyptian king and his forces had finished their campaign.

Whether one takes the lower date of the 16th of April 1468 BCE or the higher one of April 20, 1482 BCE[118] as the corresponding date for this day in the 22nd year of Thutmose III, neither is going to match to the 15th of Nisan. That would have come and gone some days previously and the Hebrew month of Iyar would have already begun.[119]

---

seem to imply that an indeterminate amount of time passed, perhaps not accounted for by Clement of Alexandria.

[117] Curiously, according to Joshua 5: 10-12, the Israelites began their foray into Canaan at Passover or the "Feast of Unleavened Bread", the place named Gilgal being their starting point.

[118] As argued by some modern scholars.

[119] That is, had there actually been a Hebrew calendar at that time, as we know it today. This calendar is supposed to have begun with Moses—but when?

Just a month earlier, while still in Egypt, the pharaoh's attention was called to a very strange thing in the sky by the "scribes of the House of Life,"[120] according to a spurious document called the Tulli Papyrus.[121]

"In the year 22, in the 3rd month of winter, at the 6th hour of the day[122]... the scribes from the House of Life saw a circle of fire appear in the sky... it had no head and its breath was fetid. Its body was one rod long and one rod wide... It had no voice. As the scribes were confused by this thing, they threw themselves to the ground.. they went to the pharaoh... to tell him.

His Majesty ordered... and henceforth everything was recorded in the rolls of papyrus. His Majesty meditated on and thought about this event. Hence, after a few days, these things appeared even more numerous in the sky. They shone in the sky, brighter than the sun, and extended to the limits of the four pillars in the sky... The position of the circles of fire was powerful. The Pharaoh's army contemplated them."

His Majesty stood in the middle. It was at supper time. Then these circles of fire rose higher in the sky and towards the South. Fish and poultry fell from the sky. A marvel never before observed since the foundation of the nation. And the Pharaoh had incense brought, which was burned in order to bring peace on earth... And these events were inscribed on the Pharaoh's orders in the annals of the House of Life... so that they would never be forgotten."

---

[120] The "Per-Ankh", a place where records were kept, presumably all the wisdom of ancient Egypt.

[121] The papers of Egyptologist Professor Alberto Tulli, connected to the Vatican Museum, are reported to contain references to a UFO sighting at the court of Thutmose III. The papyrus to which Tulli refers and the translation of it have been declared a hoax—justly or unjustly.

[122] Mid-day.

Whether true or invented, the "sighting" is interesting because it would have occurred at a period when, by the testimony of the Bible, such things were hardly rare. The timing of the departure for Canaan might be significant—mid-April! Was there anyone remaining in the eastern Delta who thought it best to flee before the king of Egypt, fearful of his intentions, as he made his way there on the way to Tjaru with an army large enough to face a tremendous enemy host? Manetho , the Egyptian priest, thought so.

And why does God say to Moses in Exodus 32: 34 *"And now go, lead the people unto the place of which I have spoken unto thee; behold, Mine angel shall go before thee..."*? The fact is, the Torah abounds with angels/extraterrestrials and strange phenomena. Even today, the small country of Israel continues to have a disproportionately large number of reports of such goings on.

The annals of Thutmose III, copied onto the walls at Karnak, in which he gives the date of the start of his Levantine campaign, contain an intriguing but dismayingly damaged section of text:

> *"Now this was a [long] time in years...plunder, while every man was [serving] before....But it happened in later times that the garrison there was in the town of Sharuhen, while from Yerdi to the outer ends of the earth had become rebellious against his majesty."*

This enigmatic passage has been interpreted in various ways. Kurt Sethe, for one, thought it said that the Hyksos had ruled Egypt from Avaris and were driven to Sharuhen by Ahmose I, these same people now being in revolt against Thutmose III. Others have interpreted the text as indicating that the Asiatic rebels had pushed the Egyptians from their more northerly garrisons so that the soldiers of the pharaoh remained posted only at Sharuhen, which was at the extreme south of Canaan.

But we see in Joshua 19:6 that Sharuhen had been apportioned to the tribes of Judah and Simeon as one of the cities that were to belong to them, so it is possible even this fortress was no longer under Egyptian control. However, in Judges 1:1, it is noted that these same tribes formed a pact to go to fight the Canaanites and made a general slaughter wherever they went. It may have been that, in Year 22 of Thutmose III, Sharuhen was emptied of its men of valor, making it an easy first stage for the pharaoh's invasion of Canaan.

For us to imagine that a new wave of Hyksos, made up of various types, including Minoans, preceded this pharaoh out of Egypt by treaty is highly speculative, yet it is probably our last chance to reconcile the traditional date of departure with the assertion of Manetho that the Hebrews left Egypt in the reign of "Thummosis". The next and last pharaoh by that name was Thutmose IV, a man who ruled for about a decade and seemed to capitalize on the fact that his warlike father, Amenhotep II, had subdued Canaan. In other words, Thutmose IV was not a military individual and all we know of him in that department is that he quelled a rebellion in Nubia in his Year 8.

Jewish legend has it that the king of Egypt accompanied the Children of Israel to make sure they left Egypt,[123] but there is also the notion that the pharaoh thought they were going into the desert for three days in order to offer sacrifices, no doubt the ones the Egyptians would have found offensive.[124] Within a short time, the king sent his officers after the people, who claimed they were under the impression they had been told to leave for good. A fight ensued, whereupon some of the Egyptians were wounded or killed. Those who lived went back and reported to the king what had occurred. Meanwhile, Moses instructed the Hebrews to go back to Pi-Hahirot because *"he did not desire the departure of his people to have the appearance of flight before the Egyptians."*

---

[123] Ginzberg, supra, Volume III, page 6.

[124] The rabbinic tradition holds that the Exodus took place on a Thursday. Ginzberg, supra, Vol.III, page 10.

As long as we are on the subject of Jewish legends, we may as well interject the one that tells of the Israelites living peacefully in Egypt for 180 years until Ganon, a descendant of Joseph, of the tribe of Ephraim, announced that God had instructed him to lead the people out of the land.[125]   The Ephraimites were the only ones who paid attention to Ganon and they departed, finding themselves presently at Gath, a city of the Philistines.   The Ephraimites asked the men of Gath to sell them some sheep and when they refused, there was a skirmish. This brought down the wrath of the chiefs of the other Philistine cities upon the Hebrews and only ten of the Ephraimites escaped with their lives to return to Egypt. Such is the explanation for Moses avoiding "the way of the Philistines" when it was his turn to be the leader of an exodus.

Louis Ginzberg's work contains some interesting remarks upon the mysterious place, Pi-hahirot, which has been thought to contain the Semitic word for "reeds", but which also begins with the Egyptian term "pr" (vocalized "pi") or "house/temple/place",   amounting   to   an   unlikely combination of these two tongues.

"Accordingly, they retraced their steps to Pi-hahiroth, where two rectangular rocks form an opening, within which the great sanctuary of Baal-zephon was situated. The rocks are shaped like human figures, one a man and the other a woman, and they were not chiseled by human hands, but by the Creator, Himself. The place had been called Pithom in earlier times but, later, on account of the idols set up there, it received the name Hahiroth."[126]

---

[125] Ginzberg, supra, Vol. III, page 6.

[126] Pithom would have been "Per Atum" and already dedicated to a god, that being Atum, the manifestation of Re as the setting sun. It would have been situated in the Wadi Tumilat. If the Jewish lore contains any wisdom, then "Pi-Hahiroth" must have been "Pr-Hwt-Hrty", meaning "the house of the sanctuary of the two gods". If the male deity was Baal-zephon (Baal of the North), then perhaps the female was Hathor, the chief goddess of the eastern Delta. Baal, of course, was a Canaanite god, and Hathor was identified with his feminine counterpart , known as Baalath.

Once they were out of Egypt, one might be tempted to consider the idea that some of the new wave of migrants, the former Minoans, could have settled along the coast of Canaan, near a sea that attracted them more than inland sites, taking a clue from the fact that Thutmose III, himself, never conquered any of what would become known as the strongholds of the Philistines in his subsequent campaigns, with the exception of Gaza, perhaps honoring a pact he had made with the settlers. But, of course, a "Philistine presence" in the Levant prior to ca. 1200 BCE is too tough a morsel for most people to swallow.

Curiously, the rabbinic tradition holds that the reason the Hebrews, themselves, did not attempt to conquer this fertile territory at once, nor even venture near it, was because "*Abraham had sworn a solemn oath to live at peace with the Philistines during a certain period, and the end of the term had not yet arrived.*"[127]

The difficulty is that not all those who lived in the area called "Philistia" were the same people. For instance, Abimelech, king of Gerar, with his Semitic name (see Genesis 20-21, 26) was not likely one of the Philistines of Judges even though he lived "*in the land of the Philistines*", an anachronism in the time of Abraham. According to the Old Testament (Amos 9:7; Jeremiah 47:4; Deuteronomy 2:23), the Philistines came from Caphtor, which is probably Crete. But these were not necessarily the Philistines of the Iron Age who were renowned workers of metal, as Crete is not a place to have fostered such a craft.

We have already noted that the term "Philistines" was an anachronism in the Book of Genesis and probably while Joshua lived, as well:

"*Now Joshua was old and well stricken in years; and the Lord said to him: 'Thou art old and well stricken in years, and there* remaineth *yet very much land to be possessed.*

---

[127] Ginzberg, supra, Vol. III, page 7.

This is the land that yet remaineth: all the regions of the Philistines, and all the Geshurites; from the Shihor, which is before Egypt, even unto the border of Ekron northward—which is counted to the Canaanites; the five lords of the Philistines: the Gazite, and the Ashdodite, the Ashkelonite, the Gittite and the Ekronite; also the Avvim on the south..." [128]

The list of unconquered territories continues, but one is mindful of the fact, having been advised in Deuteronomy 2:23 about the Avvim *"that dwelt in villages as far as Gaza"* until the Caphtorim (Cretans) destroyed them and *"dwelt in their stead"*, we are now supposed to credit that the erstwhile "Caphtorim", the Philistines, are living alongside the Avvim. Perhaps what Joshua 13 means is that Gaza, Ashkelon, Ashdod, Gath and Ekron had not been conquered by anyone (prior to the arrival of Thutmose III) and that the "Caphtorim" had not yet arrived to vanquish the Avvim. Who the five lords of the Philistine cities were at that time is anybody's guess.

We do not know of Egyptians battling the Philistines until the 20th Dynasty when Ramesses III, the last truly great pharaoh, defended Egypt, in his Year 8, from an attack by a coalition of "Sea-Peoples", including the "Peleset":

"I extended all the boundaries of Egypt. I overthrew them who invaded them from their lands. I slew the Denen [who are] in their isles, the Tjeker and the Peleset were made ashes. The Sherden and the Weshesh of the sea, they were made as those that exist not, taken captive at one time, brought as captives to Egypt, like the sand of the shore I settled them in strongholds bound in my name."

Because of his beneficence to these enemies, some scholars believe that it was Ramesses III who used them as mercenaries in his garrisons in places such as Gaza, Beth Shean, and Dor. When Egyptian imperial power waned and

---

[128] Joshua 13:1-6

the soldiers of the forts became free agents, the Philistines were born. Perhaps, but if the Peleset were not *already* the Philistines, who were they and where from? Even though they were allied with other islanders, Ramesses III does not actually say the Peleset lived on an island, anymore than did the Tjeker, who were probably sea-pirates quartered in the port of Dor.

During the childhood of Thutmose III, something had happened to the Israelites. They had begun to mingle. Judges 3:5-6 discloses: *"And the children of Israel dwelt among the Canaanites, the Hittites, and the Amorites and the Perizzites, and the Hivites and the Jebusites; and they took their daughters to be their wives, and gave their own daughters to their sons, and served their gods."* That is why, the Bible asserts, a king of the north, called "Cushan-Rishathaim" obtained dominance over them.

The Gebel Barkal Stela, erected by Thutmose III in his 47th Year, contains an extract from his first war with another northern enemy referred to only as "that wretched enemy of Kadesh". We will remember Josephus quoting Manetho regarding an Egyptian king named "Thummosis" setting out with 480,000 men, a very great army in those times. The following might explain why:

> *"He (Amen-Ra) entrusted to me the foreign countries of Retenu on the first campaign, when they had come to engage with my majesty, being millions and hundred-thousands of men, the individuals of every foreign country, waiting in their chariots—330 princes, every one of them having his own army"*

The annals of Karnak give the same and other details:
> *"That wretched enemy of .Kadesh has come and entered into Megiddo. He is there at this moment. He has gathered to him the princes of every foreign country [which had been] loyal to Egypt, as well has those of Naharin and*

Mitanni, them of Hurru, them of Qode, their horses, their armies [and their people]."

These rebels against the domination of Egypt had decided to gather in Megiddo, a fortified place. In Year 23, first month of the third season (Shomu) on the feast of the day of the "true new moon", King Thutmose appeared in a golden chariot at dawn. The siege of Megiddo lasted for seven months.

"Then they saw his majesty prevailing over them and they fled headlong [to] Megiddo with faces of fear. They abandoned their horses and their chariots of gold and silver...."

Thutmose made the observation, to his men, that the capture of Megiddo *"is the capturing of a thousand towns"* due to the fact that all the rebel leaders had taken refuge within it. They could not outlast the strong-willed pharaoh and decided to surrender. This battle or siege is what gave rise to the term "Armageddon" (Megiddo), for it was *the* showdown of showdowns, the day of reckoning for the people of the Levant. The Egyptians carried off a tremendous amount of booty from the place and made the princes swear an oath:

"We will not repeat evil against Menkheperre [Thutmose], who lives forever, our good lord, in our lifetime, inasmuch as we have seen his power, and it has pleased him to give us breath. It was his father who did it—[Amen-Ra]—it was not the hand of a man!

Then my majesty ordered them given leave to go to their cities. They all went on donkey-back, so that I might take their horses. I took captive of the townspeople thereof for Egypt, and their possessions likewise."

It is not difficult to understand, with the intervention of the mighty warrior, Thutmose, how the long period of peace mentioned in Judges 3:11 became possible and even mandatory, as the king returned to Canaan on several more occasions to quell rebellions or simply to replenish his coffers, taking back inhabitants to be enslaved every time. His "Hymn of Victory" to the god, Amen, in the temple at Karnak boasted, probably not very idly:

"I bind the barbarians of Nubia by the ten-thousands and thousands, the northerners by hundred-thousands as living captives....I cause thy victories to circulate in all lands. The gleaming serpent, who is upon my brow, is thy servant, so that there shall arise none rebellious to thee as far as that which heaven encircles."

Portrait of Thutmose III as a young man by the author

As a matter of fact, the king led campaigns every April for the next twenty years. One suspects that this is the time other pharaohs passed through the eastern Delta and the fortress of Tjaru on their way to Asia, as well, making April the optimum time for the author of the Book of Exodus to date the departure of the Hebrews from the Delta—for that is the month a king of Egypt and his army would normally have been in proximity to pursue them. Arthur Weigall, one of the more gifted writers involved with Egyptology at the turn of the 20th Century said it with great flair:

"Thutmose III went regularly every summer[129] to the wars, and returned to Thebes at the end of September or beginning of October, bringing with him the wealth he had captured in Syria[130] or the Sudan. It was then that the people of Thebes obtained their glimpses into the outside world, and learned to admire the luxury of conquered Syria and to despise its people. Each year the fleet of war galleys moored in front of the city discharged onto the crowded quays the wretched, bedraggled prisoners who had been brought here to work for the rest of their lives as slaves. Each year the loot from the Syrian cities—golden vases, fine linens, splendid arms and armour, gilded chariots, and numbers of horses—was conducted through the thronged streets of the palace. Each year the soldiers of the victorious army paraded through the city, and the sounds of martial music were heard as frequently as were the chants of the priests."[131]

One might ask—why did King Thutmose tell the foreigners to leave Egypt's Delta precisely at the time he was planning a Canaanite campaign? Did it not occur to the pharaoh that he might have to fight all these people eventually in Asia? As incredible as it might seem, perhaps Thutmose and the "neo-Hyksos" had become allies, part of their pact being that they would be allowed to settle in Canaan once they had assisted the Egyptians in subduing the inhabitants—true mercenaries, just as some of the "Sea-Peoples" became for Ramesses III much later. And is that why they had been given leave to go from Avaris without any blood-letting in the first place—and why the Hebrew Bible doesn't mention any strife with Egyptians while the Conquest took place?

---

[129] What Weigall meant was that he departed during the season of Shomu.

[130] Read "Canaan".

[131] *Antiquities of Egypt* (London, 1910) page 64.

After 40 years, Eglon, king of Moab, "smote Israel" and the people were forced to serve him 18 years until ca. 1439 BCE—probably about the time the bellicose son of Menkheperre Thutmose, Amenhotep II, executed seven Asiatic princes and deported thousands more people to Egypt.

> "....after His Majesty had returned from Upper Retenu and had overthrown all those disloyal to him, extending the boundaries of Egypt in the first campaign of victory. His Majesty returned joyful of heart to his father Amen when he had slain with his own club the seven chieftains who had been in the district of Takhsy, they being placed head downwards at the prow of His Majesty's ship of which the name is 'Aakheperure[132] the Establisher of the Two Lands'. Then six of these enemies were hanged on the face of the enclosure wall of Thebes, the hands likewise[133], and the other enemy was shipped up to Nubia and hanged upon the enclosure wall of Napata in order to cause to be seen the victorious might of His Majesty for ever and ever."

Amenhotep II might seem an excessively cruel man, but Joshua, himself, hung the king of Ai from a tree (Joshua 8:29) and killed all his subjects. The rulers of Jerusalem, Hebron, Yarmuth, Lachish and Eglon fared no better at the hands of the successor of Moses (Joshua 10:26), becoming fodder for the crows while swinging from branches. These were brutish times.

After Year 9 of Amenhotep II, there was little trouble in Canaan and he seems to have continued as king until 1419

---

[132] The prenomen of Amenhotep II.

[133] Severed hands by the basketful is how the army determined how many of the enemy it had killed.

BCE.[134] The next pharaoh, Thutmose IV, reigned for a decade, the greater details of which we do not know, until he was succeeded by his youthful son, Amenhotep III, who sat on Egypt's throne for nearly 40 years. The latter was a canny diplomat who kept the pax Egyptiaca in the Levant. Therefore, it is easy to believe that the Israelites experienced a fairly tranquil existence for "four-score years"—after Ehud the left-handed son of Gera, the "Aod" of Clement, killed the King of Moab in Judges 3:21. Another hero, Shamgar the son of Anath, surfaced to subdue the Philistines by slaying 600 of them with an ox-goad.

1359 BCE brings us to the reign of the heretic, Akhenaten, and his ephemeral and/or rather feeble successors, including Tutankhamen, whose grip on the empire had, we have seen, loosened considerably. At this time, a certain Jabin, king of Canaan[135], with his seat at Hazor, had a captain named Sisera who commanded "*900*

---

[134] The mummy of the pharaoh shows evidence that smallpox caused his death. He was a middle-aged man of medium height with fine, slightly wavy hair, which was balding somewhat.

[135] Due to the continued existence of the Egyptian empire, it is not very likely that there could have been a "king of Canaan". In fact, Canaan consisted, at that time, of numerous city-states ruled by petty princes, who answered to the pharaoh, so Jabin's influence would have been limited to Hazor. It may even have been that Jabin was "Commissioner of Canaan", highest-ranking official of the king of Egypt in the Levant and an attested title. The name is contemporary and is probably the same as "Yabnilu" a prince of Lachish at the time of Akhenaten—but not the same person as Hazor was in the north and Lachish in the south. Not all the officers of the pharaoh in Canaan had Egyptian names, yet "Sisera" is suspiciously Egyptian, just as "Siseres" is the Greek rendering of the Egyptian "Shepseskare". ("Sisera" would be even better suited to the Egyptian name "Shepsyre", the /p/ being unlikely to be vocalized.) The Amarna Letters, the archived correspondence between King Akhenaten and his vassal princes, reveals that assassination was a hazard of serving in Canaan. An Egyptian official named "Pawer" ("the Great One") was murdered, but it is not certain whether this is a personal name or a designation. When the pharaoh was informed that his man had been killed, it was said "*The corpse was cast away. It had no one for funerary offerings.*"

chariots of iron".[136] These men oppressed Israel for 20 years until a heroine named Yael drove a tent-peg through Sisera's temple, killing him. When the era of Jabin ended ca. 1339 BCE, a forceful commander had arisen under Tutankhamen's kingship, named Horemheb.

> "*He was sent as King's messenger as far as the sun disc shines, returning when he had triumphed, when his [conquest] was effected. No land could stand before him...and he does not leave off in going north....the army, filling the storehouse of the god, (the pharaoh), who was satisfied at heart...which Syria gave to them....he was serviceable to the king.*"

Horemheb, the victorious general, eventually became king of Egypt, himself. A new Sothic Period had begun in the four-year timeframe of 1321-1317 BCE. It may be that, by 1317, Seti I was already king because he called his era that of "*wHm mswt*" or "repeating births". In other words, a renaissance. But, according to the accepted chronology, Horemheb was still pharaoh at that time. Regardless, Egypt was making a strong showing in the Levant again and it is little wonder that the prophetess Deborah was able to sit in calm judgment under her palm tree for the next 40 years until ca.1299 BCE, with a new crop of aggressive pharaohs in power.

It was in his tenth year that the Hittite king, Mursilis II, recorded an ominous portent of the sun.[137] The solar eclipse

---

[136] These give the impression of having been some type of wheeled contraptions, perhaps the world's first "tanks", from which archers could safely let loose their arrows. Although 900 of these seems an excessive number, we know that, by now, the iron-age had truly already begun because objects fashioned from this metal were discovered in the tomb of Tutankhamen. Probably, the "iron chariots" merely had iron components, just as Ahab's "House of Ivory" contained ivory decorations but was built of stone.

[137] Astrom, Paul, "*The Omen of the Sun in the Tenth Year of the Reign of Mursilis II*", in *Studies in Early Art and Archaeology in Honour of Professor Homer L. Thomas* (1993).

of April 13th 1308 BCE is most probably what Mursilis experienced. Since he probably reigned between 1317 and 1295/1287BCE, some scholars believe 1279 BCE to be the most likely date for the accession of Ramses II—known to history as Ramesses the Great.

In his Year 5, Ramesses II mobilized his army, doubtless due to the unrest described in Judges 6:1-6. Despite the presence of the king of Egypt in Canaan, culminating in the Battle of Kadesh between Egypt and the other super-power of the day, the Hittites, the Bible says the Midianites, the Arabs, oppressed the Israelites for the next seven years. But Gideon the son of Joash fought his own war, taking the very earrings from the lobes of the "Ishmaelites", not forgetting the valuable trappings of their camels. Another four decades of rest ensued during the 68-year reign of Ramesses II, whose treaty with the Hittites—whereupon they divided Canaan between them—surely contributed to this lull.

In 1252 BCE, the king of Egypt still remained firmly ensconced on his golden throne but problems arose for the Israelites during the 3-year leadership of Abimelech. Things were evidently set right through the efforts of one Tola, a man of the tribe of Issachar, who dwelt in Shechem of the hill-country of Ephraim. Clement of Alexandria calls the new judge "Boleas", instead. Twenty-three years later, it is ca. 1226 BCE and Prince Merneptah has taken over most of the duties of his aged father, officially succeeding him, according to Egyptology, in 1212 BCE. At this point[138], somewhere between 1226 and 1207 BCE, Israel is devastated, although the Book of Judges does not lay the responsibility at the feet of Merneptah, who claimed it nonetheless.

> **Judges** 10: 7- "....And the anger of the Lord was kindled against Israel, and he gave them over into the hand of the Philistines, and into the hand of the children of Ammon. And they oppressed and crushed the children of Israel that

---

[138] The "Israel Stela" is dated the 3rd month of Shomu, Year 5 of King Merneptah.

year; eighteen years [oppressed they] all the children of Israel that were beyond the Jordan in the land of the Amorites, which is in Gilead. And the children of Ammon passed over the Jordan to fight also against Judah, and against Benjamin, and against the house of Ephraim, so that Israel was sore distressed. And the children of Israel cried unto the Lord, saying: 'We have sinned against Thee, in that we have forsaken our God and have served the Baalim.' And the Lord said unto the children of Israel: 'Did I not save you from the Egyptians, and from the Amorites, from the children of the children of Ammon, and from the Philistines? The Zidonians, also, and the Amalekites, and the Maonites, did oppress you; and ye cried unto Me, and I saved you out of their hand. Yet ye have forsaken Me, and served other gods; wherefore I will save you no more. Go and cry unto the gods which ye have chosen; let them save you in the time of your distress.'"

Instead, this period of strife is designated the era of the Ammonites, who oppressed Israel for 18 years[139] until Jephthah the Gileadite led the people to make a great slaughter among them. In fact, in Judges 11:26, it is **stated that the Hebrews had now been in the Levant for 300 years since leaving Egypt**, which is, **perfectly correct**, if we accept the date of 1510 for an exodus and 1210 BCE as the date of the decimation of Israel![140] This passage from Judges has been fated to be largely ignored by scholars because it does not fit to the popular concept that there was only one Exodus during the latter part of the 19th Dynasty---which is when Jephthah seems to have taken the field. Judges 12: 1-7 imparts the information that the tribe of Ephraim picked a quarrel with Jephthah and his followers. Thus began a feud

---

[139] Is it mere coincidence that Manetho assigned 19 years to Merneptah's kingship? However, Egyptology has not been able to vindicate this number, the pharaoh's last attested year being 10.

[140] Probably, however, that is just a "round number".

between the Gileadites and the men of Ephraim. The latter were detected when detained because they could not pronounce the "sh" in the password, which was "Shibboleth" (path), saying "Sibboleth", instead. 42,000 men of the hill country were killed during this conflict and one hardly knows how King Merneptah, himself, can have perpetrated a worse carnage.

However, if we do venture to assume the date of 1210 BCE as the year of the devastation of Israel 300 years after going out of Egypt, 180 years later emerges as 1030 BCE and the time of King Solomon and the building of the Temple, like it or not.[141] I Kings 6:1 states that **Solomon built the Jerusalem Temple 480 years after the departure of the Jews from Egypt.** In fact, as was already discussed, one tradition seems to hold that an exodus occurred in 1510 BCE—even though certain ancients were adamant that "it" had happened in the time of Ahmose I. If the Book of Kings had the 1570 date in mind instead of the 1510 year, then Solomon would have had to exist as early as 1090 BCE! Needless to say, 480 years from 1482 BCE as Year 22 of the reign of Thutmose III, Manetho's "Tethmosis", lowers the date for Solomon's greatest achievement to around 1000 BCE.

---

[141] Bible experts have assigned 968 BCE as the date of the construction of the Temple and 922 BCE as the year of the death of Solomon, surely on the assumption that there was one exodus during the reign of the 19th Dynasty of ancient Egypt. As for relevant Egyptian chronology, David Rohl has convincingly argued, in *Pharaohs and Kings*, supra, that the Third Intermediate Period of Egyptian history, which conventionally is supposed to last from 1069-525 BCE, ought to be reduced by 141 years.

Chapter Four

After this glimpse into the future, we must revert to the beginning of the 18th Dynasty and the expulsion of the Hyksos. Egyptology believes King Ahmose drove them out—and certain ancient historians agreed. Manetho disagreed and certain others took their cue from him. Manetho wrote that, when a pharaoh named Thutmose finally persuaded them to leave, they were only 240,000 strong—falling very short, indeed, of the figure provided in the Book of Exodus.[142] Probably, **all** are correct when they claim that a mass evacuation of foreigners took place in the early part of the 18th Dynasty. Whenever it was these people left, they had to go somewhere, in peace or in hostility, and there is every reason to believe they settled in Canaan, whether or not archaeologists have managed to find a significant trace of them. With the exit of this large number, those who considered themselves "ethnic Egyptians" felt that they were not only masters of the whole of Egypt again but immediately acquired the confidence to sally forth and conquer most of their neighboring countries. Thanks to some new additions to the paraphernalia of battle, adopted from the Hyksos, the Egyptians were now much better equipped to do so.

Weapons of bronze, the deadly composite bow and the horse-drawn chariot were part of the arsenal at the beginning of the 18th Dynasty. King Kamose was the first Egyptian ruler to have himself portrayed wearing the khepresh[143], the blue "crash helmet" of chariot fighters, soon to become one of the standard crowns of the pharaohs. By making vassals of these surrounding nations, the Egyptians

---

[142] Which, at 600,000 would have constituted roughly half the population of Egypt. (Redford)

[143]Semitic, meaning "cover the head".

hoped to turn themselves into the most powerful and feared entity in the Near East, preventing a recurrence of the debacle with the Hyksos. However, since the agenda of war in those days included decimating the vanquished populations by enslaving them, a situation was created that eventually amounted to a circuitous result.

> "Lo, the miserable Asiatic! It is a difficult life in the place where he is, suffering from lack of water, hidden by many trees, the paths thereof difficult because of the mountains. He does not reside in one place, but the tracks of his feet wander around. He has been fighting since the time of Horus, without conquering nor yet being conquered. He does not announce a day for fighting, like an outlawed thief or a gang of marauders."

Thus, we begin to see that the continued subjugation of Canaan was not without its downside for the Egyptians. While the pharaoh could boast of his conquests on the walls of the buildings he erected and the reckless heroes of the day could receive their reward of slaves, land and gold, it was the ordinary soldier who paid the dreary price:

> "Let me tell you the woes of the soldier, and how numerous are his superiors: the general, the troop-commander, the officer who leads, the standard-bearer, the lieutenant, the scribe, the commander of fifty, and the garrison-captain. They go in and out of the barracks, saying "Get volunteers!" This last is awakened at any hour. One is on his back as though he were a donkey. He toils until the sun-disc sets in the darkness of night. He is hungry, his belly aches; he is dead while yet alive. When he receives a grain ration, having been released from duty, it is no good for grinding.
>
> He is called up for Syria. There is no rest for him. There are no clothes, no sandals. The weapons of war are assembled at Djaru. His march is uphill through mountains. He drinks water every third day; it is smelly

91

and tastes of salt. His body is wasted with sickness. The enemy comes, surrounds him with missiles, and life recedes from him. He is told: 'Forward, on the double, valiant soldier! Win for yourself a good name!' He has no idea what he is supposed to do. His body is weak, his legs fail him. When victory is won, the captives are handed over to his majesty, to be taken to Egypt. The foreign woman faints and she is slung about the soldier's neck. His knapsack drops, another grabs it while he is burdened with the woman. His wife and children are in the village; he dies and does not reach home. If he emerges alive, he is worn out from marching.[144] Whether he leaves or stays, the soldier suffers. If he bolts and joins the deserters, his whole family is imprisoned. He dies on the edge of the desert, and there is none to perpetuate his name. He suffers in death as in life. A big sack is brought for him; one does not know his resting place."

The next text describes the "joys" of being stationed in some insufferably hot Levantine backwater or another:

"If ever a flask full of beer of Qode is opened, and people go out to get a cup (of it), there are 200 large dogs as well as 300 jackals, 500 in all, and they stand in readiness every day at the door of the house as often as I go out through their smelling the liquor when the jar is opened."

Yet another asks the question of a soldier:

"Tell me how you can go to sleep each evening with only a piece of sack-cloth over you. You slumber only because you are so exhausted. Some knave takes away your bow, your girdle-dagger, and your pair of quivers. Your reins have been severed in the darkness, and your team runs off

---

[144] Elsewhere it is written "If he comes home to Egypt, he is like a worm-eaten stick. He is ill and must lie in bed."

careening over the slippery ground as the road extends ahead of it. It smashes your chariot and makes [such a crash ?] that your leather canteens fall to the ground and are buried in the sand. They become part of the scorched earth. Your aide begs for sustenance for your mouth. 'Now that I have arrived safely, you people should give a bit of food and water.' But they play deaf and do not hearken. They take no notice of your litany of woes."[145]

Nevertheless, it was the warlike kings of the Thutmosid dynasty who waged their campaigns in the east and bedecked themselves with gold taken from subjugated Nubia, setting the stage for the next exodus. These kings brought many thousands of captives from Canaan **back to Egypt** where, as it happened, a Golden Age occurred for these displaced people within a century, some of them achieving the highest offices in the land.[146]   That was the situation by the time Akhenaten was crowned king.

And so, like all the other good periods for Semitic peoples in Egypt, it would follow that this one, too, came to an end. At the outset, the Book of Exodus tells us exactly what the problem was from the Egyptian point of view: the people from Canaan became too numerous, especially in the Delta—shades of the Hyksos of times past. Also, the Egyptians felt threatened by what would happen if these "foreigners" should decide to ally themselves with the foes of Egypt. That is what the Bible tells us, but other sources assert that this fear became a reality.

If Egyptologists claim that there are no Egyptian records to corroborate such an occurrence as is described in the Book of Exodus—that is not strictly true, as we have seen and shall see further. The pharaohs of dynastic Egypt put

---

[145] Papyrus Anastasi I.

[146] "*...the policy of deporting to Egypt...large numbers...reached its epogee under Amenophis II, who carried off 85,000 men, women and children of all social strata.*" Donald Redford, *Egypt, Canaan and Israel in Ancient Times*, Princeton University Press, New Jersey (1992).

their historical records on the walls of their temples and on stelae, tablets of stone, which they erected in various spots. But we only are advised of their victories—never their defeats. If they ever suffered adversities, they only hinted at them in a cryptic fashion, and it is these subtle messages that cause the experts to gnash their teeth. Yet one factor that can be gleaned from Egyptian texts is something that is not even hinted at in the Bible. The Book of Exodus, for some reason, would have us believe that all persons of foreign extraction residing in Egypt were impoverished and exploited, doing nothing but making bricks and otherwise laboring on the king's building projects. Ever since the era of the late Thutmosids, the Egyptian evidence increasingly tells a different tale. From it we glean that people of Semitic background, Egyptianized to a point that is difficult to determine, were more empowered than oppressed—so much so that, in the end, one of them was able to place a king on his throne and by implication run the country for and through him. We are forced to credit this contradiction of the Biblical text because it is more in keeping with the position of the Jews whenever they lived in Egypt. They did remarkably well, beginning with the legendary Joseph, himself, but their "otherness" always defeated them in the end. Somehow, the excuse to strip them of their power and possessions always conveniently presented itself, and this pretext sometimes was that "they couldn't be trusted". The words that appear at the beginning of the Book of Exodus could have been uttered by Egyptian president, Gamal Nasser, of the Twentieth Century CE when he began to arrest Egyptian citizens of the Jewish faith on suspicion of espionage for Israel:

> "Now there arose a new king over Egypt, who did not know Joseph. And he said unto his people: 'Behold, the people of the children of Israel are too many and too mighty for us; come, let us deal wisely with them, lest they multiply, and it come to pass, that, when there befalleth us any war, they also join themselves unto our

enemies, and fight against us, and get them up out of the land.'" **Exodus 1:8-10**

As was mentioned, apparently there is an Egyptian version of the events that played themselves out, featuring a man called Moses, but these accounts come to us from Egyptians who lived long after the last native king of Egypt had died.   They will be examined shortly.

I now quote historian, Eugen Weber, in his description of the anatomy of history:

> "*The events of a time very often seem chaotic at the time. Later they seem clear enough; their general lines appear evident and so do the principles of their development. And this may be because we, as it were, invent them and invest them with coherence. But it may be, too, because there really is such a thing as a general trend, a dominant tendency or climate of opinion at any one time, and that this only becomes apparent in the perspective lent by distance. Still, invented or perceived, history remains an artifact, the work of our minds and imaginations.*"[147]

Thus, history is not a totally subjective creation.   Your experiences are not mine, even though we were at the same place on a given day.   We can come from different perspectives.   Additionally, as German Egyptologist, Jan Assmann, author of *Moses the Egyptian*[148], makes the point:
"*The present is 'haunted' by the past and the past is remodeled, invented, reinvented, and reconstructed by the present.*" Antonia Fraser, in her *The Lives of the Kings and Queens of England*, asserts that "*all written history is a form of distortion*" and quotes Robert Birley, who analyzed myths in *The Undergrowth of History* and who wrote:

---

[147] From *The Western Tradition* (Lexington, Mass., 1995)

[148]Harvard University Press, Cambridge, Mass., 1997.

95

"...*apocryphal stories generally survive because they encapsulate a true facet of an historical period, however false the facts on which they are based. Thus the story of Alfred and the cakes expresses the extreme destitution of the (English) monarchy at that date, just as the story of Elizabeth, Raleigh and the cloak illustrates the chivalrous hold on her subjects' imagination which the Virgin Queen had been careful to cultivate as a measure of government.*"

There is no such thing as "absolute history", that is to say history without bias, totally devoid of chauvinism or national viewpoint. Therefore, it is hardly surprising that, while the Bible portrays Moses as a deliverer of the oppressed Hebrews, the Egyptian version makes him the chief of a gang of oppressors.

If one accepts that both sides must be taken into consideration, one will have to conclude that the Book of Exodus is a romanticized version of the events and that the Egyptian version has its defects as reliable history, as well, and both of these accounts contradict one another in fascinating ways.

For example, Exodus 8:22 says that Moses was concerned about offending the Egyptians because, in the Hebrew version, Moses is a solemn, well-intentioned, proper prince who is supported and aided by God in his every move—just the instrument of the Almighty.

> "*And Pharaoh called for Moses and for Aaron, and said: 'Go ye, sacrifice to your God in the land. And Moses said: 'It is not meet to do so; for we shall sacrifice the abomination of the Egyptians to the Lord our God; lo, if we sacrifice the abomination of the Egyptians before their eyes, will they not stone us?'*"

However, the Egyptian version does not hesitate to reveal that the "mixed multitude" that was giving the pharaoh a difficult time was looting the temples of Egypt, throwing the priests out naked, and "*roasting the sacred animals*" without any worries about being stoned, whatsoever. Not only, in this version, were the companions of Moses *suspected* of siding with Egypt's enemies—but Moses is clearly accused of allying himself with the people of Canaan[149], this enemy being only too glad to meet Moses in the Delta, which of course they took over in the manner of the Hyksos of yore—behaving even worse, as the Egyptian version is quick to point out. This chaotic time will be described in detail in a subsequent chapter of this book.

Regardless, according to Josephus, none of the negative accusations had detracted from the appeal of Moses in Egypt and one has to wonder exactly what was behind his universal popularity. Josephus, a Jew who gave us what we know of the Egyptian version of the exodoi, gleaned from the histories of the Egyptian savants, Manetho and Chaeremon[150], wrote of his ire at the way these authors portrayed Moses. Josephus found it difficult to comprehend why anyone who had formerly been an Egyptian priest, as these men claimed Moses was, would instruct his followers "*not to worship the gods nor to abstain from the flesh of the animals reverenced in Egypt*" and dismisses their entire account of Moses as a rather stupid fiction. "*The Egyptians regard him as a wonderful, even divine being, but wish to claim him as their own by an incredible calumny...*"

Yet Josephus gives no reason why Manetho and Chaeremon would want to make Moses an Egyptian, if he was not, or why the Egyptians would idolize him in the first place.

The Hertz Edition of the Pentateuch eloquently remarks, in a commentary:

> "*With the death of Joseph, a large portion of the Israelites in time forgot the religious traditions....The greater portion of the people, however, must have kept*

---

[149] The Canaanites were probably still smarting from the indignities the Ramesside dynasty had inflicted upon them in recent times.

[150] Circa First Century CE, librarian of Alexandria and later tutor of Nero. Chaeremon wrote a history of Egypt and other pieces that have not survived.

alive in their hearts the memory and hope of Israel. Otherwise it is quite impossible to understand how they maintained their separate existence during generations of oppression and still more during centuries of prosperity in a highly civilized society like the Egyptian."

It is a difficult question—without a facile answer. While some people who are enslaved may desire freedom or those who feel alienated may harbor a wish to live in a place where they feel they "belong", Egypt was simply not a country that people quit voluntarily without good cause. On the contrary, people came to Egypt because there was food there that did not depend upon sufficient rainfall to be produced. Also, the Egyptians had the foresight to make a habit of storing grain in case the Nile flooding, the source of fertile silt, failed to live up to expectations. Life in Egypt may not have been easy, but one could eat there. It was a very rich and prosperous land compared to most, the wealthiest and most progressive on earth. Even though today Egypt is a third-world country, its former exalted status among the peoples of the ancient world give modern Egyptians a native pride that transcends the reality of the poverty they must deal with on a daily basis.

Many have preferred to imagine the "Israelites" in Egypt as being rather like the Jews of Eastern Europe, for example, steeped in religion, their lives regulated by the Law despite being "strangers in a strange land". But, as Moses was the one who "laid down the law", we cannot really know what sort of people our long-ago ancestors in Egypt were prior to that—or even if they were monotheists in any sense that can be compared to our Judaism of today. On the contrary, many were probably worshippers of Canaanite gods and, as the Book of Exodus makes plain, adopted Egyptian ones, as well. Still, as some of their names contain the element "El"[151], we have proof that this deity was honored, perhaps

---

[151] As in the case of one Aper-el, a northern (Memphite) vizier of the era of Amenhotep III/Akhenaten, whose huge tomb was discovered by French Egyptologist, Alain Zivie. The son of Aper-el and his wife Taweret was called "Huy", however, short for Amenhotep.

even exclusively, by a segment of the population of Canaanite origin.

If the Israelites managed to keep their identity while in Egypt, it may have been largely due to the fact that the Egyptians preferred foreigners to remain different from themselves. Other nations were known by various appellations but only Egyptians were called "men". Egyptians were nothing if not chauvinistic, but it is too much to expect that they did not inter-marry with strangers at all. They certainly did, and so did their kings, who took foreign wives even at the time of Abraham, the Bible tells us.

Even so, the implication remained that this was not altogether desirable and an Egyptian novel, "*The Tale of the Two Brothers*", portrays the alien queen of a nameless pharaoh as a bad, scheming woman, who had seduced him with her alluring perfume. Although it is true that Ramesses the Great married at least two foreign women in order to cement a political alliance, a story from a bit of pseudo-graphia called the "Bekhten Stela" makes it appear as though one of them had been an unbalanced creature, inhabited by a demon, who required an Egyptian exorcist before she was in any shape at all to join her sister as the bride of the mighty pharaoh, whose desirability as a husband was, naturally, beyond question.

Whether such women would be allowed, like Jezebel, the queen of Ahab of Israel, to worship her own, imported gods is uncertain, but it is unlikely to have been a great problem as, by the New Kingdom, Canaanite deities were a part of the Egyptian pantheon, as matters stood. How much foreign queens had influenced this is the real unknown quantity, but their input is clear in other areas. For instance, Thutmose IV wed a daughter of the king of Mitanni, a land whose situation is rather a mystery, but it is during his reign that women's fashions change dramatically. Dresses that were formerly portrayed as tight-fitting shifts held up by two breast-revealing straps, suddenly become voluminous gowns of pleated, saffron-colored material. More jewelry is sported than ever before, including lots of bracelets and huge, medallion-like earrings. But, within the next two generations, the way women looked and dressed changed again and the art of Egypt underwent a total revolution.

During the 18th Dynasty, there came a time when monotheism was the official religion of Egypt. This was due to the reformation of Amenhotep IV, who changed his name to Akhenaten, and who was married to the famous beauty, Nefertiti. Many persons currently believe that Akhenaten exerted such an influence as to create the basis of modern Judaism and some even feel that the legendary Moses was actually none other than Akhenaten, himself. More about him anon.

While this book cannot agree with such extreme romanticism or hope to "unmask" the real Moses, other "candidates" for the honor will be brought forward. The Ten Commandments were supposedly incised in stone, but the true history of the Exodus seems to be written in sand. Yet sands are known to shift and, of course, the discovery of new material can alter history that has been reconstructed from the evidence at hand. Lacking any new building blocks, we have the option of taking apart the old edifice and reassembling it in a different shape.

Hopefully, I have by now demonstrated that an Exodus from Egypt was more than possible. It was almost guaranteed, and **for only one to have occurred in all of dynastic Egypt would have surely been too few**. Time is a vast canyon and sometimes the echoes of past voices grow faint. Nowadays Jews set aside a day in the calendar to lament the Holocaust and another to celebrate the founding of the state of Israel—these things having happened within the lifetime of our oldest generation. That is the way that things are done in Jewish life. Records are finite, but tradition has proved more durable. How far do we have to travel in that canyon before we reach the point where we can no longer recall exactly the precise details surrounding those days of commemoration? And will we still be there to debate such questions?

Chapter Five

Although human existence in ancient Egypt or Kemet—the Black Land—was primitive almost beyond modern Western comprehension, the Egyptians were not a primitive or backward people. While this appears a great contradiction, it was nevertheless true. Their accomplishments, ingenuity, artistry, and complexity are awesome to us even now. We still can't figure out how they actually built the pyramids or raised their towering obelisks and we may never know.

The ancient Egyptians have left us quite a legacy of art and writing, some of it great. We are even privileged to look upon the actual embalmed faces of these people who lived so long ago. We have so many books about ancient Egypt with so many pictures in them that we feel certain we have been able to form a good idea of how they lived. But have we really? Did the ancients merely leave us a tank-full of red herrings from which we have tried to make a meal? Were they a nation of artists and scribes so hide-bound by convention that all they portrayed, every sentence they wrote, lagged so far behind the reality of their actual culture that they might have been depicting their own ancestors instead of themselves and mimicking their language instead of writing their own? We already know that the language[152]

---

[152] "It is true that the new modes of parlance which came into existence from time to time were by no means adequately reflected in the contemporary hieroglyphic inscriptions; for in Egypt the art of writing was always reserved to a conservative and tradition-loving caste of scribes, upon whose interests and caprice it depended how far the common speech of the people should be allowed to contaminate the *mdw nTr*, ' the god's words'." Sir Alan Gardiner in *Egyptian Grammar*. Additionally, the Egyptians had a number of dialects, some of which were barely mutually intelligible, if we go by this passage from the Papyrus Anastasi I: *"....(your utterances) there is no foreign-speaking one who can interpret them. They are like the talks of a man from the Delta with a man from Elephantine."*

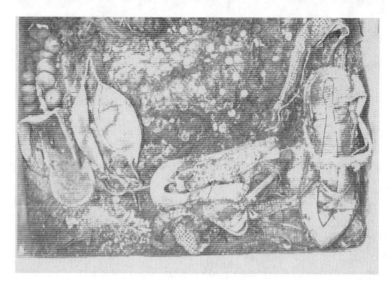

used on monuments and official documents didn't jibe with what was spoken in the streets of Thebes, in the fields, or even in the court of the pharaoh by the time of the New Kingdom.[153]

The tomb of Tutankhamen, discovered in 1922, offered further proof of how different the reality was from the iconography. A single chest from the dazzling tomb treasure told the story. In case you haven't seen it, I will show the contents of the chest to you. The photograph was taken just as it was opened. Not long afterward, much of the contents crumbled into dust. Beautiful things were carelessly thrown into this box, probably disarrayed by the robbers who stole an unknown quantity of the funerary goods before their crime was interrupted. Magnificent wearing-apparel of the ruler of all Egypt was stirred together in that chest as in a washing machine. One can make out an entire marvelous sandal so intricately fashioned that it is at once apparent that shoe-making in the 18th Dynasty was as highly evolved an art as gold-smithing. In the chest, the sandal was still near-perfect. On whose foot in all of ancient Egyptian art do we ever see a shoe such as this one? In one corner of the chest were some large beads as are usually seen hanging about the necks of Bedouin women in *National Geographic* magazine, but not the ladies of dynastic Egypt. Next to them lies a strange bit of gear that I wouldn't even hazard a guess

---

[153] According to Peter Clayton, in his *Chronicle of the Pharaohs*, this was the period from 1570 – 1070 BCE.

as to what it was—but it looks for all the world like one of the skimpy bras that constitute the top half of modern bikinis.

Whatever this is, I've never seen it depicted on an Egyptian of antiquity. There is a lot of cloth—never tested so we don't know for sure what sort—at that time still encrusted with sequins—some in the shape of stars, some discs and some squares. Some of the material is as heavily sequined as certain evening dresses of today and edged with beading like garments that are manufactured in modern India. One of the interesting items in the chest was an imitation cheetah pelt like priests and "heirs" of dead monarchs are shown wearing with a wooden head attached to it and spots made from sequins.

The contents of this box tell me that we have no real idea at all how Tutankhamen and his court dressed in spite of all the paintings, statues and reliefs. No sequins there.[154] Likewise Egyptian art never prepared us for the level of craftsmanship and design of the furniture and jewelry from the tomb. Nobody had ever imagined such wonderful and strange objects could exist.

That, I think, is the trouble. When I look at a photo of that chest I know that we can't envision how ancient Egypt really was because our imaginations are limited. And we have been misled by the art into thinking that all was streamlined simplicity and white pleated linen when it could all have been as rococo as a French queen's boudoir. Most Egyptians are shown with their faces half-obscured by heavy wigs, presumably covering shaved heads, but there are mummies of women with hair past their shoulders and once-beautiful men with hair as long as a rock star's. We have a royal lady with neatly-arranged, upswept sausage curls—some hairdresser's last effort before the bandages were

---

[154] Except possibly on the kilt of Ay, the successor of Tutankhamen, as shown in a painting in the tomb. Ay is also the first pharaoh known to me to have been portrayed wearing a red kilt instead of the usual white one. These pictorial innovations are surely due to the changes brought about by Akhenaten, Tutankhamen's putative father, in whose reign we see not only a religious and iconographic reformation but also changes in the written language.

carefully wound around the coiffure. Where do things like this fit into our conception of ancient Egypt? Where are the other paintings of red leather gloves such as we are allowed to see but once (and never, ever such wonders of glove-making as King Tut wore) and where are all the green shoes (yes shoes, not sandals, and green was the favorite shade) that have come down to us?

That's why, every once in a while, I look into that disordered box. It's just to remind me that the image I have of ancient Egypt isn't real. It's fascinating, it's attractive—but it's false. The truth was in that box—but most of it has disintegrated. Actually, we still have one of Tutankhamen's embroidered shirts or "dalmatics". It looks nothing like anything he's wearing in any of his portraits. In fact, it's the same shirt men wore in western civilization up to about the 15th Century CE and are still wearing in some parts of the world today. Probably, the people of King Tut's time would have shocked us had we been able to see how exotic they actually appeared, how different from the familiar concept of an ancient Egyptian that we have formed in our minds. Outside of those few things from the boy-king's tomb, a whole way of life is lost to us. Of this I feel quite sure. Yet there are certain facts we do know:

The Egyptians of long ago had no conveniences at all as we define them. We cannot even imagine what it was like to be poor in ancient Egypt, unless perhaps one knows what poverty means in rural India of today, using one example. Teeming metropolitan areas such as are seen in Calcutta did not exist in the Land of the Pharaohs, although there were great cities up and down the Nile. The overall population of Egypt was far less than it is now and such squalid overcrowding was not known. Cairo, with its overwhelming populace and ever-worsening pollution, was not even a real city back then and, of course, inconceivable in its present state. There were quite simply fewer people everywhere on earth.

Most Egyptians lived in homes or perhaps hovels that contained only the bare necessities. Nobody but the privileged had a bed that was also a piece of furniture. If a poor man happened to own a chair it was likely because he had somehow found the wood and made it himself. Wood was scarce in Egypt and it was not burned for fuel. Ordinary folk sat or slept on the floor. There was not a great deal for the average subject of the Crown to call his own and nothing, really, to make life easier or more appealing except drink, as usual, and perhaps some types of opiates. Absolutely no one had a piece of soap, a toothbrush, a sanitary pad, a hairbrush, deodorant, an aspirin, a condom, an ice-cube, eye-glasses, coffee[155], sugar, chocolate, a candle, a coin, a match or a watch to tell the time. Nobody smoked anything except possibly fish. Try to imagine yourself doing without all of the above for even a week and, on top of it, eliminate the electricity and plumbing modern man takes so for granted.

Certain Egyptians were able to build fine homes, one of which is described in the Papyrus Lansing, "In Praise of the Scribal Profession", by one Wenemdiamun and is owned by his superior, the scribe and Chief Overseer of the Cattle of Amen, Nebmare-Nakht, known as "Raia":

"Raia has built a beautiful mansion, it lies opposite Edjo.[156] It is constructed like a work of eternity.[157] It is planted with trees on all sides. A channel was dug in front of it. The lapping of waves sounds in one's sleep.

---

[155] Tea, which is essentially a beverage brewed from anything that can be steeped in hot water, was probably drunk. We have no way of ascertaining whether actual tea leaves, the kind we know, were imported from the Indian sub-continent. Chamomile was known in ancient Egypt and a tea made from it was probably imbibed for its soothing effect on the digestive system.

[156] The capital of the 10th Nome of Upper Egypt (Aphroditopolis).

[157] That is, something intended to last, like a temple. A canal was excavated in front of the mansion so that there would be a source of water , diverted from the Nile, the vegetation of the grounds being irrigated by means of a shadoof. It seldom rains in Egypt.

One does not tire of looking at it. One is gay at its door and drunk in its halls. Handsome doorposts of limestone, carved and chiseled. Beautiful doors, freshly carved. Walls inlaid with lapis lazuli. Its barns are supplied with grain, are bulging with abundance. Fowl yard and aviary are filled with geese; byres filled with cattle. A bird pool full of geese; horses in the stable. Barges, ferryboats, and new cattle boats are moored at its quay. Young and old, the poor have come to live around it. Your provisions last; there is abundance for all who come to you."[158]

Some fortunate people did have perfumes, cosmetics, a sit-down toilet (which concealed a pot that had to be emptied), books (scrolls), lamps (oil-burning), footwear, gloves, salt and pepper, honey, wines, a chariot, board games, tweezers, spoons (no forks) that were used for dispensing ointment but probably not in eating, animals (including horses and oxen), wigs, musical instruments, meat, a way of pressing clothes, and perhaps even a means of measuring time. Time was important mainly to the temple priests, who had to regulate certain rituals. This was done by using a clever mathematical invention, the clepshydra or water-clock. The rising and falling-away of the river was also measured by a Nilometer, which was basically markings on a rock near the river by which the Egyptians were able to predict an abundant crop or a famine. There were three seasons- Inundation, Winter and Summer—each containing four months. When events were recorded, they were put in the context of the year of the current pharaoh's reign. These years were counted up, but when the king died, it became "Year 1" all over again for his successor. At times, the pharaohs were not above appropriating each other's regnal years—padding their own eras, as it were.

Egyptian men liked to be clean-shaven, although it is hard to believe the peasant working the land bothered about his facial hair every day. Men did not actually shave their own

---

[158] Miriam Lichtheim, *Ancient Egyptian Literature*, Vol. II, page 173.

beards but frequented the village barber—or their servants shaved them. Ladies had their own razors but to what extent they used them we do not know. To be found in every home were beer, fish, fowl[159] (less often than fish), onions, dates, clay pottery, a knife (copper or stone), a needle (bone), some flaxen thread, and a comb. If one wanted any kind of flour, one ground it oneself at home with a stone. Bread, the dietary staple of Egypt, was usually baked flat like the Middle Eastern bread of today.

When darkness descended, people went to bed. With blackness all around and no smog, the night sky appeared to be lit by a million stars. The ancient Egyptians were much taken with this nightly canopy and the stars and constellations figured in their religion and art. The best painted tombs have starry ceilings and even signs of the zodiac overhead. Astrology was quite a preoccupation and writers like Diodorus Siculus praised the efforts of the Egyptians in this field:

> *"To this day, they have preserved records concerning each of the stars over an incredible number of years..... and as a result of their long observations they have prior knowledge of earthquakes and floods, of the rising of comets...."*

Beyond love-making, there was not a great deal to do after dark. Fire and light were expensive, unless one burned dung. Those of us who are able to obtain a flame with a flick of a lighter or the turn of a knob, never think about how elusive fire can be unless we have gone camping and the matches have gotten wet. The ancients had to make fire in

---

[159] The chicken, however, was not raised in Egypt until the New Kingdom. Since the original home of domestic fowl is southwestern Asia and all breeds can be traced to a single wild species, the red jungle fowl, which is found in the wild in India, perhaps the Egyptians imported it from there. Or perhaps they obtained the chicken from Canaan where it had been brought by Indo-Iranian people who had settled there.

one or two laborious ways that depended on a spark catching onto some dry material like straw.One could talk, naturally, even in the dark, but rural Egypt rose early so as to get things done before the day grew too hot, so many persons kept farmer's hours. At any rate, scarcely anybody retired with a book for few people knew how to read or write. Such matters belonged to the scribal profession and to the sons of the privileged, who had been educated to literacy. There was little to read, in any case, although tales, poems, and songs[160] were set down on papyrus. Papyrus, the first form of paper, took time to make and was not easily affordable, so most writing that was not meant to last was done on a potsherd or broken-off piece of limestone. Papyri, however, could be very lengthy when they contained versions of the Book of the Dead, a large corpus of incantations, hymns, and litanies for the benefit of the deceased, interred with same. These scrolls unrolled to over one hundred feet, at times. That is a lot of ink, too, which was made of soot mixed with water and sometimes other ingredients to prevent fading. Colored inks were available as well, in cakes such as are seen in a child's paintbox of today. To be a scribe, a learned man, was considered a very important and honorable profession.

Everyone had to know how to do something in order to survive. Even though the State governed everything in an organized political system, it was definitely not a welfare state. Yet nobody believed in being independent. In fact, it's an alien concept in Egypt even now. Children lived with their parents until they married and even afterward and one cared for one's parents in their old age, if they were so fortunate as to attain it. Not to have children, particularly sons, was considered disastrous and certainly bode ill as

---

[160]The ancient Egyptian did not employ musical notation, but we have the lyrics to a few of their songs. Song was used to lighten every sort of endeavor, just as it is in modern Egypt. In dynastic Egypt, the word "praise" was "hos", which was connected with singing. Ones praises were sung, evidently.

regards ones future. Living alone, a person might become helpless, without family to see to it they were disabled, temporarily or permanently, and then who would care for him? There was nothing resembling a hospital and, living conditions being crowded as homes were small, there was not likely to be room for a sick lone individual at the house of a relative. So one was required to stay in one's own abode and, hopefully, one would not have to shift for oneself there. Even the rich were afraid to be at the mercy of their servants, lest they be robbed blind if they became ill.

Being well-off in ancient Egypt meant having a good house, nice clothing, and probably jewelry, but one still had the problem of procuring food unless one was a wealthy land-owner like Raia. Grocery stores did not exist, although we must assume that peasants brought produce and fowl to market in the cities. We cannot be sure how things were bought in a society without coinage, but it is likely the Middle Eastern suk or outdoor bazaar, where one can find almost everything, was indispensable even in ancient times. Probably, in pharaonic Egypt, people were paid for a day's work in food. Most certainly, the king fed everyone who worked on royal projects, and one might imagine the sovereign's agents continually stocking the stores of grain and vegetables.

The Pharaoh was obliged to feed his court each day, as well, which at times must have consisted of hundreds of souls. Taxes provided all this sustenance. As Egypt was an agricultural nation then as now, it was the farmer who had to give his share to the Crown. As has been mentioned, Egypt was governed systematically with local representatives of the king ensconced everywhere.

Egypt is a long, narrow strip of arable land flanked on either side by desert—called the Red Land. Every inch of fertile soil was used for agriculture. Rural villages, even cities with temples and palaces were built on the desert or on the very edge of the cultivated land. The dead were buried in the desert, as well, the arid conditions being a big plus in their preservation for thousands of years. At any rate, one could stand with one foot on the Red Land and the other on the black soil, so abruptly did the fertile ground end. As one might imagine, sand blew about and got into everything. It caused lung problems and dental trouble, too. Sand got into the bread, wearing down tooth enamel, which resulted in abscesses that often turned to fatal systemic poisoning.

In fact, the people of Kemet were unhealthy as a whole. Their mummies and skeletal remains tell a pathetic story. Many ancient Egyptians appear to have suffered from malnutrition, arthritic conditions and bilharzia, a debilitating disease contracted by walking barefoot in contaminated water. Bilharzia is caused by a snail that remains a problem in the irrigation canals of Egypt to this day. Eye diseases were also much in evidence, partial or total blindness being not nearly as rare a condition as it is in our own culture.

We know that, despite a leaner diet than ours, ancient Egyptian arteries hardened, too. Stress, not fat, was probably the culprit. Heart attacks, strokes, and cancer were not the main causes of death in those days, however, because the risk of these problems increases with age and most people never made it to sixty. Without antibiotics, infection killed off a great many ancient Egyptians. Added to that, there were no remedies against such afflictions as tetanus (lockjaw), diabetes and tuberculosis. Operations of any type were seldom performed, even tooth extractions. Mummies have shown evidence of smallpox and polio and, of course, there were plagues the nature of which we do not know. Each year, during the season of the inundation, the monsoon rains of Ethiopia caused the Nile to overflow its banks, and pestilence seldom failed to follow behind the flood from the south.

Yet there were physicians who employed a mixture of magic, folk medicine, and learned skill. Egyptian doctors knew a great deal for their time and were well-trained, as medical papyri attest. They even did a bit of brain surgery, miraculously not always with fatal results. Egyptian doctors were in demand all over the known world. In those days, if an Egyptian healer could not keep you alive, no one could.

Think of the first life-threatening illness you suffered and when it occurred, and you will know approximately how

110

long you would have lived in ancient Egypt. Probably not even that long, as you were immunized in childhood against various maladies that could and did kill Egyptian children. Infant mortality was very high, indeed, and that was a significant factor in keeping the population low even without birth control.

It is a striking fact that most Egyptian mummies in museums are people who were cut down in the prime of their beauty and strength, probably by something that could easily be treated today. On the other hand, among the royal mummies, a little prince or princess is a rare find, too, so perhaps the children of the rich and mighty lived longer than most. No doubt, the kings of Egypt were a tremendously privileged group. They lived in magnificent palaces, ate well, dressed gorgeously, and had every need attended to, yet their mummies show us that they, like the rest of the people of Kemet[161], seldom reached the age of sixty. Death, it appears, was an equal opportunity destroyer in ancient Egypt.

Nevertheless the Egyptians were a joyful people, who loved to tell stories, enjoyed a good joke and even were known to draw a bawdy picture or two. Music and dance were always part of the Egyptian culture and, in those days before mass entertainment, an individual who knew how to relate an interesting tale was much esteemed. An example of the imaginary powers of the ancient Egyptians is the description of the "Benu-bird" given to Herodotus:

"Another sacred bird is the one called the phoenix. Now, I have not actually seen a phoenix, except in a painting, because they are quite infrequent visitors in the country; in fact I was told in Heliopolis that they appear only at 500-year intervals. They say that it is the death of a phoenix's father which prompts its visit to Egypt....There is a particular feat they say the phoenix performs; I do

---

[161] The Egyptians' name for their own land, pronounced something like "*Kameh*", and meaning the "Black Land" due to the fertile soil on both sides of the river. The desert was known as "DSrt" ("*troshe*") or the Red Land.

not believe it myself, but they say that the bird sets out from its homeland in Arabia on a journey to the sanctuary of the sun, bringing its father sealed in myrrh and buries its father there. The method it uses for carrying its father is as follows. First, it forms out of myrrh as big an egg as it can manage to carry, and then makes a trial flight to make sure it can carry the egg. When this has been tested, it hollows out the egg and puts its father inside, and then seals up with more myrrh that part of the egg which it had hollowed out to hold its father. The egg now weighs the same, with its father lying inside, as it did before it was hollowed out. So when the phoenix has sealed the egg up again, it carries its father to the sanctuary of the sun in Egypt."[162]

That the Egypt of antiquity was particularly fond of folklore about its pharaohs is reflected in the writings of the ancient historians. These legends of the kings grew much embellished over time and took on a mythological quality. The exploits of one monarch tended to get mixed up with those of another. Yet it is astonishing how many mnemonic anecdotes, backed up by archaeological evidence, have managed to survive. And so it is the collective memory of the people of Egypt that gives us insight into the mysteries of their land. However, in the words of the author, Thomas Mann, *"The well of the past is very deep"* and sometimes only patience and the ever-evolving world of science will reveal to us those things upon which Time has set a seal.

---

[162]Heliopolis. Rolf Krauss suggests that, from the New Kingdom onward, the Benu-bird symbolized the planet Venus.

Chapter Six

Kings and queens have been portrayed in splendid garments throughout the ages, yet, somehow, I don't think anyone has ever looked as majestic or as elegant as the Pharaoh of The Two Lands in his pleated, bleached kilt or whatever embroidered or sequined tunics he normally wore, his streamlined crowns, the cobra rearing on his brow, his body covered with gold and bright stones, blazing like the sun, his belt and apron heavily encrusted with gleaming threads, beadwork and studs—even his sandals being works of art.

During his time on the throne, the king's existence seems to have been strictly regulated—at least as Diodorus Siculus[163] was given to understand:

> *"Of primary interest is that the life that the kings of the Egyptians lived was not like that of other men who enjoyed unfettered power and do in all things exactly as they please without being held to account, but all their acts were regulated by provisions of law, not only their administrative acts, but also those that had to do with the way in which they spent their time from day to day, and with the food which they ate. In the matter of their servants, for instance, not one was a slave, acquired by purchase or born in the home, but all were sons of the most distinguished priests, twenty years or older and the best educated in the land, so that the king, having the most exemplary men to attend to him throughout both day and night, might be exposed to nothing base; for no*

---

[163] Greek historian (circa 90-21 BCE), born in Agyrium, Sicily. Diodorus's great work, the *Bibliotheca Historica* (Historical Library), was a history of the world in 40 books, of which the first five are extant in their entirety. The next five are lost; the next ten are complete, and many fragments of the others have survived.

ruler advances far along the road of evil unless he has those about him who will abet his perversities. The hours of both the day and night were planned according to ritual, and at all times it was absolutely required of the king that he should do what the laws stipulated and not to follow his whims. As an example, in the morning, as soon as he was awake, he first had to receive the letters that had been sent from all over, so that he might tend to all business as a priority and be accurately informed about everything that was being done throughout his kingdom. Then, no sooner had he bathed and decked himself out in rich garments, including the insignia of his office, he was ready to sacrifice to the gods.

When the victims had been brought to the altar[164] it was the custom for the high priest to stand near the king, with the common people of Egypt gathered somewhere nearby, and declaim in a loud voice that health and every advantage of life be given the king if he uphold justice towards his subjects. And public proclamation had also to be made of each and every virtue of the king, the priest extolling his piety toward the gods and his concern for men, inasmuch as he was temperate and just and truthful and generous with his possessions. In a word, the king was superior to every desire, and magnanimous in that he punished crimes less severely than they deserved and rendered to his those who served him well a gratitude exceeding the benefaction. After reciting much more in a similar vein the priest concluded his oration with a curse upon misdeeds and errors, exempting the king from all blame therefore and

---

[164] Perhaps Diodorus intended animal sacrifices in this passage. Evidence for the Egyptians ritually killing humans is lacking—even though it is claimed by Porphyrius that "Amosis put an end to the custom of human sacrifice in Egyptian Heliopolis, as Manetho testifies in On Antiquity and Religion. Human beings used to be sacrificed to Hera, and they were inspected, just as the pure calves that are sought for and marked with a seal. Three were sacrificed each day. Amosis ordered life-size waxen images to take their place."

114

praying that evil consequences should fall upon those who had advised him in error and led him astray.

All this he would do for the purpose of encouraging the king to fear the gods and serve them, and also to force him into a proper manner of conduct, not by sharp admonitions, but through praises that were so agreeable as to commit him to virtue. After this, when had performed the divination from the entrails of a calf and had found the omens good, the sacred scribe read before the assemblage out of the holy books some of the wise counsels and deeds of their most distinguished sages, so that he who held the supreme leadership keep in mind the most excellent principles as he went about his prescribed functions. For there was a set time not only for his holding audiences or rendering judgments, but even for his taking a walk, bathing, and sleeping with his wife, and, in a word, for every act of his life. It was customary for the kings to partake of delicate food, eating no other meat than veal and duck, and drinking only a limited amount of wine, which was not enough to make them ill or drunken. In general, their whole diet was ordered so conservatively that it had the appearance of having been drawn up, not by a lawgiver, but by the most skilled of their physicians, with only their health in view.

Strange as it may seem that the king did not have the entire control of his daily fare, far more remarkable still was the fact that the kings were not allowed to render any legal decisions, transact any business at random or to punish anyone maliciously or for any unjust reason, but only in accordance with the established laws relative to each offence. In following the dictates of custom in these matters, far from feeling constrained by them, they actually held that they led a most happy life; for they believed that all other men, in thoughtlessly following their personal inclinations, commit many acts which lead to no good. Oftentimes some who realize that they are about to commit a sin do so anyway when overpowered by love or hatred or some other passion, while they, by virtue of their having been chosen before all others by the most prudent of all men, were insulated from making mistakes. And since the kings followed so righteous a course in dealing with their subjects, the people demonstrated a good will towards their rulers that surpassed even the affection they had for their own relatives. For not only the priests but, as it happened, all the inhabitants of Egypt were less concerned for their wives and children and their cherished possessions than for the safety of their kings. Consequently, during most of the time covered by the reigns of the kings of whom we have a record, they maintained an orderly civil government and continued to enjoy a most felicitous life so long as the described system of law was in force. Not only that, they conquered more nations and achieved greater wealth than any other people, and adorned their land with monuments and buildings never to be surpassed, and their cities with costly dedications of every description."

But an Egyptologist of bygone years, Adolf Erman, tells of a darker aspect to the Egyptian pharaoh's existence in his book, *Life In Ancient Egypt*,[165] and is quite eloquent about "the heavy crown":

"Around the king were the old counsellors who had served his father, and to whom the clerks and officials were accustomed blindly to obey, as well as the generals with the troops in their pay, and the priesthood with their unlimited power over the lower classes. In the small towns the old rich families of the nobility, residing in their country seats, were nearer to the homes of the people than the monarch dwelling in his distant capital. The king was afraid to offend any of these powerful people; he had to spare the sensitive feelings of the minister; discover a way of gratifying the ambition of the general

---

[165] Macmillan and Company (England, 1894)

116

without endangering the country; watch carefully that his officers didn't encroach on the rights of the nobility; and above all keep in favor with the priests. It was only when the king could satisfy all these claims, and understand at the same time how to play off one party against another, the he could expect a long and prosperous reign. If he failed, his chances were small, for there lurked close to him his most dangerous enemies, his nearest relatives. There always existed a brother or an uncle, who imagined he had a better claim to the throne than the reigning king, or there were the wives of the late ruler, who thought it a fatal wrong that the child of a rival rather than their own son should have inherited the crown. "

Then Erman talks about the situation of the royal sons and the positions they held:

".....officiated as high priests in the temple of Heliopolis, and others again, bearing the title of 'erpat" or "prince of the blood', became the "chief judges" or the 'scribes of the divine book' and nearly all of them were, in addition, 'Chief lector-priests of their father' and belonged, as 'governors of the palace' to his inner circle of courtiers. Under the New Empire, when the army came more to the fore, they preferred to be invested with military titles, and were called generals of their father."

Erman has some more to say about the duties and privileges of the princes but, despite his pessimistic overview of the Egyptian court, he does not say anything about any possible bloodbaths that occurred among his sons when the reigning monarch died.

117

Chapter Seven

For a long time, it was not considered very important to regulate the activities of Thutmose III of the 18th Dynasty. On the contrary, according to him, not much honor or attention was afforded him at all. He had lost his father when he was a very small boy, perhaps even a baby. Although Thutmose was the legitimate heir to the throne, he was too young to rule and so his father's half-sister and principle wife, Hatshepsut, became the boy's regent. One can imagine the lonely little boy trailing after the gardeners of the palace grounds, who may have had a genial way with him and fostered what was to be a lifelong interest of the king in botany. An inscription in the Theban tomb of the architect Ineni says:

> *"(Tuthmose II) ascended to heaven and united with the gods, while his son stood in his place as king of the two lands, having assumed rulership over the throne of the one who begat him, and while his sister, the god's wife Hatshepsut, was conducting the affairs of the country, the two lands being in her care. With Egypt in obeisance she is served, the beneficent divine seed who has come forth before him, the prow-rope of Upper Egypt and mooring post of the southerners."*

After seven years lapsed in this fashion, the ambitious queen suddenly decided to assume full pharaonic titles and to enter a phase in her life where she was privately a woman and publicly a male. Instead of taking his place as rightful king assisted by trusted counselors, young Thutmose was now forced to play the role of "junior partner" to "the woman who would be king", this situation inexplicably lasting until Thutmose was in his twenties.

18th **Dynasty:** Thutmose III (relating his predicament under the rule of his aunt, Hatshepsut):

" It is no fable. So long as I was a child and a boy, I remained in his temple (Amen); not even as a seer of the god did I hold an office."

Thutmose III (on Hatshepsut):

"What I relate is no invention: she was astonishing in the sight of men, and an enigma for the hearts of the gods who knew it all. But she did not realize it—that no one was for her except herself."

The inability of the king to get out from under the thumb of his aunt would possibly make sense if Thutmose had been mentally deficient or weak and cowardly in his nature, but time would prove him to be just the opposite. There came the day when Hatshepsut either died or was ousted by her nephew and suddenly Egypt found herself ruled by the greatest pharaoh she had ever known.[166] A man of superior intellect and military acumen, Thutmose III subdued all the surrounding lands that may have been perceived as a threat to his country and a few extras while he was about it. When an Egyptian pharaoh said he "laid waste" to a certain area, he meant that his army virtually denuded it like a swarm of southern locusts. Even the botanist had little regard for the foliage, even though we know that he sometimes brought interesting specimens back to Egypt.

"Now his majesty destroyed the town of Ardata, with its grain. All its pleasant trees were cut down. Now (his majesty) found the entire land of Djahi, with its orchards filled with their fruits. Their wines were found lying in their vats, as water flows, and their grains on their threshing floors, being ground. These were more plentiful than the sands of the shore. The army overflowed with its possessions...Now his majesty's army was as drunk

---

[166] That is not to say that the "woman king" was inept. In fact, Egypt seems to have prospered under her guidance.

119

and anointed with oil every day as if at feasts in Egypt."
Fifth Campaign, 29ᵗʰ Year of King Menkheperre Thutmose.[167]

In the following year, King Thutmose turned his attention to a place called Kadesh on the river Orontes. As usual, trees were felled and grain cut down.

"List of the tribute brought to the glory of his majesty by the princes of Retenu (Syria) in this year: Now the children of the princes and their brothers were brought to be hostages in Egypt. Now, whoever of these princes died, his majesty was accustomed to make his son go to stand in his place. List of the children of princes carried off in this year: 36 men; 181 male and female slaves; 188 horses and 40 chariots, worked with gold or silver or painted." And...*"All the mysterious marshes of Asia from which his majesty carried off living prisoners while he made a great slaughter within them—lands which had not been trodden by other kings except for his majesty. The reputation as a valiant man is from what he has done, not being eradicated on this earth forever."*

The personal barber of this mighty king was named Si-Bastet. One day, during one of the ruler's sixteen campaigns in Asia, Si-Bastet approached his master for a favor. The tonsorial artist had managed to take a captive, a Canaanite male, whom he wished to bring back to Egypt. One can imagine Thutmose's amusement, perhaps jokingly asking his servant if he had threatened the captive with his razor. We can see   Si-Bastet smiling calmly as he expertly drew the instrument of his profession over the pharaoh's lean cheeks, perhaps even grasping the latter's majestic nose as he shaved his upper lip, knowing he would get his way because it served every man well to indulge his barber, the person who held a sharp blade to his throat every single day.

---

[167] Since Thutmose III ruled for a total of 54 years (including the period when Maatkare Hatshepsut overshadowed him) and his mummy indicates that he was only a middle-aged man when he died, he may have been a mere baby when Thutmose II passed from the scene.

Perhaps Thutmose even asked to see the Canaanite prisoner the civilian, Si-Bastet, had somehow seized. Probably the king was not surprised to discover that the new slave of the barber was no more than a boy verging on manhood, perhaps an orphan that he, himself, had created. One would imagine that the intellectual Thutmose even managed to address the lad in his own West-Semitic dialect and that the captive made responses that pleased the pharaoh, who may have recalled what it was like to be young and without friends. For his part, the Canaanite boy beheld the most impressive man he had ever seen in his life. Rather frightening eyes beneath heavy eyelids assessed him with the gaze of a general who is accustomed to taking the measure of his men but a little smile played about the king's thin lips in a way that signaled one need not fear him. Between the keen eyes was a great curving beak of a nose. When the boy was asked his name, he probably replied "Levi-El".[168]

"Levi," we may imagine the pharaoh saying, "it is our wish that you come to Egypt to live there under our protection and serve our barber well. Henceforth, you shall be called 'Iuwy-Amen'."

"Iuwy" was a word that sounded something like "Levi". Since most Egyptian men had a nickname, Iuwy-Amen was probably called "Yuya". Si-Bastet proved to be a kindly master and not only taught the young Canaanite to become a barber and a surgeon but treated him like the son he lacked. Yuya often accompanied Si-Bastet when he went to shave King Thutmose and, in time, he, himself, performed this service for members of the king's household. Because Yuya was a foreigner who spoke Egyptian with an accent, Si-Bastet had this "letter of introduction" written for his slave to give to the captain of the king's guard, a document signed by five witnesses of the court in Year 27 of the ruler:

---

[168] In fact, Levi-El was either the name of a town in Canaan, along with Jacob-El and Joseph-El, or the name of a tribe—these being included on a roster of sites under the Egyptian empire.

"I have a slave who is assigned to me whose name is Iuwy-Amen. I captured him myself when I was following the Ruler (on campaign)...He is not to be beaten, nor is he to be turned away from the door of the palace. I have given the daughter of my sister Nebetto, whose name is Takamenet, to him as wife. She shall have a share in (my) inheritance just like my wife and my sister."

It is obvious that the presence of the Canaanite in his household had not only provided Si-Bastet with an apprentice but had solved the problem of a husband for his sightless niece—for that is what "Takamenet" means in Egyptian—"the Blind Girl". Hopefully, she had another name, as well.

In order to be deemed worthy of being a royal barber's nephew-in-law, Yuya must have been clever and amiable, perhaps even quite presentable-looking. In fact, he may have been an outstanding character in many respects. Since he had access to the palace, even King Thutmose may have grown to like him.

What eventually became of Si-Bastet's nephew? Certainly, he had been placed in an ideal position to make something of himself. Did his sterling qualities enable him to achieve a position that no longer involved shaving? What we know for certain is that intermarriage between the foreign captives and Egyptians did occur and perhaps not infrequently.[169] In fact, there is probably another even more famous case of it a generation later.

A gentleman of rather alien appearance, also nicknamed "Yuya"[170], for some reason became one of the most exalted

---

[169] The mirror-image situation is described in 1 Chronicles 2:34. *"Now Sheshan had no sons, but daughters. And Sheshan had a servant, an Egyptian, whose name was Jarha. So Sheshan gave his daughter to Jarha his servant to wife..."*

[170] We don't know the actual name and even "Yuya" is variously spelled in his tomb, indicating no one was quite sure what glyphs to use. Ahmed Osman thinks "Yuya" is short for "Yusuf" but "Yahya" is Persian for Johanna, another Hebrew appellation.

men in Egypt, complete with copious titles, of a lofty status seldom seen in the land. He was known as the "four-times great", something quite remarkable, as even the god of wisdom, Thoth, himself, was normally not referred to as more than "three-times great".[171]

Theodore Davis, an American millionaire and amateur excavator, found what seemed to be an upper-class tomb in 1905. The occupants were an elderly couple whose names were Yuya and Thuya. These names were recognizable at once, because they had been seen before on a commemorative scarab of King Amenhotep III, who, by his Year 2, had married a girl named Tiye.

> "Life unto the Horus, the strong bull, crowned with Truth
> Lord of the North and the South, establisher of laws
> Pacifier of the Two Lands, Horus the Golden, mighty of valor, smiter of foreign lands
> King Neb-maare-re, son of the sun, Amenhotep, Ruler of Thebes,
> Giver of Life and the Royal Spouse, the mighty   lady, Tiye, as she lives.
> The name of her father is Yuya; the name of her mother, Thuya
> This is the wife of a powerful king, his southern frontier is as far as Karoy. His northern frontier extends as far as Naharin"

The burial of Yuya and Thuya was not intact, but it was obvious from their elaborate nested coffins and the few fine pieces that remained in their tomb, that every honor had been shown the pair. But the most impressive aspect of this burial was the mummies of Yuya and Thuya, which were well-preserved, the features of Yuya, particularly, being almost the same as they must have been in life. Thuya was

---

[171] Whence derived "Hermes Trismegistus", purported author of the *Corpus Hermeticum*, the wisdom of Thoth, written some time between the first and fourth centuries CE.

pronounced a familiar Egyptian type but Yuya's face seemed to indicate a different ethnicity. The fact that his name or nickname was spelled several different ways on the items in the tomb seems to point to it being an unusual appellation to the Egyptians.

These are among the arguments offered by Ahmed Osman, a modern Egyptian author, to support his theory that Yuya was none other than the Biblical Joseph (Yosef or Yusuf in Semitic)[172]. However, as has been mentioned, some ancient writers evidently believed that Joseph came to Egypt, not in the 18th Dynasty, which is when Yuya lived, but during the Second Intermediate Period, the time of the Hyksos—or even earlier than that. No matter what the actual background of Yuya was, it can't be disputed that some set of circumstances brought him to the attention of the royal family and caused him to prosper.

Most Egyptologists still think the reason was that Amenhotep III, as a youth, fell in love with the commoner's daughter, Tiye, the whole affair being a Cinderella story with Tiye ending up as the pharaoh's Chief Wife. To my way of thinking, a very young heir to the throne (as this particular Amenhotep surely was[173]) never had the sort of freedom that allowed him to choose his queen for romantic reasons. A suitable girl would have been selected for him and certainly not out of the masses. There is little doubt in my mind that Tiye was related to her husband, at least on the side of her mother, Thuya.[174] Whoever old Yuya was, he had managed

---

[172] *Stranger In the Valley* (London, 1987)

[173] His father, King Thutmose IV, reigned only 9 years and was about age 30 at death, judging by his mummified remains. Amenhotep III was the great-grandson of Thutmose III. He was married to Queen Tiye by his Year 2.

[174] It has been proposed that "Thuya" is a hypochoristicon for "Nefertari", Thuya being a descendant of the revered Queen Ahmose-Nefertari, whose male line was promised the title of Second Prophet of Amen forever by King Ahmose. Indeed, Thuya's son, Aanen, was Second Prophet (i.e. second in authority next to the High Priest).

to marry a high-born lady.   That such a thing was possible is contained in the Bible in the examples of Hadad the Edomite (1 Kings, 11:18-20), who was permitted by the pharaoh of the time to marry his wife's sister.   Their son, Genubath, was reared in the palace with the sons of the king. I Chronicles 4:18 has a Hebrew named Mered, of the tribe of Judah, marrying a certain Bithiah, the daughter of a king of Egypt. And, of course, Joseph, himself, became the husband of Asenath, the daughter of a powerful priest.

How shall we account for the character in the Book of Genesis called Joseph? Was there actually such a person—or is the story of a Semitic-speaking nomad becoming Pharaoh's "right-hand-man" just a novel?[175] If Joseph is purely an invention by a Jew who wished to create a larger-than-life Hebrew success-story, then one might say the writer, himself, had an unparalleled literary success (unless the character, Moses, is a mere fiction, as well].

That Asiatics rose to positions of considerable power in Egypt is an established fact.   Their names, gleaned from various sources, show that this phenomenon can have occurred in any phase of Egyptian history.   Nevertheless, if there was actually someone called Joseph who was extraordinarily prominent in his adopted land, there certainly seems to have been quite a bit of confusion regarding him even among the writers of antiquity.

Flavius Josephus mentions that an Egyptian historian, Chaeremon, said that the Egyptian name of Joseph was "Peteseph" and that he was a contemporary of Moses, both of them having been "sacred scribes".[176] While Manetho gives

---

[175] Which might be a sterling example of Egyptian literature were it written in the Egyptian language.

[176] However, "Peteseph" is a type of name not seen before the latter part of the 19th Dynasty. Curiously the name "Potiphar" or "Petepre" comes up one other time in connection with Moses. Two men who were known in legend as magicians in the court of the pharaoh and whose names were recalled as "Jannes and Jambres" (or Mambres), opposed Moses. It is

the original name of Moses as having been "Osarseph", Chaeremon supplied that he had been called "Tisithen", instead. Since all the Egyptian chronographers, including another bete noir of Josephus, the anti-Semitic Apion, appeared to believe Moses was an Egyptian from Heliopolis, it is not surprising that Manetho gave him the name of an Heliopolite god. "Osar-sepa" seems to be a combination of Osiris and Sepa, the latter being a protector-deity of the former (and of the necropolis) who assumed the shape of a centipede, ultimately merging his identity with Osiris. Josephus rightly observed that the names Osarseph and Moses are not interchangeable, implying that the substitution of one for the other makes no apparent sense.

Chaeremon's identification of Joseph as "Peteseph" does make sense under the circumstances—even though it is erroneous. "Peteseph" means "One Given By the god Sepa". The Book of Genesis relates that, as a minister of the pharaoh, Joseph married the daughter of a priest of On (Heliopolis) called Potiphar, bearing the same name as Joseph's former master, the captain of the guard. What could be more fitting than the son-in-law of a priest of Heliopolis, himself named "Petepre"("One Given By the god, Ra"), being called "Peteseph", after the god, Sepa? Doubtless, Chaeremon was attempting to find a corresponding Egyptian name for "Joseph". However, the Chief Librarian at Alexandria may not have known that "Joseph" means "God has increased" in Semitic and that the proper Egyptian translation would have included the Egyptian cognate, "spA", a verb meaning "to increase or double", resulting in "spA -pA-nTr" (nTr, pronounced "noute", being Egyptian for "god") and not the name of the god, Sepa.

Many adhere to the idea that the books of the Hebrew Bible, otherwise called "The Old Testament", were not written until after the Jews went into exile after the destruction of the first great temple in Jerusalem in 587 BCE. True or not, the Joseph story must surely have been authored by

---

written that their father was named "Balaam the son of Potiphar". These will appear in a subsequent chapter.

someone familiar with older Egyptian literature, like "The Tale of the Two Brothers"[177], a story in which a young man encounters much the same situation of seduction attempted by the wife of Potiphar in her lust for Joseph. In other words, the author could read and write Egyptian.

Ancient Jewish and Christian writers, such as Ecclesiasticus, Josephus, Philo, and Origen all seem to agree that the first five books of the Bible were authored by Moses.[178] However, few modern Bible scholars subscribe to this belief.

The chronology of the Exodus is set, in the view of many, by the mention of Pithom and Raameses, the cities which the Hebrews built for Pharaoh, this needing to happen in the 19th Dynasty. However, the last city is also part of a passage in the Book of Genesis![179]

> "And Joseph placed his father and brethren, and gave them a possession in the land of Egypt, in the best of the land, in the land of Rameses, as Pharaoh had commanded."

This wholly anachronistic reference to the area of the eastern Delta as "the land of Rameses" serves to indicate that the "Pithom and Raameses" of the Book of Exodus is meaningless as an historical marker. More significant is the fact that whoever wrote the books of Genesis and Exodus

---

[177] The "short-story" genre started in ancient Egypt. This tale, the Papyrus D'Orbiney, is dated to the 19th Dynasty, written in the hand of the scribe, Innana, perhaps the "Jannes" of folklore, to be introduced in the second half of this book.

[178] Recent studies have suggested that the origins of Egyptian Christianity (the Coptic Church) has its roots among the Jews living in Alexandria in the 1st Century CE. By the end of the 2nd Century in Alexandria, the major city of Hellenistic Egypt, the Christian catechetical school was headed by Clement of Alexandria, who was succeeded by Origen, the founder of Greek Christian theology and biblical science.

[179] Gen: 47:11

had to live after the latter part of the 19th Dynasty, that is after Ramesses II built the city named after himself—or he cannot possibly have known about it.

Beyond Genesis, Exodus and Numbers, the area known as "Ramesses" (as I would spell it) does not come up again in the Bible. The Delta is alluded to on several occasions, but always with regard to other cities, notably "Zoan"[180] or Tanis, a place strategically located on the east side of the Tanitic branch of the Nile and which replaced Per-Ramesses-Meryamun as a pharaonic capital of Lower Egypt. The first recorded builder at Tanis is Psusennes I (1039-991 BCE) of the 21st Dynasty. Stones and statues from "Raamses" of the Torah were taken to Tanis and reused there. Therefore, the inclusion of the name of Tanis in the Pentateuch makes it difficult to believe these first five books were written prior to the 21st Dynasty.

Since two of the Christian preservers of Manetho's *Aegyptica* say of the reign of "the Shepherds": "*It was in their time that Joseph was appointed king of Egypt*" or "*It was in their time that Joseph appears to have ruled in Egypt*", perhaps Manetho, himself, actually wrote this. Still, in Egypt the tradition is that the Bahr Yusuf, a long canal that was dug as an irrigation project from the Nile to the Faiyum, is associated with the Biblical Joseph. Diodorus Siculus described the Bahr Yusuf, attributing it to a certain "King Moeris":

> "*For since the Nile did not rise to a fixed height each year and yet the fruitfulness of the country depended on the constancy of the flood-level, he excavated the lake[181] to receive the excess water, in order that the river might not,*

---

[180] Modern San el Hagar (San of the Stones). Numbers 13:22 claims that Zoan was built seven years before the very ancient Canaanite city of Hebron, which is very odd as the spies sent by Moses stopped at Hebron!

[181]Now called Birket Qarun, a lake that occupies part of the depression that was once the ancient Lake Moeris. The Faiyum is one of the most fertile areas of Egypt.

by an excessive volume of flow, immoderately flood the land and form marshes and pools, nor by failing to rise to the proper height, ruin the harvests by the lack of water. He also dug a canal, eighty stades long and three plethra wide,[182] from the river to the lake, and by the canal, sometimes turning the river into the lake and sometimes shutting it off again, he furnished the farmers with an opportune supply of water, opening and closing the entrance by a skilful device and yet at considerable expense; for it cost no less than fifty talents if a man wanted to open or close this work. The lake has continued to serve the Egyptians down to our time, and bears the name of the builder, being called to this day the Lake of Moeris."

Since "Moeris"[183] is supposedly the Greek version of the prenomen of Amenemhat III, which was Nymaare, and if Joseph was connected to him and his canal, that would mean Joseph would have lived during the 12th Dynasty.[184] Manetho wrote that the alien people, the Hyksos, had become a considerable force in the Delta by the time of King "Tutimaeos" of the 13th or 14th Dynasty, about seventy or eighty years later. Moreover, this 12th Dynasty date for the arrival of Joseph does make sense in light of the Semites already being a source of labor during the succeeding 13th Dynasty, as the Brooklyn Papyrus attests.[185]

I think it quite reasonable to believe that, like the slaves in the Brooklyn Papyrus, Joseph was known by two names

---

[182]Approximately nine miles long and three hundred feet wide. The canal was restored by Saladin, sultan of Egypt in the 12th Century CE.

[183] Also known as "Mares".

[184] Amenemhat III is thought to have ruled from 1842 to 1797 BCE.

[185] Ten kings are listed for the 13th Dynasty, which lasted approximately 70 years, but the years in which these men ruled are not known for certain.

and that he lived sometime before the first exodus, the expulsion of the Hyksos.[186] We have seen that "Sepanoute" was the first element and I think it not farfetched to conclude that "Ankhu" may have been the second name[187], with the masculine article "pA" (the) added at a later time when such a prefix was the vogue. If Moses was 80 years old in 1570 BCE, and if Joseph died 170 years before the birth of Moses (according to Flavius Josephus), then Joseph would have had to be dead by 1820 BCE—which, indeed, would put his service in the time of Amenemhat III and his predecessor, Senusret III. However, since some of the ancients did not agree that Moses was a part of the expulsion of the Hyksos, the era of Joseph cannot be so precisely fixed. In fact, he was also associated with a certain king "Chenephres"—that is to say Sobekhotep IV.

It may be recalled that the Brooklyn Papyrus, with its list of "Apiru" slaves, is dated to the reign of King Sobekhotep III, who sat on Egypt's throne ca. 1745 BCE at a place called "Ity-Tawi"[188], also near the Faiyum, the verdant spot where the Bahr Yusuf ends. There was a very interesting vizier attached to the court of Sobekhotep III, who should not escape our attention and who went by the name of "'Ankhu".

In the Brooklyn Papayrus, Sobekhotep III issues a written command to Ankhu. He is also represented on a stela in the Louvre that records restorations made in the temple of Abydos by a priest named Amenysonb. The pharaoh of the time of the Louvre stone was Khendjer, his strange name

---

[186] Some maintain that Joseph must have served a Hyksos king in order to have gained such a high degree of acceptance as a foreigner and because he rode in a chariot, a conveyance not in use in Egypt until the Hyksos period. I feel that the first contention is disproved by the knowledge that people of Semitic background grew prominent under native kings and the chariot can be an anachronistic element like the 19th Dynasty name of Potiphar.

[187] Or possibly "Ipiankh", as suggested by Kenneth Kitchen. The "ankh" element was, in reality, probably vocalized "anakh".
[188] Modern Lisht.

perhaps denoting foreign origin. Gardiner remarked that there were possibly even two Khendjers, one in the north and one in the south—or one had simply changed his prenomen at some point.

At any rate, one of the Khendjer prenomina is listed with certainty in the Turin Canon and since it is probably Sobekhotep III who appears four places farther on, Sir Alan Gardiner wrote:[189]

> " ...we might have the strange phenomenon of a single vizier holding office during the reigns of five ephemeral and possibly hostile monarchs."

In fact, the 13th Dynasty seems to have been "the era of the king's right-hand man". For quite some time, it was believed that the actual power lay with a series of viziers and that the kings were nothing but figure-heads, but it is not possible to know why this would have been the case.[190] Nevertheless, in Genesis 41:40, Pharaoh says to Joseph *"Thou shallt be over my house and according unto thy word shall all my people be ruled"* and Genesis 41:44 has him pronouncing *"I am Pharaoh, and without thee shall no man lift up his foot in all the land of Egypt."*

A rumor insists that it is a 13th Dynasty ruler, one following closely after Sobekhotep III, who was connected to an exodus in a rather round-about way, as we shall see in due course. Not many details are known of the reign of Khaneferre Sobekhotep IV (1730-1720 BCE?), called "Chenephres" by those who wrote in Greek, but he has left the impression of being a powerful monarch due to his many

---

[189] *Egypt of the Pharaohs*, pages 153-154.

[190] Aidan Dodson, in his *Monarchs of the Nile* (London, 1995), asserts that *"More recent work has cast doubt this interpretation, and it is unclear how far, if at all, matters diverged from normal Egyptian governmental practices."* Page 68.

surviving monuments. Soon after him the 13th Dynasty petered out in a nebulous fashion.

Not least, we are also mindful of that piece of pseudo-Manetho, *The Book of Sothis,* claiming that Joseph arrived in Egypt in Year 4 of the 15th Dynasty ruler, Apophis, and becoming grand vizier in the 17th year of that Hyksos king, who reigned for 40 years somewhere in the timeframe of 1663 and 1555 BCE, according to Clayton's chronology.

So the jury must still be out regarding just when Joseph lived, but he remains one of the most interesting and appealing characters from the Torah. There is a certain romance, exceedingly popular in ancient and medieval times, the most complete title of which is *"Life and Confession of Asenath Daughter of Pentephres, priest of Heliopolis, and how Joseph the Handsome took her for Wife"*. It was supposedly *"written in Greek during the Roman period by a Jew of Egyptian origin,"*[191]although it could date to the end of the 2nd Century BCE, which would make it the oldest Greek novel. The text has been translated into Latin, Syriac, Armenian, Slavonic, Romanian, Neo-Hellenic, Anglo-Saxon, Ethiopian and Arabic.[192] In this work, based on the story in Genesis, Asenath lives in a tower, like Rapunzel,[193] and disdains all the young men who wish to marry her, including the king's sons.

When Joseph comes along in his chariot, dressed in fine robes, the young Egyptian girl falls in love with him at first sight and has no other thought but to marry him. Her parents are delighted because Joseph is the favored courtier of the pharaoh. When she learns that Joseph refuses to wed a pagan, Asenath goes into mourning, dressing in black and covering her head with ashes. After a few days of pining

---

[191] Marc Philonenko.

[192] Joseph Meleze Modrzejewski, *The Jews of Egypt,* (Paris, 1992; English vers., Philadephia, 1995).

[193] And also like the king's daughter in the ancient Egyptian novel, *The Tale of the Doomed Prince.*

away, an angel appears to Asenath at the rising of the morning star, who is even more beautiful and luminous than Joseph. Among other things, the angel tells the girl to put on a wedding gown and that her name would be called "City of Refuge" henceforth, instead of Asenath.[194]

Of course, Joseph returns and the pair are married, with Asenath converting to the religion of her husband. In fact, the author of the tale carefully points out that Asenath looks more like a Jewish girl than an Egyptian, to begin with. The most remarkable aspect of this story, in my opinion, is the name that the angel gives to Asenath. Can the writer of this romance have possibly known that Haware/Avaris means "Place of Refuge" in Egyptian?

A legendary figure like Joseph can be put into any era just as easily as Biblical personages could be painted by Renaissance artists dressed like their contemporary nobility. Ahmed Osman maintains that for Joseph to have lived during the 18th Dynasty (circa 1386 BCE) is sufficient to render him already forgotten by the pharaohs of the time of a late 19th Dynasty exodus—even if he had been the father-in-law of Amenhotep III. Nor does it necessarily mean Joseph is a fictitious creation because he encounters, in his story, the same sexually-charged situation as the hero of the Egyptian novel, "The Tale of the Two Brothers". Besides, to place real people in make-believe situations is not unknown in Demotic literature, the fiction of the Late Period of Egyptian history. Of course, knowing these things brings us no closer to understanding who wrote the book of Genesis and/or the tale of Joseph—except that, judging by the personal names given to the characters, the author can hardly have lived before the end of the 19th Dynasty. In other words, if Moses wrote the tale, he cannot have lived at the time of King Ahmose of the early 18th Dynasty.

---

[194] This serves to indicate, in my opinion, that the name "Asenath" already had the meaning of "place", perhaps being "Ist-n-nTr", the place or seat of the god and would be changed to "place of refuge".

Chapter Eight

Returning to Yuya, the father-in-law of Amenhotep III, mention cannot be omitted that, while everything about the tomb of this personage indicated that he followed Egyptian polytheistic religious practices, he is nevertheless connected to monotheism by those who believe that his grandson, Akhenaten, was somehow influenced by him. The fact  remains that exactly what prompted this king of Egypt to select the manifestation of the sun, the Aten, as the object of his rather obsessive worship, is obscure. Above is the mummy of Yuya.

Akhenaten was, indeed, a monotheist to the extent that his existence as an ancient Egyptian and a pharaoh allowed him to be. He reasoned, quite accurately, of course, that there could be no life without the sun, which rose every morning without fail and bestowed its benefices upon the earth. My own belief is that some phenomenon, perhaps a lengthy solar eclipse, instilled a fear in the heart of the young Amenhotep that perhaps the sun was sending an ominous message that it was displeased and might not be so predictably generous with its life-giving rays in the future. In his Year 5 or 6, Amenhotep IV altered his name to Akhenaten and decided to build a new city, Akhetaten[195], where he could rule and dedicate himself to adoring and propitiating the solar disc.

---

[195] "Horizon of the Aten", now Tell el Amarna.

However, long before taking this step, the royal heir had been fixated on the Aten. In a way, Akhenaten was rather like the passenger in an airplane who feels on a conscious or subconscious level that, if he relaxes and stops worrying about the plane, it will crash. In his anxiety, he is "concentrating" on the machine and keeping it aloft. The other passengers, who are more relaxed, do not exactly believe nothing bad can happen to them, but prefer to bet on the odds in favor of them arriving safely at their destination. In short, I think Akhenaten ceased to have confidence in the reliability of the sun and also, in his egotism, felt he was the man who could make it keep shining if he paid it sufficient attention.

King Akhenaten, in my opinion, was a neurotic individual but certainly a progressive ruler in some ways.[1] In his eagerness to please his god, whom he evidently felt was a jealous one, he began to persecute what he concluded were the useless gods of Egypt, who were as much a part of life in the Two Lands as the Nile, itself. Lest one is tempted to think that the veneration of animals, which is what many of the established deities basically were, is totally harmless if decidedly unsophisticated, one must be reminded that such a theology can sometimes cause difficulties. The roving sacred cows of India, for example, cannot provide meat for the hungry poor but they do constitute a hazard to every kind of navigation on the streets and roadways, and do nothing for sanitation there, either. The ancient writers have informed us that the worship of the sacred cats of Egypt posed a much more serious potential threat, as anyone suspected of harming one was put to death by the ordinary people around him. Even a cat that died of natural causes was supposedly mourned by the Egyptians by the act of

---

[1] In order to preserve his brand of monotheism and still be a god, himself, Akhenaten and his chief wife presented themselves as Shu and Tefnut, two deities who formed a sort of "holy trinity" with the sun-god, having sprung from him in the first place.

shaving off their own eyebrows. Felines being presumably numerous under such conditions, they procreated apace but it was not the custom to give them names. Dogs, however, were sometimes treated as individuals and named by those who cared to own them. The museums of the world possess mummies of the various animals that inhabited ancient Egypt. Hundreds of them have been found.

> "*Compel an Egyptian to consume milk of a sheep; if you have the power to do so, impel an inhabitant of Pelusium to eat an onion. Almost every city in Egypt worships its own animals and monsters, and whatever they revere is regarded by them as inviolable and sacred.*"[2]

Diodorus, however, gives some more, rather charming details of the attention paid to the zoomorphic deities:

> "*These cut up flesh for the hawks and calling to them with a loud cry toss it up to them, as they swoop by, until they catch it, while for the cats and ichneumons[3] they break up bread into milk and calling them with a clucking sound set it before them…*

Even though the subjects of Akhenaten were forbidden to worship any gods in animal form, the primary animus of the pharaoh was directed at the idol that was represented as a man, called "Amen".[4]   By the 18th Dynasty, this was the chief deity of Egypt, and was served by a powerful priesthood. Eventually, at least by his Year 9, Akhenaten stripped the priests of their influence by shutting down the

---

[2] Jerome, *Adversus Iovinianum II.*

[3] A kind of mongoose, called "Pharaoh's cat" (*kutt Faraon*), worshipped as a god due to its aiding humans by being the fearless enemy of snakes.

[4] Probably more properly written as "Amun", but I endeavor to keep consistency with the spelling of the name "Amenhotep", which is always written thus.

temples. Whereas previously the First Prophet of Amen had been rather like a pope, now Akhenaten filled that role, himself, in the cult of the Aten.

While some modern Egyptophiles like to think of Akhenaten as an introspective dreamer, one suspects he was more like Henry VIII of England in that he enjoyed pomp and  grandeur, being convinced that there were no restrictions on his personal behavior. Actually, King Hal realized there were limits but preferred to work around them. Akhenaten did not need to divorce or execute any of his wives because the pharaoh of Egypt traditionally kept as many women as he could afford. His queen was a lady of exceptional beauty, Nefertiti, whom he perhaps loved as much as he claimed to on his monuments, but he had at least one other wife that we know of, named Kiya. And we cannot ignore the evidence that Akhenaten, in time, married his eldest daughter, Meritaten, and had a child by her. There is also the suspicion that this religious reformer had sex with others among his six daughters and even his own widowed mother.[5]

Just how much the Egyptians disapproved of their ruler's comportment with regard to the females in his family, we have no way of knowing, but we can safely guess that the "heretic's" worst act, in their eyes, was the desecration of the name of his late father wherever it was cut into stone— precisely because the name contained the element of the taboo god. Amenhotep III had been a kind of god, himself,

---

[5] The character of Oedipus, the king of Thebes who unwittingly killed his own father and married his mother is thought by some to be modeled on Akhenaten or what remained of him in Greek mnemohistory. Along these lines, the dramas, *Seven Against Thebes* and *Antigone* would represent the post-Amarna period.

and had occupied Egypt's throne for nearly 40 years. The social structure of the country was based on the family, just as it is in our own land today. Most men had only one wife at a time and polygamy was left to those who could support such indulgences. On the other hand, numerous children, particularly sons, were preferable and much depended on these sons being dutiful. An ungrateful son was considered an aberration and so Akhenaten wholly disgraced himself in the eyes of his people, who no doubt found his religious zeal no excuse at all for having his father's cartouches mutilated with chisels. A man's name meant everything in ancient Egypt. Without it written intact somewhere, immortality was lost to him.

Sigmund Freud, the author of *Moses and Monotheism*, believed that the roots of anti-Semitism are to be found in Egypt, in the reaction to the deeds of Akhenaten, everything about him being suspiciously un-Egyptian, from his philosophy to his appearance. In fact, this pharaoh commissioned uglier-than-life portraits of himself that were, in some strange sense, rather like anti-Semitic cartoons. Certainly, these images stressed and even exaggerated the ways in which the king differed from the Egyptian ideal and leaned toward the artistic convention used by Egyptians to represent their Asiatic foes.

In pursuit of his own legacy to posterity, Akhenaten followed the pharaonic occupation of erecting impressive monuments—although this seemed more of a compulsion earlier in his reign, in his pre-Akhetaten days (after that he concentrated on beautifying his model city[6]). Gebel el Silsila and its great quarry is not at the southern extreme of Egypt as is Elephantine or Aswan, but it is pretty far south at that. There a traveler could find a four meters high stela of Akhenaten that declared how the commanders of the soldiery mustered a large corvee to hew sandstone for the great Ben-Ben, the obelisk at Karnak. At Gebel el Silsila, the king is called Amenhotep, although he already worships the Aten on his stela and is styled "high-priest" of that deity. For the first five years of the reign of Amenhotep IV, there was a great deal of activity in all the quarries of Upper and Middle Egypt in order to supply his building projects. Not the least important aspect of Gelbel el Silsila and the other quarries of the pharaoh is that they were the "penal colonies" of Egypt.

According to the great Amarna scholar, Cyril Aldred:

> "*an excised portion of the text on the stela refers to a Master of Works who is made responsible for all new construction of the king, and the most likely candidate for this office is May, whose tomb at Amarna (No.14) shows him to have been the Superintendant of All the Works of the King, and in addition to other duties, the Scribe of the Elite Troops and the Commander of the Soldiery of the King, offices that would have put him in charge of the labor corps.*"[7]

The name of May had already been excised in antiquity.

Also intriguing is the fact that there was already another May, First Prophet of Amen, beginning of Amenhotep IV's

---

[6] Akhenaten inscribed on his "Boundary Stele", that he never wished to leave Akhetaten, dead or alive. "*These fourteen monuments*", to quote Donald Redford, "*were carved in rock, extending in a great arc across the Nile and the Bahr Yussef to the western desert edge and back again, thus defining the boundaries of "greater" Akhetaten.*" *Akhenaten the Heretic King* (New Jersey, 1984).

[7] *Akhenaten, King of Egypt*, (London, 1999)

reign, as witnessed by his two graffiti at the Wadi Hammamat quarries dated to Year 4, 3rd month of Inundation. No higher ranking prisoner at this place is imaginable. Thus we see how an Egyptian king rid himself of those individuals he perceived as dangerous, disloyal, or in some other way undesirable, irrespective of that person's station in life.

Yet there were others who went out of their way to demonstrate their fealty to Akhenaten. These were the vassal princes of the Egyptian empire, who ruled the various city-states of Canaan. They wrote letter after letter to the pharaoh in the Akkadian language, the lingua franca of the ancient Near East, their missives being tablets of fired clay. Akhenaten kept them in an archive at Tell el Amarna and many are preserved to this day.

The princes regularly implored the Egyptian king to send them troops in order to aid them in their squabbles with one another, all the while hinting broadly that Akhenaten could only keep his empire as long as his vassals were willing to serve him and promote his interests. They also exhorted the pharaoh to protect them from some of the cheeky and arrogant Egyptian officers, swaggering about with their wooden batons under their arms, who were stationed in Canaan and who failed to show them proper respect. Not least, the local princes repeatedly warned Akhenaten about the "Apiru", the people who seemingly deferred to nobody and posed a considerable threat. Their chief was one called "Labayu" (the Lion), who had taken the "land of Shechem" (the highlands of the north of Canaan) for the Apiru. A frequent correspondent, the vassal Abdu-Heba, wrote:

> *"The arm of the mighty king [Akhenaten], conquers the land of Naharaim and the land of Kush, but now the Apiru capture the cities of the king. There is not a single governor remaining to the king, my lord—all have perished!...Wherefore does the king not call them into account? Let the king take care of his land."*

For some reason, Akhenaten failed to act or make a sufficient show of strength and the Egyptian position in the Levant began to ascend to its lowest point since Thutmose I, Akhenaten's ancestor, took it upon himself to conquer these territories. Was the monotheist merely a poor administrator or was his attention diverted by a pestilence that was one of several virulent visitations to occur within the next century?

Whatever the cause of the loosening of the pharaoh's hold over the empire, it was surely not a sympathy with the rebellious Apiru that kept him from sending his army to crush them. Nevertheless, there are some people today who insist that Akhenaten and Moses were one and the same!

The name Moses or, in the Torah, Moshe, has proved problematic as to its origin. It is not really a Hebrew name and neither it, nor Aharon (Aaron), are attested again in the Bible, but were used in the Diaspora. Moshe has been surmised to come from the Hebrew mashah or "drawing out". The Bible does say of Pharaoh's Daughter "*And she called his name Moses and said 'Because I drew him out of the water.'*"[8]

Still, it doesn't make much sense for an Egyptian royal lady to have called her adopted son after a Semitic word even if she realized he was a Hebrew. Moreover, it is not unheard of for baby boys to be discovered floating in reed cradles covered with pitch in the literature of the Ancient Near East, (Sargon I of Akkad claimed this as a feature of his biography) so this part of the history of the man called Moses is perhaps just a means to Hebraicize this foreign name as being associated with water. Clement of Alexandria offered the following explanation in his Stromata[9]:

---

[8] Exodus 2: 10

[9] *Miscellanies.*

"Thereupon the queen gave the babe the name of Moses, with etymological propriety, from his being drawn out of "the water,"—for the Egyptians call water "mou,"—in which he had been exposed to die. For they call Moses one who "who breathed [on being taken] from the water."

Evidently, Clement sought an Egyptian rationale for the great leader's appellation, attempting to combine the elements "mw" and "zz" (breathe)[10], without contradicting the Biblical text. Even though Clement was probably a Greek, born in Athens, he appears to have known some Egyptian, which was then still a viable tongue.[11] Yet he did not seem to know (or perhaps care) that there had once been a name "ms" (written "Mose" for popular Egyptological consumption), that was quite popular during the 18th and 19th Dynasties.[12]

In fact, it seems to have been taken for granted among the classic sages and historians that "Moses" was not the formal name of the law-giver—and perhaps was not a "real name" at all--but some sort of epithet or descriptive. Josephus, a Jew who wrote in Greek, was disturbed by this and was actually greatly incensed by the notion of some Egyptians that Moses, himself, was an Egyptian. In his treatise, *Against Apion*[13], Josephus quotes two authors,

---

[10] As they are transliterated from Egyptian writing.

[11] But not in Alexandria, where Greek reigned supreme.

[12] This word element has the meaning of "born" and, while often joined with the name of a deity as in Thutmose (the god Thoth is born) or Ramose (Ra is born), was a name by itself, too. Exactly what Mose was supposed to imply when it stood alone cannot be exactly known, but it can have meant "prince" or simply "man-child". The Rosetta Stone is a prime example of how well Middle Egyptian, the language of the monumental texts of Egypt for centuries, could still be utilized by certain people in Ptolemaic times. Manetho, himself, claimed to have studied "the ancient records". Yet no one in antiquity that we know of—least of all Manetho— ever suggested this etymology for the name of Moses.

[13] A work intended to refute the writings of Apion and other Egyptian historians, all of whom Josephus viewed as anti-Semitic. No doubt, for the most part, Josephus was correct.

Manetho and Chaeremon, who evidently had some opinions regarding Moses. Manetho was cited as claiming that his true name was "*Osarseph, after the god, Osiris*" and that he had changed his name to Moses only after he, as the leader of a disenfranchised group of rebels, joined forces with some people from Canaan and made war on the pharaoh, turning Egypt topsy-turvy.

This seemed absurd to Josephus, who wrote:

> "*According to Manetho, Moses was called Osarseph. These names, however, are not interchangeable; the true name signifies 'one saved out of the water' for water is called by the Egyptians 'mo-y'.*"

In other words, Josephus was not interested in any other etymology than that suggested by the Torah or that Moses may have possessed a name fitting for an Egyptian— although he is, of course, correct in that "Moses" does not seem a likely substitution for "Osarseph". The writings of the Egyptian savant, Manetho, were a couple of hundred years old when Josephus read them and had probably already been annotated and corrupted by various persons with agendas of their own. So it is by no means certain whether the priest of Heliopolis changing his name to Moses was not simply a gloss added by someone who wished to reconcile the Jewish tradition of the Exodus with the "*Tale of the Polluted Ones*" of Manetho.[14]

---

[14] Another possibility is that Manetho meant that Osarseph was merely dubbed "Moses" and this did not actually constitute a name change. There is also the chance that Osarseph, himself, was a Hebrew despite being a priest of an Egyptian god. One can cite the example of a certain Yanzab, a man who actually did bear a Semitic name, who had the honor of being one of four priests who carried on their shoulders the portable shrine of the deified King Ahmose I during the reign of Ramesses II. It is interesting to note that James Hoch, in his *Semitic Words in Egyptian Texts of the New Kingdom and Third Intermediate Period* (New Jersey, 1994), believes "Yanzab" or "Yanzibu" could mean "He (a god) will establish (him)" in Semitic. (page 54)

This same story, according to Josephus, was repeated by his contemporary, Chaeremon,[15] also an Egyptian, in a somewhat different version. Chaeremon apparently maintained that the coalition of dissident Egyptians and Canaanites was led by both Moses and Joseph, whose Egyptian names were "Tisithen" and "Peteseph", respectively.

While one would think the Book of Exodus would be the first to claim a Hebrew name for Moses before he was accepted into the pharaoh's household—it makes no mention of one, even though his parents, Amram and Yocheved[16], are introduced. However, there clearly was a curiosity among the authors of antiquity about the original name of Moses, a man who was, for some reason, revered by Jews and Egyptians, alike—even though the latter viewed him, not as the deliverer of an oppressed people, but as the leader of a gang of oppressors. Josephus admitted with irritation:

"The Egyptians, who regard that man as remarkable, even divine, wish to claim him as one of themselves, while making the incredible and calumnious assertion that he was one of the priests expelled from Heliopolis for leprosy."

Clement of Alexandria wrote of Moses:

"It is clear that previously the parents gave a name to the child on his circumcision; and he was called Joachim."

This is a remarkable statement, not only because it is unsupported by the Bible—but because no one else suggests it.

The name "Joachim" is also written "Yehoiakim". It was assumed by one Eliakim, in 2 Kings 24:34.

---

[15]Chaeremon lived as a pedagogue and archivist in Alexandria for some years, and after 49 CE went to Rome as the tutor of Nero.

[16] Amram having married his own aunt, Yocheved.

144

"And Pharaoh-Necho[17] made Eliakim the son of Josiah king (of Judah) in the place of Josiah his father, and changed his name to Jehoiakim..."

In my estimation, the reason for this change is the following: "Eliakim" means "Raised-up by El" in the sense of "elevated and established". However, the pharaoh, considering himself divine, was really the one who had "elevated" Eliakim and so gave him the name containing a more generic/ephemeral term for God, one that corresponded better to "nTr" (pronounced "noute"), the generic "god" of the Egyptians, applied also to their king. Thus, "Yehoiakim".

Chaeremon maintained that Moses was known, in Egyptian, as "Tisithen". The name "Tisithen" means something not quite so grand as "Joachim", as we shall see in due course.

Where Clement of Alexandria gleaned the information that the man who became popularly known as "Moses" was once called "Raised-up by God" is a great mystery, in itself. In his interesting study, *Moses the Egyptian*,[18] German Egyptologist, Jan Assmann, says of Moses:

"Seen as a figure of memory, he belongs to a kind of counter-memory. By counter-memory I mean a memory that puts elements to the fore that are, or tend to be, forgotten in the official memory."

I would agree, and even out of this "mnemohistory" there have emerged certain bits and pieces that have been overlooked.

The ancient authors associated the name, Moses, with a pharaoh, a plague and a time of general upheaval. Manetho

---

[17] Nekau, having the throne-name of Wahemibre and supposedly reigning 610-595 BCE.

[18] Harvard University Press, 1998.

and Chaeremon, both Egyptians who wrote in Greek, did not see him as a prince but as a priest/scribe who, becoming cut off from Egyptian society, emerged as the leader of a mixed multitude that caused a great deal of trouble within Egypt and lost a pharaoh his throne.   The tale they tell is what some of us refer to as "the Egyptian version of the Book of Exodus" and this will be discussed in detail in a subsequent chapter.

A Roman, Publius Cornelius Tacitus, offers:

"Most writers, however, agree in stating that once a disease, which horribly disfigured the body, broke out over Egypt; that king Bocchoris, in search of a remedy, consulted the oracle of Hammon[19], and was advised to cleanse his realm, and to transport to some foreign land this race detested by the gods. The people, who had been collected through diligent searching, found themselves stranded in a desert. For the most part they sat in a stupor of grief, until one of the exiles, Moyses by name, warned them not to look for any relief from God or man, having been forsaken by both, but to trust in themselves. He advised they should accept for their divinely-appointed leader that man who should first contrive a way out of their present misery. They agreed, and in utter ignorance began to advance at random. The worst of their problems was the scarcity of water, and they had sunk ready to perish scattered over the terrain, when a herd of wild asses was seen coming from their pasture to a rock shaded by trees. Moyses followed them, and, beckoned by what seemed to be a grassy area, discovered an abundant spring of water. This furnished relief. After a continuous journey for six days, on the seventh they possessed themselves of a country, from which they expelled the inhabitants, and in which they founded a city and a temple."

The "Bocchoris", mentioned by Diodorus Siculus, as being "*a man who was altogether contemptible in personal*

_____

[19] That is, "Amen".

146

appearance", and the "Bocchoris" of Tacitus was not just another corruption of a pharaoh's prenomen or "throne-name" but something more complex. Josephus accused Lysimachus, for example, of inventing a whole new royal name when the latter wrote of "Bocchoris" but this is not strictly true, as will be explained.[20]

Abraham Ibn Ezra[21], in his commentary to Exodus II:10, states that Moses was called "Monios" by the Egyptians. Was this some sort of epithet? If so, what was it? Given that the passage in Exodus is "*And Moses and Aaron did all these wonders before Pharaoh; and the Lord hardened Pharaoh's heart, and he did not let the children of Israel go out of his land*", perhaps we are looking for the Egyptian "mnyt" (with a silent /t/), which means " foe, opponent". Alternatively, there was a term in Egyptian, written "mn", which had the meaning of "So-and-So", an avoidance of identification. That a similar word was an important title of the court ca 1510 BCE will be demonstrated shortly.

There seems to be no disagreement as to the place of Moses's birth, Heliopolis, in Egyptian called "On". While not exactly disagreement, some confusion may have existed on this point: Heliopolis was a city dedicated to the worship of Amen-Ra, the sun-god. It was on the edge of what the Bible calls "the Land of Goshen", the oasis of the eastern Delta. However, there was yet another "On", not far from Thebes,

---

[20] Bakenrenef, a king of the 24th Dynasty, was called "Bocchoris" by the Greeks. Seemingly, there was an older "Bocchoris", who was a man known for his strange appearance, but his name was only written this way in imitation of Bakenrenef, as the Greeks believed this to be a real Egyptian kingly name. The older "Bocchoris" was actually no name at all but a familiar Egyptian reproach.

[21] Ibn Ezra, Abraham ben Meir (1092-1167 CE), Spanish Jewish scholar, poet, and author. Ibn Ezra is best known for his biblical commentaries, especially those on the Pentateuch, which are often included in Hebrew editions of the Old Testament.

where Montu, the war-god, was the chief deity. This was sometimes called the Southern On to distinguish it from Heliopolis, which was the Northern On. On-Montu survives today as "Arment" and Arthur Weigall, an Egyptologist at the turn of the 20th Century wrote:

> "Amongst the inhabitants of modern Arment there is a firm belief that Moses was born at this spot. In the absence of any definite knowledge regarding this event, one may say that it is quite within the bounds of probability that the law-giver really was born here. Hidden among the rushes to the north of the town, his cradle would have been within a mile or so of the ordinary bathing place of the princes and princesses living in the palaces near Medinet Habu. Indeed, one may go so far as to say that there is no more likely spot for a royal bathing-place than the west bank of the river, halfway between Luxor and Arment..." [22]

So a confusion of these two sites would be understandable—not by the ancient Egyptians, who would have been quite clear as to which was which—but by later classical writers. Those who believed Moses was a priest who ran afoul of the bureaucracy may have preferred that he was, like the father-in-law of the patriarch, Joseph, a "priest of On", ensconced at Heliopolis. Those who imagined him a prince may have thought it credible that fate had brought him to Thebes to be raised there in the court.

Actual history can be drab, but memory cannot support the commonplace, so it follows that only those situations and persons, around which can be constructed some type of legend or romance, will survive in unrecorded recollection. Unadorned facts, like unwrapped gifts, are seldom brought forward. The real Moses remains as elusive as a shade. One gets the idea that this was even true a few centuries before the start of the Common Era, although it is obvious that nobody in antiquity asserted, not even anti-Semites,

---

[22] *Antiquities of Egypt* (London, 1910)

that Moses had never existed and was a figment of some author's imagination.

Akhenaten as Moses makes no sense to me because Akhenaten's form of monotheism is nothing like that of Moses. Akhenaten has always reminded me, in certain ways, of the Flower Children in the America of the Seventies, who affected a sensitive demeanor and who studiously avoided a "glamorous" appearance, while at the same time espousing the crede "anything goes". Akhenaten appeared to see beauty in nature, judging by his "Hymn to the Aten", but evidently insisted on having himself, his children, and often even his lovely queen, portrayed in a decidedly bizarre— albeit affectionate--manner. Unless he is very much maligned in this area, signs seem to point to Akhenaten not worrying about any boundaries to his personal behavior. It appears he probably slept with his daughters and may have even caused the premature death of one of them in childbirth. If, as some believe, Akhenaten was the being from whose life and reign the legend of Oedipus was derived, that means he also slept with his own mother. This suspicion about the pharaoh is fueled by the fact that a little girl named Baketaten, who seems to have been the youngest child of Akhenaten's mother, Queen Tiye, was not given the title "king's sister" in her portraits at el Amarna, thereby eliminating Amenhotep III as her father. Since Baketaten is, however, styled "king's daughter", the only other man who can possibly have been her sire was Akhenaten.[23]

There are indications that a plague raged in the latter part of the reign of Akhenaten and beyond it, one that, in the

---

[23] In order to absolve Akhenaten of carnal relations with his mother, some Egyptologists have maintained that Baketaten was the king's daughter by his secondary wife, Kiya, who died, the little girl being then adopted by her grandmother, Tiye. This, of course, is a perfectly plausible explanation. Still, a man who showed himself capable of "eradicating" his father by mutilating his name cannot be, psychologically speaking, beyond suspicion of seeing him as a rival to be vanquished and replaced in every sense.

usual manner of fierce pestilences coming out of Africa, spread over a wider area and decimated other populations.[24] One has the feeling that this particular contagion was so memorable that it was supposed by some to have been one of the plagues described in the Book of Exodus.

If one leaves out the names, the story of Oedipus the King, gleaned from several Greek sources, boils down to the following: A baby prince, condemned to die because of an oracle proclaiming that he would slay his father and marry his mother, is sheltered by a shepherd and, upon reaching manhood, unwittingly fulfills the prophecy in a place called Thebes. A plague is visited upon the land and so the brother of the mother/wife of Oedipus is sent to a distant place in order to ascertain why it had occurred. From another oracle, the uncle of Oedipus learns his shocking secret. When all is revealed, the mother/wife of Oedipus learns the truth about Oedipus' past. Devastated, the lady commits suicide and Oedipus, taking some pins from her clothing, blinds himself by sticking them into his eyes.

Oedipus has two sons and two daughters. The king is forced into exile, accompanied by one of the girls. The uncle becomes a regent for the two princes and, when they are sufficiently grown, it is decided that they should rule the kingdom jointly by turns. But one son grows overly ambitious and attempts to push out his brother. The injured sibling seeks out Oedipus in exile and attempts to enlist his aid in unseating the selfish brother. But Oedipus, still angry with his sons for allowing him to be exiled in the first place and usurping his prerogative, curses them both. They kill each other in accordance with the malediction wished upon them by their father.

---

[24] Shortly after the passing of Akhenaten, Egypt engaged in a confrontation with the Hittites, the latter leaving records saying that their land was in desolation because they had caught the plague from Egyptian prisoners of war, which continued to kill people after twenty years had lapsed!

The uncle of the two heirs now makes himself king, while at the same time proclaiming one of his nephews a hero and the other a traitor. The former is given a lavish burial while the latter is denied any burial but is to be left out for the vultures. However, one of Oedipus's daughters takes pity on her brother and secretly buries him. But she is found out and incurs the wrath of her uncle, the king. Her cousin, the king's son, is in love with Oedipus's daughter and wants to marry her. Father and son have a falling out and the daughter of Oedipus is condemned to be entombed alive. Meanwhile, the Thebans hear of these goings on and believe the royal family and its scandals are causing the pestilence to worsen. There is a riot and the princess's tomb is broken into. She is found hung by her scarf therein, her heartbroken cousin being with her but still living. The young man at first threatens to kill his father but then falls on his own sword. His mother, the present queen, plunges a knife into her heart in her grief and the king, realizing the folly of his pride, abandons himself to the Fates.

There are a number of parallels here to what we know, or what is suspected about, the Amarna age. There is no sign that Akhenaten actually killed his father, Amenhotep III, but he certainly committed crimes against the memory of his predecessor. Just how close the heretic was to his widowed mother, Queen Tiye, can only be a matter for speculation. We also do not know for certain that Akhenaten had any sons, but Egyptology does believe that two young men followed him in rapid succession. One of them, Tutankhamen, was given a fabulous burial while the other, Smenkhkare, was deprived of his funerary articles and may be the mummy found in that make-shift tomb, KV55. Scholars tend to believe that the next pharaoh, Ay, was the brother of Queen Tiye. It is thought that he had at least one son, a general named Nakhtmin, but he had no apparent heirs when he died. Exactly what happened to Akhenaten's remaining daughters[25], no one can say. It is not impossible

---

[25] One of the six died in her father's reign.

that one of them, Meritaten or Ankhesenamen[26], is the mummy in KV55. The report was that the body was found with its left arm raised to its chest in the queenly pose and a solid gold vulture pectoral was twisted about its skull in mocking imitation of a queen's headdress.

The Aten, no matter how great a force Akhenaten perceived it to be, was not an entity to suggest a code of ethics to the king. On the other hand, the monotheism of Moses goes hand in hand with the Law defined in Leviticus. Without this code the religion of Moses would not have done any more to shape the lifestyle of the Hebrews than the monotheism of Akhenaten, simply substituting an ephemeral God for the solar disc. The final result, Judaism, is based more on the Law of Moses than on the God of Moses, who isn't even defined, except that in later days He was made into a kind of majestic father figure (Avinu Malkenu).

Atenism, as far as one can tell, expected nothing of the average individual except that he refrain from worshipping other gods. Akhenaten, himself, was the intermediary through which others received the benefits of the Aten—the High Priest of its cult. How he justified this to himself and others is difficult to understand because it would seem fairly obvious that the sun does not play favorites with its benefices—nor does it discriminate as to whom it gives sunstroke. Nevertheless, the caressing hands of the Aten do not seem to touch anybody in the art except the royals.

It was the Law of Moses that enabled the Hebrews to live as a civilized people and act as keepers of the Golden Rule, which other peoples also adopted, having seen it as a sensible way of life. The Ten Commandments and the rest of the requirements and prohibitions spelled out what "boundaries" Jews needed to observe in order to live in harmony with one another and their environment, whether they were king or commoner. The Law of Moses is very clearly against incest and it strains credibility that

---

[26] Who became the queen of Tutankhamen.

Akhenaten could suddenly have dreamed up a whole new code of behavior that is contrary to his entire lifestyle—if, in fact, the deeds of the pharaoh have been correctly interpreted—during his time as king of Egypt.

Even more generally, assuming Akhenaten never committed incest at all, how does he suddenly become an altruistic human being, someone with so much social conscience that he is willing to free the Hebrews from the yoke of his own bondage as an emperor and give them a code, besides? My suspicion is that the man spent most of his reign in elegant idleness, indulging his fancies and accepting the flattery of the parvenus he raised to important positions at Akhetaten because they had followed him there. Akhenaten's priority seems to have been to exercise his new powers as sole king by forcing all of Egypt to follow his own mindset when it came to religion—or one might find ones new address to be the quarries.[27]

That the ancient writers connected Akhenaten to a plague and to an expulsion/revolt will be demonstrated here. It is thought by some that everyone left his city, Akhetaten, immediately his kingship was terminated, but that probably isn't true. His most important officials all had tombs made near the city, but there is no evidence any of them had been used for actual burial. It is difficult to credit that none of these civil servants had passed on in the 11 to 12 years of residence at el Amarna. We do not know exactly who these men were or of what ethnicity. Is it possible some were Hebrews and left or were expelled? Perhaps, at least initially, the worship of one god was something that had appealed to them. Can Moses have been among them? Did he grow up with Akhenaten?

Since the incident of the baby boy in the reed basket is surely wholly apocryphal, the alternative must be that Moses

---

[27] Actually, the quarries were more habitable places than one might imagine. Huge sections were cut out of the rock that were as roomy as large caves and these probably made no worse homes than the ruined temples and plundered tombs in which the Egyptians squatted in the last few centuries of our modern era.

was, indeed, "adopted" into the royal family for some more commonplace reason—perhaps because his father or mother may have been a functionary of the court.

Chapter Nine

If the Book of Exodus combines perhaps four exodoi of the proto-Jews from Egypt, the major question must be "To which expulsion did the character named Moses actually belong"?

Moses, who claimed his father was "a wandering Aramean",[29] was said by Flavius Josephus to have been of the seventh generation of Hebrews who had migrated from Ur of the Chaldees.

"And he was, by the admission of all, according to God's prediction, no less for his greatness of mind than for his contempt of difficulties, the best of all the Hebrews, for Abraham was his ancestor of the seventh generation. For Moses was the son of Amram, who was the son of Caath, whose father Levi was the son of Jacob, who was the son of Isaac, who was the son of Abraham."

That means that even Amram was hardly a new-comer and should have had an Egyptian name in addition to his Semitic one—as was already the case with the 13th Dynasty slaves of the Brooklyn Papyrus. In fact, Jews of today, no matter what else they are called, have Hebrew names that are used on special occasions, when they are summoned to the Torah to read from it, for example.

However, what Moses' father was called in Egyptian may never be known. The Book of Numbers seems to contain very few Egyptian names among the persons who left Egypt.[30] It would stand to reason that, when the census was

---

[29] Deuteronomy 26:5 traces Hebrew ancestry to the Arameans, but perhaps it is meant in a broader sense than the actual father of Moses being a wanderer. The father of Moses was born in Egypt, surely.

[30] One Egyptian name that comes to mind is "Phineas", probably "PaNehes" or "the Cushite".

taken after the Exodus, the Hebrew names of the Israelites would have been the only ones of any importance as their Egyptian ones would no longer be used.

Josephus also maintained that the Exodus occurred 430 years after Abraham. My own father was born in 1917. I, his eldest child, married and reproduced quite early and my eldest daughter had her children a bit later. By the year 2000, during a span of 83 years, our family had managed to beget only three more generations after my father. However, if I had managed to be born by 1933 when my father was 16 and if I had had my eldest child at 16, as well, this pattern continuing until 1997, five generations could have arisen in about the same number of years. That is why the ancient historians were correct when they claimed that 20 generations can occur over a 400-year time span.

Seven generations, in actuality, are by far too few and the reproductive pattern of the family of Moses is quite unrealistic. If the ancestors of Moses had resided in Egypt for four centuries, the likelihood of Amram, Moses's father, being still a slave or anything but thoroughly integrated into Egyptian society is very remote.

. If we place Abraham in the time of Amenemhat I/Senusret I, the early 12th Dynasty, 430 years later would perhaps arrive at a feasible timeframe for the reign of Ahmose I, using as his first regnal year 1570 BCE.[31] Now Moses, supposedly being a man of already 80 by the time he led the Israelites, would have been far older than Ahmose, the Theban prince, who was a very young man at this stage. Moses would have

---

[31] Sir Alan Gardiner, for one, warned that Manetho's dates for his dynasties must be taken cum grano salis because "*to abandon 1786 B.C. as the year when Dyn. XII ended would be to cast adrift our only firm anchor* [meaning the Sothic date in the El-Lahun papyrus], *a course that would have serious consequences for the history, not of Egypt alone, but of the entire Middle East.*" In other words, the Sothic dating allows only 216 years between the beginning of the Second Intermediate Period and King Ahmose I.

been old enough to be Ahmose's grandfather or even great-grandfather, which means the former would have had to have been born ca. 1650 BCE by our chronology. Because the expulsion of the Hyksos was held to be the time of an exodus of the Hebrews, as well, Moses was connected to Ahmose I, but not all the ancient authors agreed with the conclusion that the great Hebrew prophet and Ahmose were adversaries.

Syncellus, otherwise known as "George the Monk"[32], wrote that he had seen convincing evidence that **Moses was still young in the time of Ahmose.** Syncellus was referring to the work of Eusebius[33], which echoed the writing of Artapanus, a Jewish historian. Artapanus claimed to know the name of the pharaoh who knew Moses in his youth, writing of the era in which he believed Moses lived "*at that time there were many kings of Egypt*". Not only does Artapanus not adhere to the notion that Ahmose was the Pharaoh of the Exodus, **he seemingly places the event ca. 1510 BCE.** The Christian writer, Eusebius, subscribed to this idea, as well,[34]and so did Bar Hebraeus[35], a man who wrote a history of the world in Syriac.

It is certainly true of the Second Intermediate Period, the time before the advent of Ahmose I as the "sovereign of all

---

[32] Circa 800 CE, an attendant of the Patriarch of Constantinople, utilized Manetho's text, as transmitted by Julius Africanus and Eusebius, in his history of the world from Adam to the emperor Diocletian. He had doubtless had access to more corrupt forms of Manetho, as well.

[33] *Praeparatio Evangelica.*

[34] In fact, Eusebius warned that Manetho's king list should not be read as always being in sequence from predecessor to heir, since it probably included the names of dynasties which ruled concurrently in several different parts of Egypt. But this warning has been largely ignored.

[35] The son of a Jewish physician, Bar Hebraeus became a Jacobite monk and bishop called Gregory, although his original name had been Yochanan. His major works are his *Makhtebhânûth Zabhnê*, a history of the world, and his *Al-Mukhtasar Fî 'd-Dawal*, an Arabic recension of political history. Bar Hebraeus died in 1286 CE in Persia.

Egypt", that the land was ruled by numerous petty kings[36], but Artapanus does not appear to have had the 13th Dynasty in mind at all.

Clement of Alexandria wrote:

> *"And so Artapanus, in his work **On the Jews**[37], relates 'that Moses, being shut up in custody by Chenephres, king of the Egyptians, on account of the people demanding to be let go from Egypt, the prison being opened by night, by the intercession of God, went forth, and reaching the palace, stood before the king as he slept, and awakened him; and that the latter, struck with what had taken place, bade Moses tell him the name of the God who had sent him; and that he, bending forward, told him in his ear; and that the king on hearing it fell down speechless, but being supported by Moses, revived again'".*

Woe unto the reader now, for you are about to encounter a tangled web woven by some very perplexed ancient writers! Some of the characters connected to the account of Artapanus are familiar to us from Manetho's 18th Dynasty, even though "Chenephres" is conspicuously absent. Small wonder, as Khaneferre Sobekhotep IV existed toward the end of the 13th Dynasty when *"there were many kings of Egypt"* and he more likely had dealings with Joseph instead of

---

[36] A 13th Dynasty came into being due to the fact that the 12th Dynasty died out, it's last representative being Sobekneferu, a woman pharaoh. According to Peter Clayton's *Chronicle of the Pharaohs*, the 13th Dynasty consisted of 10 rulers who lasted for 70 years—from about 1782-1720 BCE. But Clayton remarks: *"The true chronology of the 13th Dynasty is rather hard to ascertain since there are few monuments dating from the period; many of the king's names are known only from an odd fragmentary inscription or, a little later in the period, from scarabs."* I take that to mean that neither the order of succession of the 13th Dynasty nor how much of it overlapped with the 14th or 15th Dynasty is so well understood.

[37] *Peri Ioudion.*

Moses! According to the Book of Genesis, Joseph was the one who was imprisoned. It is most unfortunate that Moses was probably confused with that other great Hebrew, at times, and we have seen that Chaeremon, for one, even believed these men were contemporaries.

Artapanus further disclosed that the wife of his "Chenephres", *"who was king of the regions beyond Memphis"*, (namely the area of Ity-Tawi near the Faiyum) was named "Merris,"[38] and that she was the daughter of another king, "Palmenothes". Bar Hebraeus, who wrote a similar account, calls this king "Amonpathis". [39]

"Merris", according to Artapanus, adopted "Prince Mousos", a child of the Hebrews. As an adult, this prince was an officer of "Chenephres" and led a military campaign against the Ethiopians. In fact, Moses became so popular that "Chenephres" grew jealous of him and induced someone named "Chanethothes" to kill him[40], but Moses slew Chanethothes, instead, fleeing the wrath of the pharaoh to go to live with Raguel, a Midianite, and his tribe.

It is apparent that Artapanus was talking about the son or son-in-law of a king of Egypt whose name resembled "Amenhotep", but could not recall the former's true name and simply gave him another. Without a doubt, he is referring to the 18th Dynasty.

When Moses returned to his native land, he confronted a new pharaoh. A text known as *Pseudo-Dionysius* informs us that:

---

[38] Also called "Damaris", evidently Egyptian "TA-mrryt" or "The Beloved".

[39] In the Syriac version of Michael the Syrian, the pharaoh's name is given as "Amenophnathis". My source is *The Apocryphon of Jannes and Jambres the Magicians*, by Albert Pietersma (Leiden, 1994). This man was supposedly king of Heliopolis, a city north of Memphis. In some sources, Chenephres is called the "king of Mapas" (Memphis).

[40] Or "Khanothis".

"In year 490 [of the era beginning with Abraham], the king of Egypt died and Chencheres reigned for sixteen years. This was he who waged a contest with Moses, with the help of Jannes and Jambres the magicians. It was about this one that Moses said: 'He drowned Pharaoh and his army in the Red Sea.'"

Chenephres, once again, was not sole king but concurrent with Palmanothes, these supposedly reigning from years 400 to 430 and Chencheres does not ascend the throne of Egypt until 490, after two intervening kings, Oros and Achencheres. Moses is said to have fled under Oros and returned under Chencheres. Apparently, Moses was protected from Chenephres by the latter's wife, Merris, until she died. It was while Chanethothes and Moses were arranging the burial of the royal lady that Chenephres commissioned the Egyptian to murder Moses.[41] Just when Oros enters the picture is not clear.

Even though we are aware that 490 of the Jewish Era should be about 1510 BCE, ninety years before that was 1600 BCE—and we are back to the Second Intermediate Period, before Ahmose I (presumably). Apparently this is when Artapanus believed that "Chenephres" or Sobekhotep IV reigned.

Unfortunately, these rulers of Artapanus et alios are the very ones who have most puzzled the analysts of Manetho's kinglist in the 18th Dynasty. It is all really quite a muddle, a result of the ongoing confusion among the various exodoi of the Semites from Egypt. The date we are given for the reign of "Chencheres" probably belongs to an **earlier exodus**, (1510 BCE), the one that seemingly involved Queen Hatshepsut, her husband, and her nephew. That is the reason Syncellus observed that it seemed to him Moses must have been young (around 20) in 1570 BCE—60 years previously! Nevertheless, "Chenephres", despite actually **preceding**

---

[41] Pietersma, page 9 of his *"Apocryphon"* who consulted several obscure ancient sources on this subject, all of which he cites in his book.

Hatshepsut by many years, represents both Thutmose II (Hatshepsut's husband) and Akhenaten, who would have come numerous years after Hatshepsut.[42] The reason for this is that these two men were both viewed as diseased villains and enemies of the proto-Jews. To be lumped in with these is Thutmose I, the conqueror of much of Canaan.

"Palmanothes" stands for Amenhotep I (father-in-law of Aakheperkare Thutmose I, who likely reigned jointly with him for a time) but also for Amenhotep III, the father of Akhenaten. "Merris" is likely a combination of Meryetamun, (sister and wife of Amenhotep I); Akhenaten's first daughter, Meritaten; Sitamen, the eldest daughter of Amenhotep III, and Hatshepsut. In other words, the tale of Artapanus is an apocryphal one, containing memories of several incidents, all of which had factors in common.

It is rather difficult to imagine the situation of the royal daughters who became the wives of their fathers, as Sitamen and (probably) Meritaten did. Were they actually spouses in every sense of the word, or were they relegated to a sort of limbo where they were not true wives but neither could they marry anyone else? Why did their fathers marry them in the first place? Was it to protect their own interests because the succession came down through these princesses and marrying them kept other pretenders to the throne from doing so? Yet it does seem that some of these daughters actually bore children of their fathers. Amenhotep III, however, had so many concubines[43] in addition to his Chief Wife, Queen Tiye, that he can hardly have had much sexual interest in Sitamen. If her mother, Tiye, had died, it may have been that Sitamen's status could have changed and she

---

[42] I think it especially significant that the prenomen of Akhenaten, "Neferkheperure", resembles "Khaneferre" somewhat.

[43] Some of them evidently specializing in "kinky" sex. See N. Reeves, *Akhenaten: Egypt's False Prophet* (London, 2001) page 61. Always in search of "new talent", the pharaoh wrote to a vassal prince in Gezer "*To Milkilu, the ruler of Gazru. Thus the king...Send extremely beautiful female cupbearers in whom there is no defect...*"

might have been elevated to Chief Wife. But Queen Tiye outlived her husband.

Perhaps this was the reason a junior queen like Sitamen would have adopted a child, knowing she was not likely to get one any other way. In Jewish legend, the pharaoh's daughter is always called "Bithiah", a Hebrew name that means "Daughter of God". So does the name "Sitamen", although the god is an Egyptian one, Amen.

The royal lady is also called "Thermutis", a name that can be associated with Hatshepsut for reasons explained further along. Hatshepsut had no son with her late husband, Thutmose II, but the king had one by a lesser wife, a fact of which Hatshepsut may have been resentful.

Akhenaten, Sitamen's brother, had a vizier serving under him, whom he called called "Tutu" for short because the man's original name contained the proscribed god, Thoth. Can this have been the "Chanethothes" of the tale?[44] As it is known that Moses married the daughter of the Nubian king, he may have been seen as a threat to the pharaoh in the event he decided to turn his coat and march on Egypt with his new wife's people.

As for Meritaten, daughter/wife of Akhenaten—it is thought she may have had a daughter by him called Meritaten Junior but there is no mention of a son—unless possibly Tutankhamen was the offspring of this incestuous union.

Most interesting is that Artapanus supplies that Chenephres *was the first to die of elephantiasis*,"[45] a striking bit of data in light of the theory of some that Akhenaten, one of the pharaohs represented by this appellation, was the

---

[44] Akhenaten also had a very distinguished servant named "Hani", a polyglot who served as his emissary to foreign courts . From what we know of this man, it would seem unlikely that he can have been an assassin.

[45] Pietersma, who informs that this item could be found in Eusebius' *Praeperatio Evangelica*. It is also Pietersma who suggests this can have been leprosy, instead.

model for Oedipus Rex, "oedipus" having the meaning of "swollen foot" or "swollen leg", the distinction not being as specific in Greek as in English.

A limestone relief from Amarna shows Akhenaten with his primary spouse, Nefertiti, after she had become his co-regent[46], probably due to the fact that he had no sons old enough to assume this position and therefore trusted nobody but the queen. That Akehnaten required a second-in-command makes sense in that he possibly suffered from Marfan's Syndrome and blindness in addition to the problem with his limb. In Egyptian art, only the lame are depicted with a foot lifted off the ground and a staff under one arm, as is Akhenaten. In the portrait, Nefertiti offers her husband a bouquet of a lotus flower and some mandrake fruit, which was thought to have aphrodisiacal properties.

However, under the circumstances, he was supposed to, perhaps, smell the yellow "apples" to calm him. In fact, it was thought that, if one smelled the fruit long enough, one became catatonic. It was once believed that mandrake possessed the magic power to heal a number of diseases and to induce a

---

46 Possibly under the name of Ankhe(t)kheperure Neferneferuaten. In her later years, Nefertiti is shown wearing, instead of her famous tall blue headdress, this round helmet that seems to be a modification of a kingly crown called the *khepresh.*

feeling of happiness. That is why the roots of mandrake used to be, in days of yore, tremendously expensive. The mandrake was used as a sedative, soporific, pain-killer and also as a treatment for ulceration.[47]

According to Eusebius[48] (as the monk, Syncellus, tells us) it was in the time of a certain "Chencheres" that *"Moses led the Jews in their march out of Egypt"* but Syncellus adds:

> *"Eusebius alone places in this reign the exodus of Israel under Moses, although no argument supports him, but all his predecessors hold a contrary view, as he testifies."*

Bar Hebraeus asserts that Chenephres founded Hermopolis[49], a city midway between Memphis and Thebes. It was also just across the Nile from Akhetaten, the capital of Akhenaten, a place that was razed to the ground by a successor but many of whose building blocks were re-used at Hermopolis, perhaps lending the impression to some that Akhenaten had actually resided there. Akhenaten, insofar as we know, reigned for 17 years. But there is more to this "many kings" business, as will be explained later. It has to do with the pharaohs' prenomina beginning to become duplicated within the 20th Dynasty.

Of the preservers of Manetho, only Eusebius claims that a Chencheres or Achencheres was king of Egypt for as long as 16 years. Yet all versions of the 18th Dynasty mention at least one pharaoh of a similar name, which may represent

---

[47] The root and plant contain Quercetin, Kaempferol, Podophyllin, Isorhamnetin, Gallic-acid, Berberine, Alpha-peltatin, that are being studied for their healing, anticancer and other properties.

[48] Circa 326 CE.

[49] Modern El-Ashmunein, a remnant of "Khnum", the actual Egyptian name of Hermopolis. In ancient Egypt, "kh" and "sh" were interchangeable according to regional dialect. It is of interest to note the "Prince Mousos" was supposed to have besieged this city in a war that lasted ten years. (D. Rohl, *Pharaohs and Kings*, page 252).

Smenkhkare[50], prenomen Ankhkheperure, an heir of Akhenaten (once called Amenhotep) who seems to have been married to the latter's daughter, Meritaten, but who may have been a female, as well! Indeed, there is evidence that there may have been two different kings with the prenomen of Ankhkheperure during this time, one of them a woman. Actually—and maddeningly— some versions of Manetho's 18th Dynasty list three separate kings named "Acencheres", the first of which is **definitely a female**.   Well, the reader was warned that all this would not be easy to comprehend. If it is any consolation, Egyptologists are perplexed by it, as well.

Since there seems to be considerable confusion in this part of Manetho's 18th dynasty and since it is quite contrary to our modern understanding of ancient Egyptian history, it is logical to assume that there was some sort of breakdown of the central government in the post-Amarna period and that several people were calling themselves "king" at various locations.   There is already a school of thought that holds Akhenaten was a co-regent with his father, Amenhotep III, for his first nine years, which means that, while the latter was in Thebes[51], his son was king over his own city, Akhetaten --now Tell el Amarna.

Let us take a look at Eusebius' version of Manetho's 18th Dynasty and see what is there.   We will start with "*Thuthmosis, 9 years*", which nearly all scholars agree is Thutmose IV, this pharaoh having reigned no longer than the nine years assigned to him, insofar as we know.   Next on the roster is "*Amenophis for 31 years. This is the king who was*

---

[50] In the Egyptian language, the terms "smnx" and "Ax" can have the same meaning of "benefitting" and may have been confused. It would be rather astonishing if Smenkhkare, whoever he really was, occupied the throne for as long as 16 years, for he/she is thought by Egyptology to have been king for only a year or so.

[51] Once again, since "Palmanothes" was supposedly a king of Heliopolis, Egyptian "On", this may have been a confusion between the Northern On and "On-Montu", the Southern On, which was at Thebes.   Amenhotep III resided at Malqata, near the "Arment" so beautifully described by Arthur Weigall.

reported to be Memnon and a speaking statue".   Although Amenhotep III was ruler of Egypt for more like 38 years, he did, indeed, erect gigantic statues of himself before his mortuary temple, which were known, since antiquity, as "the Colossi of Memnon".

So far so good. However, instead of Akhenaten, the real successor of Amenhotep III, the next monarch on the list is "*Orus, for 36 years*".[52] Who is this? Can it be a duplication of Amenhotep III—or is it "Wa-en-Re"[53], a name of Akhenaten, with the wrong number of years?" Some have suggested that "Orus" is just Horemheb, someone who is represented again a bit further on the list as "*Harmais, five years*"[54], this confusion having happened because Horemheb seems to have appropriated the regnal years of all the kings between him and Amenhotep III—those who were tainted by the Aten heresy and considered "traitors".

Actually, it is probably **none** of the above. I think "Orus" is simply a fictitious pharaoh who was interposed into the 18th Dynasty to fill in a slot, as someone knew there had to a certain number of kings within this era but could not correctly identify them all. (Because of some misunderstandings, rulers whom we know to have belonged to the 19th Dynasty were drafted to "beef up" the previous dynasty, as well.)

After that, the version of Eusebius is a bit vague about the successor of the interloper "Orus", although most other preservers of Manetho indicate "*his daughter, Acencheres*", followed him, ruling for about 12 years.[55] Because of all

---

[52] In other versions, "Orus" is assigned as many as 37 regnal years and as few as 28.

[53] Pronounced "ouoria", the Egyptian /n/ being one of those phonemes which often elides into the following consonant, like /m/ and /b/. Greek cannot approximate a "w" sound, thus perhaps "Orus".

[54] Also called "Armais".

[55] Manetho says that the woman reigned for 12 years and a month . This was probably a daughter of Akhenaten, whose name had been obliterated from memory. After her came, according to Josephus, a preserver of

166

these problems with the 18th Dynasty, according to Manetho, Eusebius found it necessary to deem that "Chencheres" ruled 60 years later than "Palmanothes", although actual Egyptian history, as re-assembled by scholars, provides for nothing like this within the dynasty in question. Also, of course, for Moses to have been young in the day of "Palmanothes/Chenephres" and an octogenarian by the reign of "Chencheres", all those years needed to pass. Are these 60 years something these authors invented to make the age of the Biblical Moses fit to the chronology of ancient Egypt? Apparently not, because these "extra years" for the 18th Dynasty had already surfaced in earlier documents from pharaonic times and had haunted the chronographers ever since, some of them accounting for the time in creative ways.

A legal record composed in the reign of Ramesses II refers to a "Year 59" of Horemheb.[56] Even though, as has been pointed out, King Horemheb is thought to have usurped

---

Manetho, "*her brother Rathotis for 9 years*". "Rathotis" is what was recalled from the erased and usurped cartouches of Tutankhamen and, indeed, those nine years are what Egyptology attributes to him, as well. In asking how it was possible for a woman to reign for 12 years prior to Tutankhamen, one must assume, if he was her brother, that this would have been illegal, against "maat". One also is not able to reconcile a Tutankhamen who was at least 12 at his succession with his earliest kingly portraits, where he appears considerably younger. On the other hand, it is perfectly possible that Tutankhamun was forced to wait this long before becoming king in his own right (even though he was the rightful heir all along) and that he was compelled to have a female regent, like Thutmose III--and that he died in his early twenties instead of at the age of eighteen. In ancient Egypt, ones brother could be ones son, as well. We know who made himself king after Tutankhamun because the successor is shown in the young king's tomb. It is Kheperkheperure Ay. In fact, Julius Sextus Africanus, quite a reliable source in some ways, **does** give a "Chebres" for 12 years after "Rathos" (Rathotis). Whether Ay actually reigned that long is problematic, but he may have ruled in one city while "Acencheres", held sway elsewhere, waiting for the King of the Hittites to send her the prince she had requested to aid her in holding onto the throne.

[56] The inscription of Mose, who won a famous court battle over some land.

the durations of his predecessors, the actual span of the Amarna pharaohs is calculated to be 33 years at most, which would leave 26 or so for Horemheb's actual reign. The trouble with that is there are no vestiges of such a long rule for him and, most tellingly, his royal tomb in the Valley of the Kings was left in a most unfinished state, showing more like a few years of progress than nearly three decades worth. Considering that Manetho's 18th Dynasty, in its latter part, varies so much from Egyptology's reconstruction of it from the archaeological evidence, I don't think it farfetched at all to conclude that there may be some missing "real" kings in the lineup, including perhaps an "Acencheres" or "Chencheres" with 16 of rule—ultimately ascribed to Horemheb. Yet it cannot be ruled out that the old age of Moses at the time of the climax of the Book of Exodus was influenced by the "extra years"[57] of the 18th Dynasty and that, when he confronted Pharaoh Chencheres he was, in reality, no octogenarian at all. Regardless, I assert that it was nothing less than a strong belief in an exodus that caused Manetho's original 18th Dynasty to become corrupted and hopelessly distorted—especially in its chronology.

Even though the rumors connecting Moses to the mid to latter 18th Dynasty are a minority voice coming from antiquity, they somehow strike one as much more plausible than Moses being part of the scenario of the expulsion of the "shepherds" by Ahmose I. Whether someone with a name like "Moses" led an exodus of Hebrews from Egypt within the later 18th Dynasty is impossible to verify, but the popularity of such a man with the Egyptians, a prince resented by Akhenaten, makes a good deal of sense. Since the heretic pharaoh was the opposite of popular, anyone who had sufficient standing to be seen as a rival to Akhenaten in any way, would have been a king of hearts.

Exodus 11:3 says *"and, moreover, the man Moses was exceedingly important in the land of Egypt."* In addition, Acts

---

[57] Meaning "double counting", that is to say some reigns had been counted twice.

7: 2 of the New Testament declares *"And Moses was learned in all the wisdom of the Egyptians and was mighty in words and deeds."*

Certainly, if one begins to search for men named Mose or May or Maya (which was a nickname for Mose[58]) in the 18th Dynasty, one will have no shortage of candidates. A man called "May" had begun a tomb at Akhetaten, where an inscription proclaims that Akhenaten had *"doubled my favors for me like the number of the sands. I am the head of the nobles, the chief of the people, for my lord promoted me because I did his teaching, because I listened unceasingly to his voice"*. Evidently May, a general, was in favor with the king at one point and vice versa. However, May was never interred at Akhetaten (el Amarna). His tomb there was begun sometime after Year 7 of Akhenaten and was still incomplete by Year 9. At an unknown time, his name and figure were deliberately erased from the reliefs in an act of damnatio memoriae. [59]

In my opinion, this man is an outstanding candidate to have been Moses. Nicholas Reeves, in his *Akhenaten, Egypt's False Prophet*[60], calls him "Maya", supplying further that he was, in addition to being *"general of the Lord of the Two lands"*, the *"overseer of the house of pacifying the Aten(?)* and *"steward of Waenre (Akhenaten) in Heliopolis"*, plus *"overseer of all works of the king, royal scribe."*

In the legend of Moses, the most important part of his career, when he stood up to a pharaoh on behalf of the Hebrews, took place when he was 80 years old. Still, the Book of Exodus indicates that Moses was much younger

---

[58] The "Tutimaeus" of Manetho provides a clue as to the pronunciation of the Egyptian "ms" and one can see why "May" was the hypochoristicon.

[59] A name, probably that of May in his capacity of Superintendant of All the Works of the King (in addition to the titles "Scribe of the Elite Troops" and "Commander of the Soldiery of the King"), was also erased on an obelisk fragment at Karnak.

[60] Thames & Hudson, London, 2001.

than that when he returned to Egypt because his father-in-law, therein called "Jethro"[61] was still alive to give him permission to leave the Midianites. Even though Moses was assured that *"all the men are dead that sought thy life,"*[62] meaning that some years must have gone by, Exodus 4: 25 seems to imply that the sons of the former Prince of Egypt were still young enough for Zipporah, their mother, to make the decision to circumcise them with a sharp flint without seeking their permission. Exodus, chapters 6 through 7, speak of generations, perhaps with the intent to convey that more time had passed and that Moses and Aaron, his brother, had now grown old. Since the king of Egypt is always called only "Pharaoh" in the account, one cannot be certain whether it is the same ruler from Chapter 5 to Chapter 7, when Moses begins his contest with the court magicians. According to Michael the Syrian and Bar Hebraeus, those were the same sorcerers, Jannes and Jambres, who had instructed Moses as a lad.

The Bible seemingly gives the Hebrew brothers unlimited access to the Lord of the Two Lands, whenever they chose to confront him. In reality, the only ones who saw the pharaoh on a regular basis were the people who attended to his daily needs, who were known as "*smrw*", in the Egyptian language, or perhaps "*Smsw*", members of the nobility known as "Companions".

The following excerpt from the tale of our friend, Sinuhe, the fugitive from the time of Abraham, gives some idea of the awe one felt in the presence of the king of Egypt, knowing that ones very existence depended on him, the man/god who owned everything and everybody in the land:

> *"When dawn came and it was morning, I was summoned. Ten men came and ten men went to usher me to the palace. I put my brow to the ground between*

---

[61] A title of Reuel/Raguel, meaning "His Excellency" in Semitic.

[62] Exodus 4:19

the sphinxes. The royal children waited in the gateway to meet me. The Companions who showed me into the pillared court set me on the way to the reception hall. I found His Majesty upon the Great Throne set in a recess (paneled) with fine gold. When I was stretched out on my belly, I scarcely knew who I was in his presence. This God greeted me pleasantly, and I was like a man caught by nightfall. My soul departed and my body shook. My heart was not in my body that I might know life from death.

His Majesty said to one of these Companions: 'Lift him up. Let him speak to me.' And his Majesty said: 'See, you have returned, now that you have roamed the foreign lands. Exile has ravaged you; you have grown old. Old age has caught up with you. It is no small matter that your corpse be properly buried, for now you will not be escorted by the bowmen[63]. Do not take on so; why did you not speak when your name was called out?'

Still I feared punishment and was afraid to respond: 'What has my lord said to me? I know I ought to answer, but it was beyond me, as God is my judge. Fear is in my body, like that which brought to pass the fated flight. I am in your presence. Life belongs to you. May Your Majesty do as he wishes.'

Thereupon the royal children were then brought in, and His Majesty said to the queen: 'Here is Sinuhe who has returned as an Asiatic whom the Bedouin have raised.[64] She let out a cry, and the royal children shouted all together. They said before His Majesty: 'It is not really he, O Sovereign, my lord.' His Majesty said: ' It is he, indeed.'

---

[63] i.e., the Asiatics.

[64] Read "nurtured".

171

Then they brought their menyat-necklaces, their rattles and their sistra with them, and they offered them to His Majesty. 'May your arms reach out to something pleasant, O enduring king, to the ornaments of the Lady of Heaven. May the Golden One give life to your nostrils and may the Lady of Stars be joined to you... Turn aside your war-trumpet, set down your arrow. Give breath to him that was stifled. Give us the happy reward, this Bedouin chief, Son of the Northwind, the bowman born in Egypt. It was through fear of you that he took flight and through dread of you that he left the land. Yet the face does not turn pale at the sight of you. The eye which beholds you will not be afraid.' His Majesty said: 'He shall not fear, he has no cause to be afraid. He shall be a Companion among the nobles and he shall be placed in the midst of the courtiers.'"

The returned was given land and an estate, endowed with wealth in the form of good things of every sort. Presumably, Sinuhe was past working, but he was elevated to a Companion of the pharaoh, perhaps with the idea that the king would enjoy hearing the old man's tales of his adventures in the wilds of "barbaric" Asia—in addition to the obvious factor that the queen had retained so much affection for her former servant that even her children had been told all about him and wanted him for their own.

Even though it does not apply to Sinuhe, the fact is that there were, at times, certain officials who were so involved in and so indispensable to some facet of the government that they wielded a power and influence, coupled with a public standing, so great as to cause even the pharaoh to be mindful of their importance. This would have been especially true in the event of a ruler who tended to be a bit on the weak side, having the disadvantage of being very young, ill, foolish, old, or a female. For example, Horemheb specifies, in his "autobiography", that he was created "idnw" or Viceroy of the entire land and goes so far as to say that he was more powerful than the king, whom he neglects to name.

The school of thought represented by Artapanus, Bar Hebraeus and Eusebius would have us know it was not until the day of "Chencheres" that Moses came back to lead the Hebrews out of Egypt. Now "Chencheres", whoever he was—and, yes, it may have been a "woman-king"—cannot have been implicated in an exodus for no reason. What a delicious irony it would be, indeed, if the chief reason the writer of the Book of Exodus did not name the pharaoh before whom Moses appeared to demand the release of his people is because this ruler was a woman! What a dilemma for an author of ancient times. A female, however strong, was simply not considered a worthy opponent for a male and chivalry had nothing to do with it. It was thought shameful to contend with a woman, a creature by nature inferior to a man in all respects except beauty, and to have her best you was the greatest ignominy of all. That is why, in the Bible, when certain heroines of Israel managed to bring down a male foe it was considered the worst sort of defeat this enemy could undergo. On the other hand, when Abimelech, a "prince of Israel" was mortally wounded by a woman letting fall a millstone upon his head,[65] he ordered his armor-bearer to put him to the sword so that no one could say he had been killed by a mere female.

And so, for a man like Moses to have as his antagonist a woman-king would have been seen as ridiculous rather than remarkable, something to downplay as much as possible—and possible it was as, technically, there was no such thing as a female pharaoh, there being not even a word in the Egyptian language for "queen". What sufficed was "Hmt nswt", or "royal woman".[66] Even though, in the event of the lack of a male heir, women had been allowed to succeed since the 2nd Dynasty, they were called "king", the same as if

---

[65] Judges 9:53

[66] Pronounced "hime insi"—hence the "Amensis" of Manetho, a woman who ruled in her own right in the middle of his 18th Dynasty (thought to represent Hatshepsut).

173

they had been a man. Some, like Hatshepsut, even dressed the part.

Regardless of her sex, one would not have liked to cross Hatshepsut, from what we know of her, and there are many who would offer the opinion that only a fool or a truly brave man would pit himself against a woman wearing a crown.

Moses, of course, cannot have been a fool under any circumstances. We recall Flavius Josephus commenting that the Egyptians, even in his day, considered Moses to be practically divine and this was surely not due to the fact of his being a hero of the Jews. The mystique of Moses doubtless included that he was on a par with other great officials such as Imhotep and Amenhotep son of Hapu, both of them revered as saints, just as was Moses. A reputation for tremendous intellect, wisdom and nobility of character qualified one for sainthood in pre-Christian Egypt, but it was a canonization reserved for those who were also powerful while they lived—so great, in fact, that one hoped their seemingly super-human qualities could still benefit others after their physical demise. Dead people can, after all, be appealed to at leisure, which is more than one can say for the living.

That is why, even if it happened that Moses was an opponent of an unpopular king like Akhenaten and was persecuted for that reason, he could scarcely have wielded sufficient clout, in a subsequent regime, to be of any benefit to his people, the Hebrews, unless he had resumed his status as a man of affairs, a servant of the pharaoh renowned for a dedication to righteousness. And that is the reason it would have been quite extraordinary for Moses to have waited until he was 80 years of age to return to Egypt. If Artapanus et al are correct, then the actions of Moses had to do with some policy of King "Chencheres"—but what it was remains mysterious and surely entails more than causing people to "make bricks without straw", a metaphor for "unfairly punishing the helpless". After all, one fashioned bricks for the pharaoh, to whom flimsy ones were of no benefit whatsoever.

We have seen the example of Sinuhe, the harem official who exiled himself from Egypt for many years and then was given the great honor of a situation as a "Companion" to the king as soon as he returned. But Sinuhe, as far as we know, is merely a character in an Egyptian novel. Still, in the post-Amarna period, there actually may be a case of a man who succeeded in making a comeback after being rendered persona non grata by Akhenaten. Some believe that May, the military commander, who was at first elevated and then denounced by this king, returned, in a subsequent regime, to become "Maya the Treasurer".

Maya, who lived to be an old man, served pharaohs Tutankhamen and Horemheb—at least. He taxed the entire land in the reign of Tutankhamen because revenues were needed to repair the temples, which had fallen into neglect due to the decrees of Akhenaten. That Maya was very well-regarded by the new order cannot be disputed. The tomb of Maya at the Memphite necropolis, Saqqara, was excavated by Egyptologists, Geoffrey Martin and Jacobus van Dijk. It, also, was never finished. The statuary, reliefs and paintings associated with it are of the highest artistry. One of its discoverers felt that the owner of the tomb was so important that he was treated almost as if he were a king, there being no other burial like his in all of Saqqara. A certain impressive section of relief, in particular, portrays Maya in such a way that he seems to personify the terms "patrician" and "authority", holding his staff of office in the same way that Moses always does in imaginary portraits. Geoffrey Martin, himself, asks the question relative to Maya: "Can he even have been a minor member of the royal family?" The Treasurer's tomb points out

"...the governance which came into being through me, as something that was ordained for me by my god since my youth, the presence of the King having been granted to me since I was a child. I happily reached the end, enjoying countless favors of the Lord of the Two

Lands...In the beginning I was good, in the end I was brilliant, one who was revered in the temple of Ptah.[67] *I carried out the plans of the King of my time without neglecting anything he commanded...[I made splendid ?] the temples, fashioning the images of the gods for whom I was responsible. I entered face to face to the August Image....* " [68]

Martin was struck by the fact that Maya was reticent in disclosing any information about himself in the tomb, other than his official titles. The Egyptologist also notes that the Treasurer seemed loathe to specify the name of a former master.

"Maya seems rather unwilling to spell out his name, and there is the distinct possibility that it is none other than the heretic ruler Akhenaten. During this later epoch his name was anathema (it certainly was in the succeeding Ramesside period), and it would have been distinctly impolitic to mention him in a tomb inscription."[69]

It is interesting to note that we learn, from another source,[70] that the parents of Maya were "Iawy" and "Weret" and that the name of his brother, "Nahuher", is nearly an anagram of Aharon, the correct Hebrew spelling of the name of the brother of Moses. The wife of Maya was called "Meryt", and she appears to have predeceased him. The Treasurer also had a "step-mother"[71] depicted in his tomb by the name of "Henutiunu".

---

[67] The patron deity of craftsmen and builders.

[68] *The Hidden Tombs of Memphis* (Thames & Hudson, London, 1991).
[69] Page 173.

[70] The plundered tomb of Thutmose IV, which Maya inspected in the 8th Year of Horemheb, writing an inscription on its wall.

[71] According to G. Martin—although perhaps she is his mother-in-law, who also predeceased him.

In the film, "*The Ten Commandments*", it is portrayed that the reason Moses saw an Egyptian applying the lash to a Hebrew is because he was in charge of buildings projects for Pharaoh. It was none other than Apion, the object of the scorn of Flavius Josephus, who supplied the information in the third book of his History of Egypt:

> "*Moses, as I have heard from old people in Egypt, was a native of Heliopolis, who, being pledged to the customs of his country, erected prayer-houses, open to the air, in the various precincts of the city, all facing eastwards; such being the orientation of Heliopolis. In place of obelisks he set up pillars beneath which was the model of a boat; and the shadow cast on this basin by the statue described a circle corresponding to the course of the sun in the heavens.*"[72]

When Tutankhamen died, Maya had an ushabti[73] fashioned for the young king's funeral, inscribed

> "*Made by the servant who is beneficial to His Majesty, who seeks what is good and finds what is fine, and does it thoroughly for his lord, who makes things in the Splendid Palace, overseer of building works in the Place of Eternity (the necropolis area), the royal scribe, overseer of the Treasury, Maya...*"

In fact, there exists in the British Museum a cubit rod, a measuring device used by builders, upon which is inscribed

---

[72] Since an obelisk was supposed to represent a phallus, presumably that of the ithyphallic god, Min, Akhenaten would have stopped erecting obelisks once he turned his back on the orthodox pantheon of Egypt. Therefore, Moses can have raised the pillars in the time of this pharaoh.

[73] Ushabtis are smallish mummiform figures, sometimes beautifully crafted, which were meant to act as substitutes for the deceased in the afterlife in case in the event he was called upon to do any manual labor.

a text to the effect that, if someone should use this rod, he should recall the policies of "Maya".

> "*Standard bearer on the right of the King, Royal Scribe, Overseer of the Treasury of the Lord of the Two Lands, Maya, he speaks - 'O, you Prophets, Purifiers and Lector Priests of this Temple, the gods of your city shall listen to all your prayers and will pass on your offices after a pleasant old age if you pronounce my name and act on my behalf as one favoured by his Lord.'*"

Martin and Van Dijk believe Maya died in the time of Horemheb, a warlike pharaoh whose own commoner tomb, constructed while he was only still a general, depicts, with obvious and gratuitous relish, foreign captives being subjected to blows, humiliation and scorn. The impression one receives of Horemheb from this sepulcher of his in addition to his ruthless dismissal of his predecessors is that he was certainly cold-blooded enough to be the Pharaoh of the Book of Exodus, even if he wasn't. (At least no ancient historian accuses him of being this despot.)[74] In addition to destroying the city of Akhenaten, Horemheb did his best to render that king as though he had never existed and applied the same nullification to all those who happened to reign between himself and the heretic—whoever they were. He is suspected of arranging the murder of a Hittite prince, who was sent by his father to marry a widowed queen of Egypt and rule beside her. This is the famous letter that was written to an astonished King Suppiluliumas and is from the annals compiled by his son, Mursilis, who wrote:

---

[74] Mysteriously, a seal impression was discovered deep within the tomb of Tutankhamen that could easily be interpreted as containing the name "Horemheb". Since the tomb of young Tut had presumably been sealed when Ay, Horemheb's predecessor, made himself king, this would represent quite an anachronism—unless Horemheb had been the "idnw" or deputy for Tutankhamun at some point before the latter's death. Probably, Horemheb was the powerful "servant" that the Egyptian queen did not wish to take for her husband.

"While my father was down in the country of Karkamis (Carchemesh) he dispatched Lupakkis and Tessub-zalmas to the country of Amqa. They proceeded to attack the country of Amqa and brought deportees, cattle and sheep home before my father. When the people of the land of Egypt heard about the attack on Amqa, they became frightened.[75] Because, to make matters worse, their lord Bibhururiyas[76] had just died, the Egyptian queen who had become a widow, sent an envoy to my father and wrote to him as follows: "My husband died and I have no son. People say that you have many sons. If you were to send me one of your sons, he might become my husband. I am loathe to take a servant of mine and make him my husband. I am afraid!" When my father heard that, he called the great into council, saying: "Since of old such a thing has never happened before me". He proceeded to dispatch Hattu-zitis, the chamberlain, saying: "Go! Bring you reliable information back to me. They may try to deceive me: As to whether perhaps they have a prince bring reliable information to me!"

During Hattu-zitis' absence in the land of Egypt my father vanquished the city Karkamis...The Egyptian envoy, the Honorable Hanis, came to him. Because my father had instructed Hattu-zitis while sending him to the land of Egypt as follows: "Perhaps they have a prince; they may try to deceive me and do not really want one of my sons to take over the kingship," the Egyptian queen answered my father in a letter as follows: "Why do you say: 'They may try to deceive me'? If I had a son, would I write to a foreign country in a manner which is humiliating to myself and to my country? You do not trust me and tell me even

---

[75] Believing they were next. A kind of uneasy truce had existed between Egypt and Hatti at this time and the Egyptians believed the Hittites had broken it by invading what was considered Egyptian territory.

[76] Probably a writing of "Nebkheperure", the throne-name of Tutankhamen.

such a thing. He who was my husband died and I have no sons. Shall I perhaps take one of my servants and make him my husband? I have not written to any other country, I have written only to you. People say that you have many sons. Give me one of your sons and he is my husband and king in the land of Egypt." Because my father was generous, he complied with the lady's wishes and decided for sending the son."[77]

We are advised by further records of Mursilis that this Hittite prince, Zannanza, never reached the widow because he was murdered somewhere en route. In another letter, the Hittite king blames an unnamed successor of Tutankhamen, who renounces responsibility. The Hittites and the Egyptians go to war over this incident and a terrible plague strikes the Hittites that lasts for more than twenty years, which they say they got from the Egyptian prisoners they had brought home. The account in the "Plague Prayers" states:

"...My father sent foot soldiers and charioteers who attacked the country of Amqa, Egyptian territory. Again he sent troops and they attacked it. When the Egyptians became frightened, they asked outright for one of his sons to (take over) the kingship. But when my father gave them one of his sons, they killed him as they led him there. My father let his anger run away with him, he went to war against Egypt and attacked Egypt. The Hattian Storm-god, my lord, by his decision even let my father prevail; he vanquished and smote foot soldiers and the charioteers of the country of Egypt. But when they brought to Hatti land the prisoners which they had taken a plague broke out among the prisoners and they began to die."

King Horemheb usurped the beautiful statues of the handsome young Tutankhamen as his own and defaced the tomb of old King Ay, a relative of Tutankhamen, who briefly

[77] From ANET (page 319) Princeton University Press, Princeton, NJ (1955)

succeeded the ill-fated youth. Perhaps Horemheb harbored some kindly sentiment toward Tutankhamen, as the latter's tomb was discovered in 1922 in all its glittering glory, intact except for some aborted ancient robbery attempts.

My own impression, based upon stylistic considerations, is that the tomb of Maya **continued to be decorated even into the Ramesside period.** This is perfectly possible, of course, because the 60 years from "Chenephres" to "Chencheres" is a chronological fabrication, just as were the 60 years of Horemheb indicated in Ramesside times. A man who was young in the reign of Akhenaten could very well have lived into the time of Ramesses the Great. It is even plausible that someone like Maya, who had once opposed Akhenaten (and possibly "Chencheres", as well), could have been revered as *"remarkable, indeed, divine"*[78] in the Ramesside era, when Akhenaten began to be referred to as *"that criminal"*.

Outside of that of Tutankhamen, we have not, apparently, found the mummy of any pharaoh of the Thutmosid Dynasty after Amenhotep III—Akhenaten and Horemheb, included. In a mysterious tomb called KV55 there was a mummy badly affected by dampness and which disintegrated at the touch, leaving only the bare skeleton. Because this individual was hastily interred in a tomb that contained a hodge-podge of funerary equipment from the reign of Akhenaten, it was at first concluded that the mummy was that of the heretic. More recently, forensic anthropologists have leaned toward a younger man than Akhenaten and now the consensus is that the remains are those of Ankhkheperure Smenkhkare. Still, there are things about this mummy that make its sex rather ambiguous and so it is not wholly impossible that the deceased is a female.

Because certain items among the funerary trappings of Tutankhamen had once belonged to a predecessor, Ankhkheperure, it may be surmised that this king was either temporary (such as a female regent who had assumed royal titulary, a la Hatshepsut) or an illegal male king who had

---

[78] Josephus, *Against Apion.*

"ruled without Maat", therefore relinquishing some of his/her elaborately prepared burial equipment to the rightful heir and being consigned to a very poor interment in KV55. However, an alternative could be that the dead body of Ankhkheperure or "Chencheres" **was never recovered** and that the mummy from KV55 is not Ankhkheperure Smenkhkare at all. What if an exodus did take place during the latter's reign, just as certain ancients believed, and "Cencheres" really did perish by drowning in some body of water? If there is no corpse, there is no need of the coffins or canopic equipment that had been prepared in advance.[79]

The whereabouts of the mummy of Maya is also unknown. We cannot even be sure he was interred in his splendid tomb, even though a portion of one calcite ushabti purportedly[80] naming him was discovered within it.

Now Flavius Josephus, like everyone else, believed that Moses was active in Ethiopia. As it happens, many famous men and heroes of Egypt had some connection to this land.

> *"Moses, therefore, when he was born, and brought up in the described manner, and came to the age of maturity, made his virtue apparent to the Egyptians; and showed that he was born for the bringing them down, and raising the Israelites. And the occasion he seized was this: - The Ethiopians, who are neighbors to the Egyptians, made an inroad into their country, and carried off the belongings of the Egyptians, who, in their rage, fought against them,*

---

[79] Just how much of a pharaoh's funerary equipment was prepared in advance of his death is difficult to know. All that is known for certain is that the tomb and the sarcophagus fashioned of a large block of stone, hollowed-out, were ready and waiting for years.

[80] Although there is every reason to believe the fragment, bearing the title "treasurer" refers to Maya, curiously enough the glyph /m/ that should begin his name is not there, even though the space where it ought to be is intact. What is there looks more like "Aya". t is believed by Egyptologists that ushabtis were not placed in a tomb until the time of the funeral of the deceased.

*and revenged the insults they had received from them.
Being overcome in battle, some of them were slain, and
the rest ran away in a shameful manner, and by that
means saved themselves. The Ethiopians followed after
them in the pursuit, and thinking that it would be a mark
of cowardice if they did not subdue all Egypt, they went
on to plunder the rest with greater vehemence; and once
they had tasted the delights of the country, they never
left off waging war. Because Upper Egypt had not
courage enough at first to fight with them, they
proceeded as far as Memphis, and the sea itself, while
not one of the cities was able to oppose them. The
Egyptians, under this sad oppression, consulted their
oracles and prophecies; and when God gave them the
advice to make use of Moses the Hebrew to their
advantage, the king commanded his daughter to produce
him, that he might be the general of their army. "*

Josephus goes on to describe how, after making the
journey to Ethiopia, Moses got himself a wife of the people
there:

*"....and at length they stopped at Saba[81], which was a
royal city of Ethiopia, which Cambyses afterwards
named Mero, after the name of his own sister. The place
was to be besieged with very great difficulty, since it was
both encompassed by the Nile and the other rivers,
Astapus and Astaboras, making it a very great task to
pass over them. The city was situated in a secluded
place, and was inhabited after the manner of an island,
being encompassed with a strong wall, and having the
rivers to guard it from enemies. There were also great
ramparts between the wall and the rivers, providing that
when the waters come with the greatest violence, the
place could never be engulfed. Besides, these ramparts*

---

[81] The home of the "Queen of Sheba", who visited King Solomon.

made it next to impossible for even those who crossed the rivers to take the city.

However, while Moses was uneasy at the army's lying idle, (for the enemies dared not come to a battle,) this accident happened: Tharbis[82] was the daughter of the king of the Ethiopians: she happened to see Moses as he led the army near the walls, and fought with great courage. Admiring the guile of his undertakings, and believing him to be responsible for the Egyptians' success, just when they had despaired of recovering their liberty. Now he seemed to be the main source of danger to the Ethiopians, when only just previously they had boasted of their great achievements. And so she fell deeply in love with him; and upon the urgency of that passion, sent to him the most faithful of all her servants to discuss their marriage. He thereupon accepted the offer, on condition she would manage the delivering up of the city. He swore an oath to take her to his wife; and that when he had once taken possession of the city, he would not break his promise to her. No sooner was the agreement made, things transpired as hoped, and when Moses had cut off the Ethiopians, he gave thanks to God, and consummated his marriage, and led the Egyptians back to their own land."

And so Egypt is saved on account of a handsome Hebrew, who will soon get himself another foreign wife, as well, in what may have been another diplomatic marriage. Possibly Moses did not wish to offend Jethro/Reuel/Raguel

---

[82] Probably not an actual name but the Egyptian "tA-rpyt" with the meaning of "the princess". Elsewhere the King of Cush is called "Zoros" and his daughter, "Ra'osa". (Pietersma) The name "Zoros" is doubtless the same as Zerah, an Ethiopian king defeated by King Asa of Judah, 2 Chron. XIV, 9—and was probably considered a good name for an Ethiopian. "Ra'osa" is perhaps simply the Egyptian term "rsyt", meaning "woman of the south".

by refusing his eldest daughter. The sheik, after all, had six others to marry off, none being marriageable until the first had a husband, after the Semitic tradition. Perhaps Moses took other wives, in addition. His siblings evidently did not sanction the idea of Moses "marrying for Egypt", for it states in Numbers 12:1 that *"Miriam and Aaron spoke against Moses because of the Cushite woman whom he had married."*

However, the Almighty, Himself, disapproved of them meddling in the affairs of their brother because he turned Miriam "white as snow" with leprosy until Moses prayed to God that she might return to her former—albeit humbled—self. Here we have a Biblical warning to in-laws for all time. It may have not been so important for Miriam to be chastised, and Aaron if only by example, had "Tharbis" not actually been with Moses at the time of the Exodus—so perhaps the implication is she had not been abandoned in her homeland. The prophet is reunited with Zipporah, his Midianite wife on the journey, as well—not forgetting his sons, Gershom and Eliezar, who have presumably been raised as "Arabians".

The one Egyptian woman who figured prominently in the life of Moses was his adoptive mother, the "Merris" of Artapanus, who is called "Thermutis"[83] by Flavius Josephus—and, of course, "Bithiah" in Jewish folklore.

"Thermuthis, perceiving him to be a remarkable child, adopted him for her son, having no child of her own. And when one time had carried Moses to her father, she showed him to him, and said she thought to make him her successor, if it should please God she should have no legitimate child of her own, remarking ' I have brought up a child who is of a divine form, and of a great intellect. I have received him as a gift of the river. It struck me

---

[83] This is the name of a deity, Renenutet, with the addition of the feminine article "tA" (the). Thus "Ta-Rennute" = "Thermutis". By the same quirk of pronunciation does the older "pn Rnnwt.t", the festival of the harvest goddess, become the later Egyptian month "Pharmouti".

185

advisable to adopt him for my son, and the heir of thy kingdom.'[84]   As she had said this, she put the infant into her father's hands.   So he took him, and hugged him to his breast; and, to please his daughter, put his diadem upon his head; but Moses threw it down to the ground, and, in a puerile mood, he sent it rolling with his feet.   This act seemed to all an ill omen concerning the kingdom of Egypt. When the sacred scribe saw this, (he was the person who foretold that his birth would be the downfall of the land)[85] he made a violent attempt to kill him; and crying out in a terrible voice he said, 'This, O king! this child is he of whom God foretold, that if we kill him we shall be in no danger; he himself has shown the prophecy correct by his trampling upon thy authority, and treading upon thy diadem. Take him, therefore, out of the way, and deliver the Egyptians from the fear they are in about him; and deprive the Hebrews of the hope they have of being uplifted by him.'

But Thermuthis intervened and snatched the child away. The king was not inclined to slay him; God himself, whose providence protected Moses, moved the king to spare him. He was, therefore, educated with great care. So the Hebrews depended on him, and were hopeful great things would be done by him. The Egyptians, on the other hand, were concerned about the consequences of such an

---

[84] Why did Josephus indicate that the pharaoh's daughter assumed that even her adopted son would be her father's successor?   Was it because the Judean knew that a certain royal woman of Egypt was always thought of as "the Heiress" and that her progeny would have precedence in line for the throne?   This is still a subject of some controversy in Egyptological circles.

[85] At this point Josephus seems to be getting information from somewhere outside the Torah.   Is he now paraphrasing the Egyptian historians and their contention that someone at the court of the king was predicting everything that had to do with the Egyptian version of the Exodus?

education. As it happened, there was no one, either kin or adopted, that had any oracle on his side for pretending to the crown of Egypt, and who showed any greater promise than Moses, so they abstained from killing him."

This last may seem absurd except to those familiar with the history of the kings and queens of ancient Egypt, a number of whom claimed, on their public monuments, that it was an oracle, a divine prophesy, which had enabled them to succeed.

Chapter Ten

After Akhenaten it would appear there was a conciliatory mood in Egypt and, although the disc was still worshipped, other gods would be tolerated again. Before very long, Amen was once more the primary deity. Here are the conditions described in the "Restoration Stela" of Tutankhamen, formerly Tutankhaten:[86]

> "Now when this majesty arose as king, the temples of the gods and goddesses beginning from Elephantine to the marshes of the Delta...had fallen into neglect. Their shrines had fallen into desolation and became land overrun with the rata-plants. Their sanctuaries were as they had never been, their halls were a trodden path The land was in seni-meni; the gods forsook this land..."

At the end of the 18th Dynasty of ancient Egypt several men[87] ruled who were either unable to sire male offspring or all their sons had predeceased them. The 18-year-old god-king, Tutankhamen, died suddenly without an heir. At once, an elderly priest seized the throne, reigned briefly, and was succeeded by a general.[88]

The general, Horemheb, also died without a living son, so he had appointed another military man to succeed him, one

---

[86] Tutankhamen came to the throne as a little boy. Perhaps he was the son of Akhenaten, although this is uncertain. Manetho seems to indicate that a sister of Tutankhamen reigned before him and was possibly his regent for a time.

[87] And a woman or two.

[88] Ay was probably the grandfather of Tutankhamen and a descendant of a past king, meaning that he was the oldest living "blue-blood" in Egypt. Horemheb, the military man, claimed descent from Thutmose III, calling him "the father of my fathers". The Egyptians did not distinguish between "father", "grandfather" and even "ancestor". The 19th Dynasty, the Ramessids, arguably came into being because the Thutmosid line had now died out in its entirety.

called Ramesses. With Ramesses I, we see the start of a long line of pharaohs with striking, sharp-featured faces who seem markedly different from their predecessors. Ramesses I probably hailed from the north-eastern Delta of Lower Egypt, the area close to the Red Sea. The Ramesside Dynasty retained a love of the Eastern Delta and maintained a residence there. Ramesses the Great eventually made his city, Per-Ramesses-Meryamen-Great-of-Victories, his capital. The "Raamses" of the Book of Exodus was praised by the scribe, Pai-Bes in a letter to the scribe, Amenemope:[89]

> *"I have reached Per-Ramesses and have found it in (very, very) good condition, a beautiful district, without its like, after the pattern of Thebes. It was (Re) himself (who founded it). The Residence is pleasant in life; its field is full of everything good; it is (full) of supplies and food every day, its ponds with fish, and its lakes with birds. Its meadows are verdant with grass; its banks bear dates; its melons are abundant on the sands....Its granaries are (so) full of barley and emmer (that) they come near the sky. Onions and leeks are for food, and lettuce of the garden, pomegranates, apples, and olives, figs of the orchard, sweet wine of Ka-of-Egypt[90], surpassing honey, red wedj-fish of the canal of the Residence, which live on lotus flowers, bedin-fish of the Hari-waters....The Shi-Hor[91] has salt and the Her canal has natron. Its ships go out and come (back) to mooring (so that) supplies and food are in it every day. One rejoices to dwell within it and there is none who says 'Would that!' to it. The small in it are like the great.*

---

[89] Papyrus Anastasi III, British Museum 10246, translated by Sir Alan Gardiner in ANET (Princeton University Press, Princeton NJ, 1955)

[90] A vineyard of the Delta.

[91] Literally, "the Waters of Horus" and the Shihor of the Bible, presumably the salt-flats of the Tanite branch of the Nile.

Come, let us celebrate for it its feasts of the sky[92], as well as its feasts at the beginning of the seasons. The reed-thicket comes to it with papyrus; the Shi-Hor with rushes....The young men of Great of Victories are dressed up every day, with sweet oil upon their heads and newly dressed hair. They stand beside their doors, their hands bowed down with flowers, with greenery of the House of Hathor and flax of the Her-canal, on the day that User-maat-Re-Setep-en-Re[93]—life, prosperity, health—Montu-in-the-Two-Lands enters in, on the morning of the feast of Khoiakh.[94] Every man is like his fellow in uttering their petitions.

The ale of Great of Victories is sweet;...beer of Qode[95] from the harbor,and wine of the vineyards. The ointment of the Segbeyen waters is sweet, and the garlands of the garden. The singers of Great of Victories are sweet, being instructed in Memphis.

---

[92]These festivals were astronomically set and included the rising of Sirius and the Feast of Opet.

[93] Throne-name of Ramesses II. *Ozymandias* is the way the Greeks heard "Usermaatre" and is the title of a poem by Shelley inspired by a ruined colossus of the former.

[94] Evidently, on the morning of this festival day the pharaoh held an open court where people came to ask favors. One may imagine that it was just such an assembly that the author of the Book of Exodus had in mind when Moses and Aaron first presented themselves with their demands. Khoiakh was the last month of the season of sowing, corresponding to November/December. The Exodus took place in what the Egyptians called their Spring, the end of the season of growing, or Prt ("Proya"), which literally means "coming forth". This would be sometime in our April. The celebration of the holiday of Passover begins after sundown on the 14th day of Nisan, the first month of the Jewish ecclesiastical year, about the time of the vernal equinox.

[95] Kode or Qedi, on the north Phoenician coast.

So dwell content of heart and free, without stirring from it, O User-maat-Re-setep-en-Re—life, prosperity, health—thou god!"

The early Ramessides were strong rulers, without a doubt. Ramesses I, originally called Paramessu, was an army colleague of King Horemheb, who eventually became Northern Vizier. When he was chosen successor, the first Ramesses was already an elderly man and reigned for less than two years, but he had a grown son who was a "super star" waiting in the wings. In fact, a pun was created on the name of this Prince Seti, which was "Star of the Land", these words being vocalized very nearly the same as the name of the heir.[96] The "star quality" of the man is apparent even in his mummy, which is possibly the most handsome to come down to us from ancient Egypt. The portraits of Seti I confirm this impression, although none seem to do him justice.

Upon unwrapping the mummy of this 19th Dynasty pharaoh, Gaston Maspero, the director of the Boulaq Museum, was moved to write:

"It was a masterpiece of the art of the embalmer, and the expression of the face was that of one who had only a few hours previously breathed his last. Death had slightly drawn the nostrils and contracted the lips, the pressure of the bandages had flattened the nose a little, and the skin was darkened by the pitch; but a calm and gentle smile played over the mouth and the half opened eyelids allowed a glimpse to be seen, from under their lashes of an apparently moist and glistening line, the reflection from the white porcelain eyes let into the orbit at the time of burial."

---

[96] In his victory scenes at Karnak, Seti I is referred to as "a circling star which scatters its flame", "a young bull, ready-horned and irresistible", "a crocodile lying on the shore, terrible and unapproachable", and "a fierce-eyed lion among the corpses in the valley".

The Nobel Prize-winning author, William Golding, observed in his book , *An Egyptian Journey*, that mummies were at one time used as fuel for Nile steamers, commenting that the idea didn't bother him as these were bodies that had lasted much longer than they were meant to, in any event. Golding said he was an Egyptophile and perhaps he made this remark at a disgruntled moment, but I certainly can't agree with him. It tends to bother me that gold lasts forever while people vanish into dust.

In my opinion, the fine face of King Seti I, for example, is worth any artistic masterpiece displayed in a museum. To me, the fact that this man and others like him were not returned to earth long ago gives us a human link to the past that ought to be as significant for us as it would have been to

them had they been able to imagine the situation. Perhaps to Seti, dying in relative youth, it might have compensated for not making it to old age had he possibly known how much he is still admired three-thousand years later.

I believe it is quite safe to say that nothing in Egyptology interests us more than the remains of the pharaohs and their ladies. They, like the mummies of Egyptian commoners, seem to represent the ancient land in the capacity of silent emissaries from another time. To all the many questions we have regarding ancient Egypt, these mummies once knew the answers, but now they are forever silent.

Yet many things about the mummies speak eloquently about what types of people they were, what they may have died of and how old they were at death. Nevertheless, the royal mummies certainly have presented more puzzles than provided answers. A good deal of the mysteries connected with them could be cleared up by doing DNA testing on the royal remains. Samples have been taken for such an analysis, but the results or findings have yet to be disclosed. It is rather ironic that, even though a lot of confusion exists about the Exodus (or exodoi), the remains of the relevant pharaohs are probably in Cairo or in a museum in another city of the world.[97] The desiccated corpses of the monarchs of Egypt have outlasted most of their riches and a good many of their accomplishments. The story of how this came to be is an interesting one:

Until the late 19th Century CE, Egyptian mummies were treated with a total lack of respect. In the 1700s adventurers and early Egyptophiles added their own mischief to that done by tomb-robbing natives over the millennia. Their methods were cavalier, to say the least. One Giovanni Belzoni of Padua, a giant of a fellow known as the "Italian Strongman" was greatly interested in Egyptian artifacts and did some good work as regards drawing the monuments for posterity, but he also wrote of wading through a roomful of mummies, crushing God-knows-whom under his great foot in order to gain purchase as he plowed his way through. Belzoni also recorded the fact that a female mummy's long hair came away from her scalp quite easily when he tugged at it! Later on it was determined that this mummy and some other ladies discovered by the Italian in a tomb called KV21 were probably queens, judging by their raised left arms[98], but now their remains are broken to pieces by vandals that came and went since Belzoni's day. Had these ladies been able to lie peacefully until discovered by science, we might have been able to add to our relatively small knowledge of the wives of the pharaohs.

---

[97] Not all of the mummies of the New Kingdom rulers have survived—or at least have not yet been identified.

[98] Donald Ryan, an American Egyptologist, made this observation upon re-examining the tomb.

But Giovanni Belzoni was almost scientific when compared with the 18th Century craze for Powdered Mummy, thought to cure various ailments. It is unknown how many long-dead Egyptians were pulverized in order to obtain this weird medicament, but one shudders at the notion. The institutes of the next century had "mummy unwrapping exhibitions," which were hardly methodical in their haste to reveal the face of a person who last saw daylight three-thousand years before.

Most of the desecration eventually came to a halt as the science of Egyptology began to define itself and take on a more serious aspect. The Egyptians, themselves, were forbidden by the government to do any more trafficking in mummies or other relics, which caution they, of course, disregarded. As a result, private collections the world over contain items that are rarely seen by anyone and which museums would love to own.

The Rassoul family of Qurnah (near the Valley of the Kings) had been tomb-robbers for generations but regarded themselves as simply mining one of Egypt's resources— ancient artifacts. They had stumbled on a cache of mummies and grave goods, the latter being sold by them piecemeal in a clever and non-greedy fashion over a lengthy period. Ultimately, the rascally Rassouls were found out and the authorities were led to the cache, which turned out to be one of the most fortuitous combinations of luck and design in the history of archaeology.

The design was the intent of the ancient priests and officials of the Valley of the Kings to save the mummies of their pharaohs, and some of the royal ladies, from further harm by putting them into one place after their individual tombs had been plundered. The shaft they were hidden in was a very well-guarded secret, indeed, as it remained undisturbed until the Rassoul brothers came upon it.

Emil Brugsch, a German archaeologist, cleared out the cache (at Deir El Bahari) in 1881 under the supervision of Gaston Maspero, a Frenchman in charge of antiquities at that time in Cairo. Expecting to find a few minor individuals, Brugsch and company were dumb-founded to learn they now had the remains of the greatest kings of the 18th and 19th Dynasties, personages no one had dreamt of ever seeing assembled all together in one lifetime. But there they were, more or less in one piece, reduced to lying in inferior coffins appropriated here and there but marked with the royal names and titles (sometimes with dubious accuracy) courtesy of those conscientious priests of old.

The mummies from the cache were transported on the river to Cairo. As this took place, the fellahin, or peasants, along the Nile set up a tremendous wail of belated mourning for the long-dead kings. Once brought to port, however, the pharaohs and queens were subject to taxation the same as any other cargo and, not knowing what existing category to list them under, the port authority decided to designate them "dried fish." Sic transit gloria mundi. Most of the royal mummies from the Deir el Bahari cache appeared to be satisfactorily labeled, but a few were not. There is no doubt as to the identification of Seti I or his son Ramesses II.[99]

A second cache of pharaohs was discovered in 1898 by Victor Loret, a French Egyptologist, in KV35, the tomb of Amenhotep II. This burial had already been plundered in modern times before Loret began his investigation but, as the kings had been given very plain replacement coffins by the ancient priests who rescued them from their desecrated tombs, the Rassouls were evidently never motivated to bother with them. They appeared very poor and the Rassouls, probably not knowing how to read ancient Egyptian, had no way of knowing these were kings. Only Amenhotep II had been placed in his sarcophagus like a true pharaoh.   Later on, however, someone messed this mummy about, as well, stealing the great bow buried with the king—the one he had boasted only he could pull.

The only account of Loret's discovery of KV35 is in the form of an article, "Le Tombeau D'Amenophis II", printed in

---

[99] A mummy is currently being investigated as a possible candidate for Ramesses I.   King Merneptah, the successor of Ramesses II, has been identified with some assurance, but less securely than his father and grandsire.

the *Bulletin De L'Institut Egyptien*. There, he tries to convey his excitement upon first realizing the importance of what he had found in the side-chamber:

> *"Everywhere cartouches! Here, the prenomen of Siptah; there, the names of Seti II; nearby, a long inscription including the complete titles of Thutmose IV. We had stumbled upon a royal cache comparable to that of Deir-el-Bahri."* And... *"After Thutmose IV, Amenophis III. Following the son of Amenhotep II, his grandson. The genealogical series continued, which had so well commenced with Thutmose III and Amenophis II, and which would finish with Akhenaten."*

Once out of KV35, the royal mummies eventually underwent unwrapping and examination by one G. Elliot Smith, professor of anatomy at the Cairo School of Medicine and author of that venerable and invaluable tome, *The Royal Mummies*, (1912). The corpse that Victor Loret had apparently judged to be Akhenaten was divested of its bandages on July 8, 1907, six years after it had been taken from the tomb! Smith says that Gaston Maspero, in his *Guide du Visiteur au Musee du Caire*, made the notation:

> *"Mummy of the Pharaoh Meneptah (sic), son and successor of Ramses II, found in the coffin of Setnakht. Monsieur Loret thought he recognized the mummy of ...Khouniatonou*[100]. *M. Groff was the first to affirm that*

---

[100] The way the name of Akhenaten was written by 19th Century Egypologists. Curiously, however, while describing the various aspects of the bandages of this corpse, Smith commented *"Not a fragment of writing, nor ornaments of any kind, were found on the mummy."* Had Smith already forgotten about the inscription on the shroud, which he had already mentioned in connection with Maspero? Throughout his work, *The Royal Mummies*, one can't help but notice that, in certain things, Smith always defers to Maspero. And it is noteworthy that, with regard to this hieratic writing, Smith has *Maspero* saying it existed, but never affirms that he saw it, himself. In fact, Smith appears to give evidence to the contrary.

this was Menephtah, and the reading of the cartouche, traced in hieratic writing on the breast of the mummy, demonstrates the correctness of his opinion."

Dr. Smith supplied the observation that *"the body is thickly encrusted with salt"*. Was this the information that reinforced the identification of Merneptah who was, as Maspero puts it *"...after a tradition of the Alexandrian epoch, the Pharaoh of the Exodus, the one who, it is said, perished in the Red Sea"*? My assertion is that, with Gaston Maspero, who was given to the romantic musings of a fin-de-siecle French novelist, one can never be sure. It is puzzling that Loret, if he was able to read hieratic script, could confuse any of the names of King Merneptah with the name "Akhenaten". Never having read any comment on this by M. Groff, I am, unfortunately, not able to relate his rationale for his decipherment, but there must exist some degree of possibility that we do not have the mummy of King Merneptah, after all.[101] Regardless, we shall see later on how ironic it was that these two kings should have been confused in modern times.

An irritating aspect of all this is that we nearly possessed a couple of monogrammed shirts that had belonged to the pharaoh who has been connected to the Exodus—but they were apparently found on the mummy of another king, the putative Seti II, a successor of Merneptah. The notes of Elliot Smith explain:

"In the lower (right hand of one, left hand in the other) corner of the front of the shirt there was embroidered in red

---

[101]The apparent old age of the mummy at death does seem to argue for its being Merneptah, who was the son of an even more superannuated father, Ramesses II, and who, it is believed, did not become king until after he was past sixty. The face of the mummy also bears a resemblance to certain portraits of Merneptah.

*and blue thread a vertical cartouche and name, which
Brugsch Pasha[102] tells me is that of Meneptah."*

And then: *"Alongside this (nearer the edge) on one of the
shirts is a vertically-placed hieratic inscription in ink: and
on the left corner, another, shorter, badly corroded
inscription...I regret that it is not possible to give a fuller
description of these shirts and of the writing upon them. At
the time when I unwrapped this mummy the shirts were
handed over to the conservator of the Museum, but when I
came to write this Catalogue they were not to be found in
the Museum."*

Regarding the inscription on the shroud in which the
mummy considered to be Seti II had been wrapped, Smith
only comments: *"There was a faint traces of the name written
(in ink) in hieratic on the front of this piece of linen."* The
anatomist does not state, for example, that Brugsch or
anyone else told him this writing positively spelled out a
name of Seti II. Once again, one is made rather uneasy by
Smith's vagueness when it comes to the inscriptions found
upon this mummy, especially since it shows none of the
physical characteristics of the Ramesside dynasty. Another
possibility must be that this mummy is truly that of Seti II—
but that he was not the son of Merneptah.

The likeness of Tutankhamen was captured by a genius of
a goldsmith in a golden mask. Gold was thought to be the
flesh of the gods and, in the way that great art has of being
more real than life, we can only view the withered face of the
dead boy as an artifact beside such artistry. On the other
hand, we are oddly certain that no artist, however great,
could have given us portraits of men such as Seti
and his son, Rameses II, that could have the impact on us
that their own dead faces have achieved.

---

[102] Emil Brugsch was present throughout the work of unwrapping" the
mummy called Seti II.

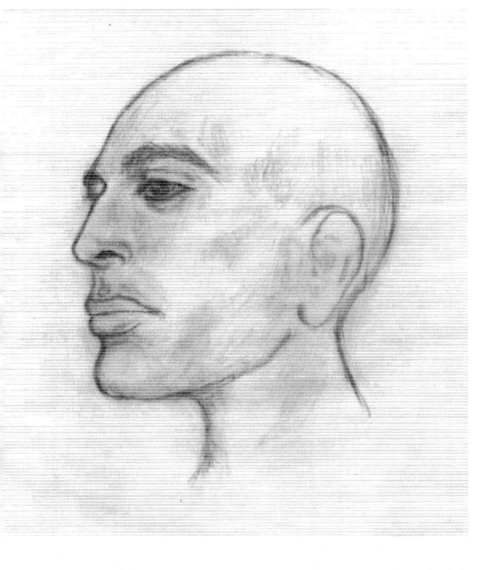

PORTRAIT OF SETI THE FIRST

By Marianne Luban *After the frontispiece in Smith's* **The Royal Mummies** *& ancient portraits*

These were very impressive men, indeed, and no one who looks upon them today can doubt it, even without knowing anything of their considerable accomplishments.

Seti I (reigned 1321-1310 BCE ?) was king for a little over a decade, but he appears to have used that time energetically. His tomb is the largest and most stunning in the Valley. Evidently this pharaoh was a patron of the arts with discerning taste, as everything from his reign bears the stamp of elegance. His temple at Abydos is decorated with reliefs that are perhaps the finest ever carved in Egypt. Manetho, according to Flavius Josephus, appears to have recorded a fascinating anecdote about a ruler of Egypt named "Sethosis":

"....Sethosis, also called Ramesses. The last named king, who possessed an army of cavalry and a strong fleet, made his brother Harmais viceroy of Egypt and conferred upon him all the royal prerogatives, except that he enjoined upon him not to wear a diadem, not to wrong the queen, the mother of his children, and to show similar respect to the royal concubines. He then departed on a campaign against Cyprus and Phoenicia, and later against the Assyrians and the Medes, and with or without a contest, through the terror inspired by his mighty army, reduced all these nations to submission.

Emboldened by these successes he, with yet greater audacity, continued his advance, subduing the cities and districts of the east. Meanwhile, sometime after his departure, Harmais, whom he had left in Egypt, unscrupulously defied all his brother's injunctions. He violated the queen, freely indulged himself with the concubines, and, at the instigation of his friends, put on a diadem and rose in revolt against his brother. The keeper of the Egyptian temples thereupon wrote a letter which he sent to Sethosis, telling him everything, including the insurrection of his brother Harmais. Sethosis instantly returned to Pelusium and recovered his kingdom."

Scholars have equated "Sethosis" with Seti I and concluded that "Harmais" was Horemheb,[103] another pharaoh of the era. While the above tale will be discussed farther along in this book, this is an opportunity to clarify that "Sethosis" cannot possibly represent Menmaare Seti I— as Manetho, himself, makes plain. Even though the reigns of Horemheb and Seti I are separated by less than two years, that the latter cannot have been crowned king before the former is proved by the tomb of a certain Amenmosi at Thebes, which contains two rows of seated statues of kings and queens depicted on a wall. Horemheb is shown between Amenhotep III and Ramesses I, the father of Seti I. That corroborates our modern understanding of the order of the succession—even though we know that Horemheb did not exactly follow right after Amenhotep III.   In between were those pharaohs associated with the Aten religion or related to Akhenaten, all of whom the Ramesside kings did not care to recognize. They were now as though they had never lived at all. Far from being considered an usurper, Horemheb was deemed perfectly legitimate by Seti I and his successors.

The real "Sethosis" and "Harmais" and their rivalry will be discussed further along. Yet it is true that Seti I had a reputation as a man of war who "....*exults at the beginning of battle, he delights to enter into it; his heart is gratified at the sight of blood. He lops off the heads of the rebels. More than the day of rejoicing he loves the moment of crushing (the foe)*", he probably was an engineer by inclination, one who was involved in his building projects.   Seti took considerable interest in the fact there was no water on the road to the gold mines in the mountainous regions.

> "*On that day his majesty inspected the desert lands as far as the mountains, for his heart desired to see the mines from which the fine gold is brought. After his majesty had gone up for many miles, he halted on the way in order to take counsel with his heart. He said 'How painful is the way that has no water!' What are*

---

103 The name of Horemheb was, in fact, written "Harmais" by the Greeks— hence the misunderstanding.

travelers to do to relieve the parching of their throats?
What quenches the thirst, the homeland being far away
and the desert wide? Woe to the man who thirsts in the
wilderness! Now then I will plan for them, I will make for
them the means to sustain them, so that they may bless
my name in the future, in years to come; that generations
yet to be may come to glory in me for my energy. For I
am indeed considerate and compassionate toward
travelers.'

Now after his majesty had spoken these words to his
own heart, he went about in the desert seeking a place to
make a watering station. And God was guiding him[104],
so as to grant the request of one whom he loved. Stone
workers were ordered to dig a well in the mountains, in
order that it might uplift the weary and refresh the heart
of him who burns in the summer heat. Then this place
was built, bearing the great name of Menmaare. It is full
of water in great quantity, like the cavern of the twin
sources at Yebu."[105]

Some time later, Seti's son, Ramesses II, pointed out that
this undertaking ultimately proved a failure (the well dried
up) and that it was he who was the successful well-digger.
From some of his texts, it is easy to see that Ramesses
idolized his father and, for some reason, did not feel entirely
capable of filling his shoes. It would seem that all through
his long life he strove to out-do his sire in everything. The
two men bore a family resemblance, although Ramesses II
was taller and more imposing in appearance. When he wore

---

[104] Even though the Egyptians worshipped numerous gods, they often
referred to God (nTr, vocalized "noute") in a cosmic sense, the active power
in the universe in whose hands rested the fate of all. This is well explained
in the chapter "The Egyptians' Ideas of God" in Sir E.A. Wallis Budge's
work, *The Egyptian Book of the Dead.*

[105] Elephantine, where it was considered by the ancient Egyptians that the
source of the Nile flowed from two springs in a cavern.

the khepresh, the tall blue crown, he surely seemed seven feet in height—and this is how people remembered him.[106] Although the visage of the mummy of King Seti appears so placid and refined, that was surely a post-mortem illusion and he doubtless gave a different impression in life. These Ramessides were no decadent, soft, late 18th Dynasty pharaohs; they could not afford to be. They knew their task was to restore the prestige Egypt had lost in the eyes of the world because the neglectful heretic, Akhenaten, had allowed the rays of the Aten to beat down on his head too long. Therefore, Seti I had characterized his accession as a "renaissance".[107]

Ramesses I and Seti I were probably genuine no-nonsense "tough guys" but, in the case of Ramesses II, one gets the nagging feeling it was all an elaborate act. The man boasted and swaggered too much; he stretched everything beyond the point of credibility.

This king was determined to leave his mark, to be thought great, and, indeed, although he has been deceased these past 3,000 years, Ramesses is still the most visible man in Egypt today. His mania for construction is in evidence everywhere; awesome, colossal edifices and images are in proportion to the inferiority complex behind them. Even the mummy of Ramesses II remains the most haughty in Egypt, frozen in an attitude of majestic disdain, like a man

---

[106] By the nickname of "Seesosis", in Egyptian "sisi". "Ozymandias" is how the Greeks heard the prenomen of Ramesses II, "Usermaare".

[107] "wHm mswt" or "repeater of births". A new Sothic period may have coincided with Seti's assumption of kingship.

who can't allow himself the luxury of letting down his guard even posthumously. The insecurity for which the pharaoh strove to over-compensate was perhaps rooted in a fact that he attempted to obliterate with fictions—Ramesses was, evidently, not the original crown-prince and may not even have been considered by his father as a future king.

Over the years, travelers in Egypt and some Egyptologists, as well, have waxed lyrical over the good looks of Ramesses II, supposing him "the handsomest man of his day". This is surely very far from the truth, although the idealized faces of the great monuments of the king appear quite benign and youthfully attractive in an oriental way. In actuality, Ramesses was probably the most intimidating-looking man in Egypt, whose gaze could turn the blood in ones veins to ice-water. Gaston Maspero had the following comments after viewing the newly-unwrapped mummy of this pharaoh:

"The chest is broad; the shoulders square; the arms are crossed upon the breast; the hands are small and dyed with henna; the feet are long, slender, somewhat flat-soled and dyed, like the hands, with henna...The head is long, and small in proportion to the body. The top of the skull is quite bare. On the temples there are a few sparse hairs, but at the poll the hair is quite thick, forming smooth, straight locks about five centimeters in length. White at the time of death, they have been dyed a light yellow by the spices used in the embalming. The forehead is low and narrow; the brow-ridge prominent; the eyebrows are thick and white, the eyes are small and close together; the nose is long, thin, hooked like the noses of the Bourbons, and slightly crushed at the tip by the pressure of the bandages; the temples are sunken; the cheek-bones are very prominent; the ears round, standing far out from the head, and pierced like those of a woman for the wearing of earrings; the jawbone is massive and strong; the chin very prominent, the moth small but thick-lipped, and full of some kind of black paste. This paste being partly cut away with the scissors, disclosed some much worn and brittle teeth, which, moreover, are white and well-preserved. The moustache and beard are thin. They seem

204

to have been kept shaven during life, but were probably allowed to grow during the king's last illness; or they may have grown after death. The hairs are white, like those of the head and eyebrows, but are harsh and bristly, and from two to three millimeters in length. The skin is of earthy brown, splotched with black. Finally, it may be said the face of the mummy gives a fair idea of the face of the living king."

In life, the eyes of Ramesses II seem to have had the expression of a calculating merchant, his small mouth rather prim above his big, puffy chin. We know all this because, in those times, the nobility and officials had statues of themselves sculpted obsequiously substituting the face of the sovereign for their own, as did the scribe, May, above.

Even so, they mostly did not trouble to flatter the pharaoh as much as he flattered himself in his own portraits, the result being that we obtain fairly accurate glimpses of how these kings actually appeared. Even the faces on many of their coffins resembled the ruler instead of their owner and occupant. The wives of the men of the court were obliged to be painted and carved with the features of the pharaoh, as well, which is rather a pity as we surely have missed seeing some lovely Egyptian women viewed through the eyes of very competent artists. Only queens seem to have reserved the right to have their own portraits, although sometimes they were modeled on their husbands.

Seti I ruled as coregent with his father for a short time. He managed to conquer Palestine by the end of his reign, restoring the stability of the Egyptian empire. He defended his western frontier against the Libyans and battled the Hittites, in addition.

His son, Ramesses II inherited the Hittites, a powerful people of Asia Minor, as his major foe and waged a lengthy war against them. The major battle of this extended rivalry for supremacy in the Near East was fought in 1274 in northern Syria at a site called Kadesh on the Orontes river. The engagement seems to have resulted in a draw, even though both nations hailed it as a great triumph.

Ramesses, predictably, went so far as to declare that he had charged the enemy all by himself, his chariot fighters having deserted him out of fear.

When he was already around fifty years old and the husband and father to several wives, numerous concubines and an impressive number of children, the Egyptian monarch managed to make a treaty with the Hittites, which he sought to cement with a marriage of state. The two major powers had decided to divide the territories that lay between their countries like a loaf of bread. For some reason, it became very important to Ramesses that a daughter of the Hittite king be sent to him and his correspondence with the shrewd queen, her mother, is rather humorous, with her procrastinating while attempting to milk the pharaoh for funds. One gets the feeling the queen was waiting for her daughter to reach the age of puberty, at least. Finally, the young girl[108] was delivered to her anxious bridegroom, who found her very much to his taste and even seems to have fallen in love with her. It was reported that the Hittite princess was "as fair as a goddess" and one can only hope that the distaff side of this political union found the imperious grandfather who was her new spouse not too appalling, for her part.[109] The charms of the young lady might have been described in the same terms as is seen in an example of the love poetry that survives from ancient Egypt:

Darling, you only, there is no duplicate,
More lovely than all other womanhood, luminous, perfect,
A star coming over the sky-line at new year, a good year,
Splendid in colours, with allure in the eye's turn.
Her lips are enchantment, her neck the right length and her
breasts a marvel;
Her hair lapis lazuli in its glitter, her arms

---

[108]In those times, no one would have considered anyone older than from twelve to sixteen a suitable bride for a king—or anyone else for that matter. The age of the groom was not considered significant and if his wealth and power had increased over a considerable number of years, so much the better. In 1618, an Englishman named Edward Terry wrote that the Great Mogul of Delhi in India did not come near his women or wives after they exceeded the age of thirty years, and neither did his nobles. One may readily imagine that the pharaohs of Egypt were of the same mindset as other eastern potentates, although the nobility of Egypt seems to have been quite modern in its view of a wife as a valued companion for the life of a man.

[109] Ramesses the Great would have been considered an "old man" at his age. The majority of men never lived to see much more than thirty years. As it transpired, the king would go on to become an "ancient man", being over eighty when he died. When this happened, there would have been very few persons in Egypt who recalled having lived under any other sovereign—just as was the case when Queen Victoria of Great Britain passed to her final reward. Working in Ramesses' favor, of course, was the fact that he was, at the time of the marriage, the richest and most influential man on earth and such power has been known to work as an aphrodisiac on females.

more splendid than gold.
Her fingers make me see petals, the lotuses are like that.
Her flanks are modeled as should be, her legs beyond
all other beauty.
Noble her walking
My heart would be a slave should she enfold me.

Naturally, such exquisite words would have been lost upon someone who did not know Egyptian and the pharaoh would have been too grand to recite them, in any case. Still, one can imagine an overwhelmed, youthful bride, not relegated to the harem but kept near her admiring husband as a balm for his sight. How did she find her glittering surroundings and the hot-eyed stares of the king's many handsome sons, the children of other beautiful wives of the pharaoh? Did she blush because she was now forced to wear Egyptian gowns as transparent as mist in a land where modesty was unknown and where wine flowed like water, drunk by people dripping with perfumed oils mixed with their sweat, which gleamed just as did the gold on their limbs?

Once in awhile she would steal a glance at her husband, the lord of all he surveyed, the one who, in her homeland, was called "the Great Dragon who dwells in his river" and hopefully be rewarded, at times, by a smile from him that showed the wonderful white, straight teeth that seemed to be a trait of the entire royal family. And, no doubt, observing his father's new favorite was a prince named Merneptah, the son of Queen Iset-nofret, who was as yet happily ignorant of the fate in store for Egypt and the manner in which it would unfold. It was quite impossible that he should then have had any inkling of how easily this abundance and splendor, enjoyed in security now, could be snatched away.

Chapter Eleven

"Those who wrote histories of Egypt, namely Manetho, Chaeremon, Apollonius Molon, Lysimachus, and Apion the philologist, make mention of Moses and the exodus of the sons of Israel from Egypt. For as Egyptians and writers about Egyptian history, they too, fittingly, relate the events that happened in their regions, but they also disparage Moses as one who provoked a sedition and who stirred up a mass of beggars and lepers and led them out of Egypt; and (they say) that once they had left for mount Sinai and Jerusalem, they called themselves Jews."

Cosmos Indicopleustes, *Topographia Christiana* XII 4[111]

Season of Summer, the Fourth Month. The monsoon rains of Ethiopia swelled the waters that made their way, with a deafening roar, past the first cataract at the southernmost border of Egypt. There they swirled around the islands on which kings had built charming little temples to the river deities, Hapi, Satet and Anuket. Soon it would be time for an eternal cycle to renew itself and the first season of the Egyptian calendar, the Inundation, known as the Akhet, would begin. By the time of Akhet, the land was parched and dry from the searing summer heat and nature had exhausted herself trying to keep vegetation alive. The trees were covered with a grey dust and the earth was cracked, colored like the hide of an elephant. The parching south-east wind blew, sometimes in great gales, from the middle of February to the middle of June and this was responsible for the grey pall that lay over the plant-life.

From December through March the air was cool in Egypt and the nights could even see freezing temperatures, but during the other eight months it was hot to very hot, July not uncommonly experiencing days of 110 Fahrenheit in the

---

[111] *Chaeremon: Egyptian Priest and Stoic Philosopher*, Pieter Willem Van Der Horst (Leiden, 1987, page 5)

shade. Yet, from June until the following winter, the Egyptians were able to breathe "the sweet wind of the north", which mitigated the intense heat of the day.

By Day 17 of the Fourth Month of Shomu[112], the rising of the waters could, in a "perfect year" be seen at Memphis and two days later, the people of the Delta observed the flooding. At first, the waters were greenish and then appeared to take on a red hue, as though tinted by blood.[113] In the coming months these waters spilled over the banks of the Nile and covered the fields of Egypt, isolating the villages, built on mounds, like scattered clusters of civilization in the midst of a shallow sea.

It was more than 300 years since King Ahmose had set out from Thebes to expel the Hyksos from Lower Egypt and the New Kingdom had begun. How many were the great and terrible things that had occurred over those centuries while the river ran endlessly and silently past!

By the Second Month of the First Season, Akhet,[114] the flood was at its highest. In the Fourth Month, or October, it

---

[112] Shomu was "summer" and June was the fourth month of this season. Even though the Egyptians believed the source of the Nile flooding was two springs at Elephantine, the "Night of the Tear-drop" was observed, which referred to "the tear from the eye of Isis that fell into the Nile and caused the Inundation" (E. Wallis Budge). In Arabic it is known as "Lelat al-Nuktah".

[113] These phenomena were called the "Green Nile" and the "Red Nile" before the completion of the Aswan Dam ceased the annual flooding of the river.

[114] August/ September. If we date another exodus to the end of the 19th Dynasty, the time of the flood would have been in its proper season. Kenneth Kitchen: "At Deir el-Medina in Western Thebes, a graffito in Year 1 of King Merneptah, Inundation Season, mentions the workmen viewing the waters of the actual Nile inundation at that time. This is only possible every fourteen centuries, because the Egyptian calendar (365 days) was 1/4 day too short, and ended a day too early every 4 years. So, its summer months had crept into winter by 730 years, and it only came right again after 1460 years or so. It was right under Merenptah in the 13th century BC, as it was in the 2nd century AD (Censorinus), and had been in the 28th/27th centuries BC but NOT at intervening times." Indeed, Merneptah's grandfather, Seti I, seems to indicate that a new Sothic Cycle was a

receded to its normal bed and shrank continually until the next summer. The time of Akhet brought the fertile silt that gave life and prosperity to the land. Without it, rainless Egypt would have become like the desert that flanked it on either side. Still, the season was not without its perils as winds, it was said, blew in pestilences from Ethiopia along with the rushing waters.

Sometimes the flooding was great and those who were in charge of the Nilometers would predict an abundant harvest of crops. In other years, there was less water and a low flood, so that the people felt the rigors of famine.[115] An inscription was carved upon a rock on the island of Sehel, near the first cataract, that was attributed to King Djoser of the 3rd Dynasty[116], telling of "seven lean years". It narrates the pharaoh's instructions to his vizier, Imhotep, to discover the secrets of the river:

"There is a city in the midst of the waters, from which the Nile rises, named Elephantine...The 'Two Caverns' is the name of the water; they are the two breasts which pour forth all good things. It is the couch of the Nile, in which he becomes young again...He fecundates the land by mounting as the male, the bull, to the female; he renews his virility, assuaging his desire. He rushes 28 cubits (high at Elephantine); he hastens at Thebes seven cubits (high). Khnum is there as a god..."

---

hallmark of his reign, which meant that the heliacal rising coincided with the beginning of the solar year. Since we know this rare event took place in 139 CE, during the reign of the Roman emperor, Antonius Pius, it makes sense that there was also a sighting of the star during the period of 1321-1317 BCE.

[115] The hunger resulting from a series of low Niles was sometimes recorded in dramatic terms, with cannibalism being the extreme resort. It is estimated that a rise of between 25 and 27 feet was required to water the entire country. The inscription of Djoser is pseudographic, dating from Ptolemaic times.

[116] 2668-2649 BCE

Then King Djoser says he saw Khnum in a dream, who foretold that the seven years of famine was about to come to an end:

"As I slept in life and satisfaction, I discovered the god standing over me. I propitiated him with praise; I prayed to him in his presence. He revealed himself to me, his face being fresh. His words were: 'I am Khnum, thy fashioner....I know the Nile. When he is introduced into the fields, his introduction gives life to every nostril, like the introduction of life to the fields...The Nile will pour forth for thee, without a year of cessation or laxness for any land. Plants will grow, bowing down under the fruit. Renutet[117] will be at the head of everything...The starvation year will have gone and people's borrowing from their granaries will have departed. .."

But something had, apparently, gone wrong in the final period of King Banire- Merneptah Hotep-hir-maat. He who had styled himself "Beloved of the gods" became deserted by them and knew not why and that is why he prayed for a nocturnal visitation of his own.

Merneptah did not become pharaoh of Egypt until he was an old man. Twelve of his elder brothers had predeceased their father, the mighty Ramesses. What happened to them all, no one knows. Most of them were handsome men and youths, the sons of beautiful queens and concubines...so many princes, both older and younger than the ultimate heir, extinguished like vanished stars in the heavens.[118]

---

[117] Goddess of the harvest.

[118] A huge tomb, known as KV5, has been excavated in the Valley of the Kings by Dr. Kent Weeks. Evidently, it was intended as a burial place for the sons of Ramesses II but, oddly, when the tomb was examined by order of King Ramesses IX, the verdict was "iw bw pwy-tw qrs im-f" or "nobody is buried in it".

For the last decade of his father's reign, the thirteenth son, Merneptah, had already assumed most of the duties of the former, who was beset with the problems connected to a great age. He had been king in everything but name and so easily fit into the role once Ramesses finally "flew to heaven". At first there had been disbelief at the announcement of the death of the old ruler, as the Egyptians had come to believe that he actually was unlike all mortal men and would simply

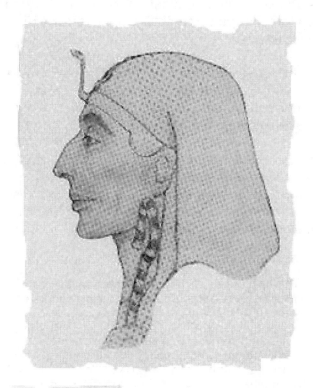

go on forever. Once the people witnessed the funerary barge of Ramesses pass up the Nile to Thebes and comprehended that the legendary monarch was truly dead, there had been some slightly-stunned jubilation at Merneptah's accession as scarcely anyone in the land had ever drunk to the health of a new pharaoh.[119]

Because a new Sothic Cycle had begun in 1321-1317 BCE, this means that, at Merneptah's accession, the summer months were still actually in summer and the Nile flooding really happened in the season of Inundation—although the civil calendar had started to slip again, of course.

The appearance of a high Nile in his first year, *apparently* prompted the Chief Archivist of the Treasury of Pharaoh, Amenemone, to write the following letter to his friend, the scribe, Pentawere:[120]

> *"Be glad of heart, the entire land! The goodly times are come! A lord—life, prosperity, health—is given in all lands and normality has come down into its place...All ye righteous, come that ye may see. Right has banished wrong. Evil-doers have fallen upon their faces. All the rapacious are ignored. The water stands and is not dried up; the Nile lifts high. Days are long, nights have hours, and the moon comes normally. The gods are satisfied and content of heart. One lives in laughter and wonder. Mayest thou know it."*

---

[119] Peden, A.J., *A Note on the Accession Date of Merenptah, GM* 140 (1994), 69. Kenneth Kitchen established the accession day of this pharaoh to be between I *akhet* 29 and II *akhet* 13. Peden further narrowed the possibility to the days 3 to 13 within II *akhet*.

[120] Even though the letter contains the standard sentiments expressed when a new ruler came to the throne, the odd thing about this missive, written in hieratic, a cursive Egyptian script, on the recto of the Papyrus Sallier I (British Museum 10185) is that the author, Amenemone, seems to have already held his office in Year 9 of Ramesses II, according to a colophon of pSallier III, which is the famous "Poem of Pentawere", the recipient. That would have been nearly 60 years prior to the accession of Merneptah! How likely is it that these two men, evidently both established adults in Ramesses' Year 9, would still be around to correspond so many years later? pSallier I also contains an enigmatic "Prayer to Thoth" by Amenemone, which coveys the impression the author is not in a very joyful mood, at all, and either about to die or go to court to be judged—and then perhaps be executed!

The "goodly times" prevailed for more than seven years. There was plenty in Egypt, more than enough for all. The treaty that the father of Merneptah had made with the Hittites was in force[121] and, when the land of Hatti experienced famine in the early years of the reign of Merneptah, he sent grain to his ally.

During his Year 5, King Merneptah underwent a crisis with his Lybian neighbors and the people of Canaan were beginning to show signs of rebellion against the Egyptian empire, as well. There was disquiet in Nubia, too. But the elderly pharaoh and his forces dealt triumphantly with all these insurrections, backed by the wonderful state of the Egyptian economy. By his Year 6, Merneptah had stabilized the situation and maintained the *pax Egyptiaca* once more.

Most remarkably, we possess a large stela, which Merneptah appropriated from Amenhotep III, incising on the verso an account of his victory over the Lybians. The final portion of the long, poetic text[122] informs of the crushing of the people of the Levant and mentions for the first and last time in pharaonic history the name "Israel". The dating of the monument is "Year 5, 3rd month of Shomu, day 3". The bottom lines read:

"The princes are prostrate saying 'Shalom!'
Not one of the Nine Bows lifts his head;
Tjehenu is vanished, Hatti is at peace,
Canaan is captured with all woe.
Ashkelon is conquered, Gezer seized,
Yanoam made nonexistent;
Israel *is laid waste, its seed is no more.*
Khor is become a widow on account of Egypt.

---

[121] Never to be broken until the Hittite empire collapsed and the Hittites no longer existed as a nation.

[122] The reign of Merneptah seems to have been blessed with a gifted writer (or writers). Even the sarcophagus that held the king's mummy contains an extremely beautiful address to the deceased king on the inside of its lid, composed in the most touching terms.

All who roamed have been subdued By the King of Upper and Lower Egypt, Ba-ni-Ra- Meramen, Son of Ra, Merneptah, Content with Maat,
Given life like Ra every day."

From Year 8, dated to the Birthday of Seth in the intercalary days, there is a report from the fortress of Khetam on the edge of the area known as Tjeku "*in the pools of Per-*

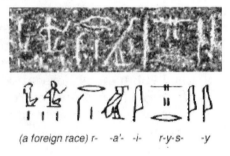

(a foreign race) r-   -a'-   -i-   r-y-s-   -y

Atum"[123], saying that "*the Bedouin tribes of Edom*[124]" have been allowed to pass "*to keep them alive and to keep their cattle alive through the great ka of Pharaoh*".   Evidently there were certain times in the months when some of these people were permitted to enter, one or more of the five days before the New Year seemingly being allocated for this purpose.

Merneptah, knowing that the chances for a long reign like that of his sire were against him, was busy excavating his large tomb and erecting his mortuary temple, taking pieces from the half-ruined cenotaph of Amenhotep III[125] in order to speed up the construction. The pressure was on to accomplish these projects before death overtook the pharaoh

---

[123] The Wadi Tumilat.   Per-Atum is the "Pithom" of the Book of Exodus.

[124] Shasu.

[125] The mortuary temple of Amenhotep III, on the west bank of the Nile near the Valley of the Kings, had perhaps already been affected by an earthquake, prior to the one in 27 BCE. All that remains of it today are the two "colossi of Memnon" that stood at its entrance, one of which emitted a moaning or "singing" sound at dawn in ancient times, a phenomenon that attracted a number of travelers until the damaged colossus was repaired by the Roman emperor Septimius Severus (193-211 CE) and the statue grew dumb.

and the workmen employed no doubt suffered as a result.[126] However, forces eventually came into play that no timetable devised by a man or even a god could control. It must be so, because Merneptah is connected to an exodus of Semites from Egypt and is considered the Pharaoh that would not let the Israelites go by an "Alexandrian tradition", as asserted by Gaston Maspero.

The Plagues of Egypt were as follows:

River of blood—in which the fish died and people could not drink its water.

Frogs—in the beds, the ovens and everywhere else. When they died, they caused a stench throughout the land.

Gnats—they seemed to arise out of the dust. Gnats are maddening to both humans and animals. But it may be that the gnats were really "ants".

Flies—pests that also are capable of spreading germs and disease. For ages, they have been attracted to the festering eyes of Egyptian children, who are prone to suffer from a particular sort of opthalmia.

Cattle murrain—causing the death of the cattle of the Egyptians.

Boils or blains—a result of a "soot" that came into contact with the skin.

Hail, rain, thunder and fire—"*such as hath not been in Egypt since the day it was founded even until now*". The flax and the barley were destroyed but not the wheat and the spelt, as they had not yet ripened.

Locusts—ate whatever the hail had not destroyed.

Darkness—people could not see one another for three days.

---

[126] Under the best of circumstances, excavating the long galleries of the tombs of the pharaohs, burrowing deep into the bed-rock with copper chisels, must have resembled a stint in hell. Even plastering and decorating these halls must have been grueling work as the ventilation was barely adequate and the only light came from little oil-burning lamps into which salt was strewn so they would not smoke.

Death of the Firstborn—of both the Egyptians and their animals. Even the oldest child of Pharaoh died. Only the Hebrews were spared.

Some of these calamities are surely related to the first exodus, when the volcano of Thera caused both panic and awe. But others are the familiar " Horsemen of the Apocalypse", namely Pestilence, Famine and War, who bring in their train the fourth rider, Death, mounted upon his pale horse. The first three horsemen act in a kind of sequence. Because of war, the farmer is afraid to venture into his field and his crops suffer. This spells famine and the populace, weakened from hunger and demoralized by the strife, are more apt to fall prey to infections. The blights of plants and diseases of animals are also factors that bring on famine and the weather is yet another element pertinent to all of it.

> "The influence of climate upon Plague is still imperfectly understood. The Great Plague (of London) occurred in a year of drought so severe that Richard Baxter, the divine, declares that winter, spring and summer to have been 'the driest that ever man alive knew, or our forefathers mention of late ages; so that the grounds were burnt like the highways where the cattle should have fed. The meadow grounds where I lived (Acton) bare but four loads of hay which before bare forty' "[127]

Even when fields appear promising, locusts are not unknown to have been harbingers of disease. For example, the plague of Orosius in 125 CE was preceded by an invasion of these creatures, who ravaged large areas of crops.

The Bible construes the plagues as pressure exerted by God upon Pharaoh so that he would allow the Children of Israel to depart from Egypt. The ancient Egyptians would also have viewed them as the work of the gods, and this leads us to the *Tale of the Polluted Ones* of Manetho and Chaeremon, as narrated by Josephus:

---

[127] Walter George Bell, *The Great Plague of London* (London, 1924).

"This is the Manetho who promised to translate Egyptian history from the priestly writings. The author begins by stating that our ancestors entered Egypt in great numbers and overpowered the inhabitants, further admitting that later on they were driven out of the country, occupied what is now Judea, founded Jerusalem, and built the temple. So far he followed the chronicles; but at this point, under the pretext of recording fables and current reports about the Jews, he took the liberty of bringing up some incredible tales, in order to represent us as mixed up with a multitude of Egyptian lepers and others, who for various maladies were condemned, as he asserts, to banishment from the country. Inventing a king named Amenophis, an imaginary person, the date of whose reign he consequently did not venture to fix (although he adds the exact years of the other kings whom he mentions), he attaches to him certain legends, having presumably forgotten that he has already stated that the departure of the shepherds for Jerusalem took place 518 years previously.

> For Tethmoisis was king at the time of the Exodus, and according to Manetho, the succeeding reigns covered a period of 393 years, down to the brothers, Sethos and Hermaeus, the former of whom, he says, took the name of Aegyptus and the latter that of Danaus. Sethos, after expelling Hermaeus, reigned fifty-nine years and his eldest son, Rampses, who succeeded him, sixty-six.[128]

> And so, after admitting that all those years had passed since our forefathers left Egypt, he now interpolates this fictitious Amenophis. This king, he states, wished to be granted, like Or, one of his predecessors on the throne, a vision of the gods, communicating his desire to his namesake, Amenophis son of Paapis, whose wisdom and

---

[128] Josephus got 518 years by adding 393 + 59+ 66. His calculation is based on a misunderstanding and is totally meaningless. Josephus is, of course, a preserver of Manetho's "chronicle", his kinglist, but one need not consider for a moment that he was actually quoting the Egyptian in his figures.

knowledge of the future were regarded as marks of divinity.

This namesake, then, replied that he would be able to see the gods if he rid the whole land of lepers and other polluted persons[129]. The king was delighted and assembled all those in Egypt whose bodies were wasted by disease: they numbered 80,000 persons.

These he cast into the stone quarries to the east of the Nile, there to work segregated from the rest of the Egyptians. Among them, Manetho adds, there were some of the learned priests, who had been attacked by leprosy. Then this wise seer Amenophis was filled with dread of divine wrath against himself and the king if the injustice done to these persons should become known. He added a prediction that certain allies would join the polluted people and would take possession of Egypt for 13 years. Not daring to make a prophecy himself to the king, he left a full account of it in writing, and then took his own life[130] The king became despondent."

Up to now, Josephus has been merely paraphrasing Manetho but, at this point, he quotes him verbatim:

"'When the men in the stone-quarries had suffered for a long time, the king acceded to their request to assign them for habitation and refuge the abandoned city of the shepherds, called Avaris, and according to an ancient theological tradition, dedicated to Typhon. [131] There they went, and, having now a place to serve as a base for revolt, they appointed as their leader one of the priests of

---

[129] Chaeremon submits that the pharaoh had "a vision of Isis in his sleep, who reproached him for the destruction of her temple in war-time". So here we must read " have a vision of the gods".

[131] Sutekh or Seth.

Heliopolis called Osarseph, and took an oath of total obedience to him.

By his first act he ordained that they should not worship the gods nor abstain from the flesh of any of the animals held in special reverence in Egypt, but should kill and consume them all. Further, they should have nothing to do with anybody except members of their own group. After laying down these and a multitude of other laws, absolutely opposed to Egyptian custom, he ordered all hands to repair the city walls and make war with King Amenophis.

Then, in concert with other priests and polluted persons like himself, he sent an embassy to the shepherds, who had been expelled by Tethmoisis, in the city called Jerusalem, setting out the position of himself and his outraged companions and inviting them to join in a united assault on Egypt. He escorted them first to their ancestral home at Avaris, to provide abundant supplies for their multitudes, to fight alongside them when the moment came, and without difficulty to reduce the country to submission. The shepherds, delighted with the idea, all eagerly set off in a body numbering 200,000 men, and soon reached Avaris.

The news of their invasion shocked Amenophis, king of Egypt, who recalled the prediction of Amenophis, son of Paapis. He began by assembling the Egyptians, and, after consulting with their leaders, sent for the sacred animals which were held in utmost reverence in the temples, and instructed the priests in each district to conceal the images of the gods as securely as possible. His five-year-old son Sethos, also called Ramesses after his grandfather Ra(m)pses, he entrusted to the care of a friend. He then crossed the Nile[132] with 300,000 of the most efficient

---

[132] The city of Memphis was on the west bank of the river. The pharaoh was headed east.

warriors of Egypt and met the enemy. Instead, however, of doing battle with them he, convinced that he was about to go against the gods, turned back to Memphis. There he picked up Apis and the other sacred animals which he had ordered to be brought there and at once, with all his army and the Egyptian population, started up country for Ethiopia, whose king was under obligation to him and at his service. The latter made him welcome and maintained the whole multitude with all the products of the country suitable for human consumption, assigned them cities and villages for the predicted thirteen years of exile. Moreover he stationed an Ethiopian army on the Egyptian frontier to protect King Amenophis and his subjects. Such was the situation in Ethiopia.

Meanwhile the Solymites[133] came down with the polluted Egyptians, and treated the inhabitants in so sacrilegious a manner that the regime of the shepherds seemed like a golden age to those who now beheld the impieties of their present enemies. Not only did they set cities and villages on fire, not only did they pillage the temples and mutilate the images of the gods, but, not content with that, they habitually used the very sanctuaries as kitchens for roasting the venerated sacred animals, and forced priests and prophets[134] to slaughter them and cut their throats, and then turned them out naked. It is said that the priest who gave them a constitution and code of laws was a native of Heliopolis, named Osarseph after the Heliopolitan god Osiris, and that when he went over to this people he changed his name and was called Moses.'"

Then Josephus continues in his own voice:

---

133 The people from Jerusalem.

134 The high-priests, called "seers".

"Such and more, which, for brevity's sake, I omit[135], is the Egyptian gossip about the Jews. Manetho adds that Amenophis subsequently advanced from Ethiopia with a large army, his son Rampses at the head of another, and that the two attacked and defeated the shepherds and their polluted allies, killing many of them and pursuing the remainder to the frontiers of Syria. That, with more of a similar kind, is Manetho's account...."

[At this point Josephus makes many sarcastic comments about the text he has supplied. We shall omit these for now and go on to Chaeremon's version.]

"The next witness I shall examine is Chaeremon. This writer likewise professes to write the history of Egypt, and agrees with Manetho in giving the names of Amenophis and Ramesses to the king and his son. He then proceeds to state that Isis appeared to Amenophis in his sleep, and reproached him for the destruction of her temple in wartime. The sacred scribe Phritobautes told him that, if he purged Egypt of its contaminated population, he might be at ease. The king, thereupon, collected 250,000 persons and banished them from the country. Their leaders were scribes-- Moses and another sacred scribe—Joseph. The exiles, on reaching Pelusium, fell in with a body of 380,000 persons, left there by Amenophis, who had refused them permission to cross the Egyptian frontier. With these the exiles concluded an alliance and marched upon Egypt. Amenophis, without waiting for their attack, fled to Ethiopia, leaving his wife pregnant. Concealing herself in some caverns she gave birth to a son named Ramesses, who, on reaching manhood, drove the Jews, to the number of about 200,000, into Syria, and brought home his father Amenophis from Ethiopia."

---

[135] These are among the most exasperating words ever written by a human.

Josephus cites another author, as well, Lysimachus[136], whose account offers a few other details—and who calls the pharaoh by the name "Bocchoris".

"In the reign of Bocchoris, king of Egypt, the Jewish people, who were afflicted with leprosy, scurvy, and other maladies, sought shelter in the temples and lived a beggarly existence.[137] The victims of disease being very numerous, a dearth ensued throughout Egypt. King Bocchoris thereupon sent to consult the oracle of Ammon about the failure of the crops. The god told him to purge the temples of impure and impious persons, to drive them out of these sanctuaries into the wilderness, to drown those afflicted with leprosy and scurvy, as the sun was indignant that such persons should live, and to purify the temples; then the land would yield her increase."

The erudite Josephus seems outraged by their stories to the point where all objectivity appears to desert him. His acrid rebuttal indicates that he views all Egyptians as the dedicated enemies of his own people and refuses to acknowledge any truth in the accounts of the Egyptian historians whatsoever. Josephus employs what he believes to be pure logic to refute the "mendacity" of the others and in this resembles modern minimalists whose so-called "practical", nay-saying view of the Hebrew Bible serves as a bar to the toleration of further investigation by others not similarly inclined.

The Jewish author is so eager to disbelieve that which contradicts his own understanding of the Exodus, drawn from the Torah, that he becomes willfully blind. For example, Josephus attempts to discredit Manetho, at the outset, by mentioning that the Egyptian thought his ancestors had already quit Egypt at the time of the expulsion

---

[136] An Alexandrian writer of uncertain date.

[137] Lysimachus apparently construed that all these "polluted ones" were Jews, even though Manetho makes it plain this was not so.

by "Tethmoisis"—so why was he saying they were driven out by a fictitious Amenophis and his son?[138]   Josephus is insensible to the fact that it is he who is being illogical, considering that he specifically paraphrases or quotes Manetho as saying that the "shepherds" had left, their former stronghold, Avaris, was deserted and half-ruined, and that Osarseph/Moses and his fellow rebels were calling on their descendants in Canaan to come to Egypt and help them fight the pharaoh.

Josephus seemingly refuses to comprehend that the king of Egypt wanted nothing more than to *understand* why the heavenly powers had turned against him, that he was willing to go to great lengths to mollify them and prayed for an oracle.[139]   The pharaoh may, himself, have had his blind spots, but Josephus' snide remark that, if the ruler wanted to see the gods of Egypt he had only to look around him, is unworthy of the intellectual.   The author of *Contra Apionem*[140], fluent in several languages and scripts, points in ridicule to the part where Amenophis admits he cannot fight

---

[138] Manetho does not mention Moses in connection with the expulsion of the Hyksos. In fact, Josephus quotes him as having written "*Some say they were Arabs*", a sure indication that Manetho did not know precisely who "the shepherds" were and did not equate them with the Jews—even though Josephus does.

[139] Over fifty years earlier, the king of the Hittites, Mursili, had written down his "Plague Prayers", invoking the gods to cease afflicting his land with a contagion that the Hittites had caught from Egyptian prisoners of war and which had been raging for twenty years. Mursili, however, thought he knew why the gods were displeased (the sins of his father), yet he wrote "*If, on the other hand, people are dying for some other reason, either let me see it in a dream, or let it be found out by an oracle, or let a prophet declare it or let all the priests find out by incubation whatever I suggest to them. Hattian Storm-god, my lord, save my life! Let the gods, my lords, prove their divine power! Let someone see it in a dream! For whatever reason people are dying, let that be found out!...*"

[140]*Against Apion*, the work in which Josephus quotes the Egyptian historians. It is particularly ironic that, in his autobiography, *The Life*, Josephus tells of having "*beheld a marvelous vision in my dreams*", which he regarded as an oracle of his future greatness.

against the gods and retreats south, without having the slightest clue that not being able to fight against the gods means the same as not being able to escape ones fate as it was already prophesied and ordained.

The reason that the goddess, Isis, is mentioned in the story is that she seems to have had a special identification with cures, even miraculous ones. So wrote Diodorus Siculus:

> "As for Isis, the Egyptians say that she was the discoverer of many health-giving drugs and was greatly skilled in the science of healing. Consequently, now that she has attained immortality, she finds her greatest delight in the healing of mankind ...for standing above the sick in their sleep she gives them aid and works remarkable cures upon such as submit themselves to her...."

That fact that Chaeremon had not neglected to mention that "Amenophis" had incurred the wrath of Isis by ruining her temple, can only mean that the pharaoh was, himself, ill but could not obtain the healing intervention of the goddess.

However, to be fair to Josephus—if he could not figure out who this "Amenophis" was and dismisses him as an invention of the Egyptians—in this he is not alone. Although he had access to Manetho's kinglist and is one of the preservers of fragments of this lost manuscript, we cannot expect him to have perceived the truth any more quickly than those of us who have stood in a long line behind him.

Even though the writings of Manetho of Sebennytos were never intended to be mysteries, certain parts, as handed down by other authors, surely contain intriguing puzzles. I have been as much led astray as anyone else who has attempted to unravel the enigmas of Manetho's history of Egypt and have, I now believe, reached some false conclusions regarding it as set forth by me in print.

To recap, according to Flavius Josephus, two Egyptian historians, Manetho and Chaeremon, wrote of a chaotic interlude that began during the reign of a certain pharaoh,

"Amenophis", who wished to "see the gods" like a predecessor, King Or. His counselor, supposedly bearing the same name as the ruler, offered some dubious advice. Basically, I think Manetho has guided us down a path filled with pitfalls because, at the outset of his remarkable account of King "Amenophis" and his persecution of the "polluted persons", he has Amenophis being advised by one "Amenophis Paapis' son". Insofar as I am aware, this has been accepted by all interpreters of the story as the legendary Amenhotep son of Hapu, and so nearly everyone who has taken any interest in the *Aegyptiaca* has tended to surmise that it was King Nebmaare Amenhotep III who wanted to "see the gods" and ended up fleeing to Ethiopia. I, personally, confess to thinking that the Amenophis referred to was really Akhenaten, who had been forced to abdicate due to opposition to his heresy, but now I feel that the entire drama, which includes a character called "Moses", is a rather cryptic and quite complex folktale, the Egyptian version of the Exodus—or at least an exodus or two.

Perhaps Manetho included Amenhotep son of Hapu due to his conviction that no Egyptian pharaoh could have a more distinguished advisor than this deified personality.[141] Those who are familiar with Manetho's kinglist will recall there being an "Amenophis" who supposedly reigned for 19 years and six months after the extraordinarily long kingship of Ramesses II.[142] Africanus, one of the Christian preservers of Manetho, calls this Amenophis "Amenophath" and it is clear, from all the quoters of the "*Aegyptiaca*", that the difference between the names Amenhotep and Merneptah was not so

---

[141] Amenhotep son of Hapu had a mortuary temple, near that of Amenhotep III, the king whom he served, and his cult seems to have been limited to the Theban area but continued unto the Roman period, when a "Hymn To Amenhotep" was inscribed on a doorpost of the temple of Ptah at Karnak. Deified, he was invoked as a god of healing. No writings of his have come down to us, a Greek fragment probably being pseudo-graphic.

[142] Ramesses Miamun, also miswritten "Harmesses" in the version handed down courtesy of Flavius Josephus.

apparent to the antique chronographers, including perhaps Manetho. The *Book of Sothis*, another pharaonic kinglist that has been dated to the 3rd Century CE[143], places an "Amenophis" with 8 regnal years following "*Ramesses, also called Aegyptus, 68 years*", (which is the precise duration of the reign of Ramesses II and probably a more correct reckoning of the years of the former) confirms the miswriting of the name of the successor, Merneptah.

Many masculine names that are seen in dynastic times were no longer used by the Ptolemaic or Greek era of Egypt. I doubt any living Egyptians of that period were called "Amenhotep". Curiously, even though Manetho was supposed to have been the leading scholar of his day, anyone who closely scrutinizes his kinglist will observe that the names of the pharaohs are mostly rendered as they might have been pronounced and are not precise transliterations, in Greek, from the hieroglyphs with which they were normally written in cartouches. From our point of view, it would seem strange that so little distinction between the names Amenhotep and Merneptah could exist in the mind of those who were "hierogrammateis", or "sacred scribes"[144]. In fact, in Ptolemaic texts the spelling is generally bad because the pronunciation of Egyptian had deteriorated and puns are made between words that, in former days, would not have been thought to have a resemblance. Now many words sounded alike to Ptolemaic priests and the graphemes /A/, /i/ and /a/, which had once been distinct, were now interchangeable and sometimes the same words were spelled differently within the same document.

In brief, there were several Egyptian names, including also Amenemope and Meremope, that, no matter how different they appear in spelling, sounded very much alike when

---

[143] By Gutschmid. *The Book of Sothis* was compiled by a monk named Syncellus.

[144] Like Manetho. To know that the name of someone like the famous Imhotep was heard vocalized as "Amouthe" by the Greeks will go a long way toward explaining the problem.

vocalized in the slurring Egyptian manner, where certain consonants, /b/, /p/, /m/, /n/, were usually elided into the one that followed.   /r/ and /t/ often were lost in pronunciation, as well.

Therefore, I propose that it became quite convenient for the Egyptian writers of the Late Period to do exactly what the author of the Book of Exodus had done—but to go one step beyond. The Egyptian version of an exodus also was made up of more than one episode but, rather than leave the Pharaoh nameless, he was called "Amenophis", an amalgam of Amenhotep IV (Akhenaten), Merneptah and Seti-Merneptah!

It is written that the King "Amenophis" in question had a little son, "Sethos also called Ramesses"[145], named after his grandfather, "Rampses". Certainly, any progeny of Merneptah would have had Ramesses II for a grandsire.[146] It has been accepted that Merneptah had a son named Seti-Merenptah who was "*Heir of the Two Lands, Generalissimo, Senior Prince and Royal Scribe*". Judging by the archaeological evidence, a king Userkheperure Seti-Merenptah appears also to have lost his throne—only to reclaim it—as in the legend of Sethos and Harmais (or Hermaeus), which apparently has Manetho as its source.

That is why Josephus suspiciously wonders why Manetho failed to assign a duration of years to "Amenophis". The Egyptian historian could scarcely do so under the circumstances.   While Josephus was justified in his conclusion that the king of the "*Tale of the Polluted Ones*" did not actually exist, he could not have been expected to guess

---

[145] Yet Sethos and Ramesses are not necessarily the same person. This may be another case of "*Amosis, also called Thethmosis*", as is stated in the *Book of Sothis*, previously discussed. However, this "Sethos also called Ramesses" could have been influenced by the story of "Sethos and Hermaeus", to be discussed shortly.

[146] But no pharaoh named Amenhotep is known to have had a son called Ramesses.

that he was a composite. Josephus, as is clear from his remarks, strongly believed in only a single exodus, taking place when the "shepherds" were evicted.

The "*Tale of the Polluted Ones*" may be apocryphal but, despite Josephus's condemnation, it is certainly not devoid of plausible elements. The story seems to recall, in part, the reign of Akhenaten when certain priests, including those of high rank, were sentenced to the quarries. In addition, it was at that time that the temples of the orthodox gods (including Isis) were shut down, soon becoming the abodes of squatters, just as was the case with the ruins of Egypt in more modern times. The name of Akhenaten had been anathema long before the day of the Ptolemies. For centuries, if one referred to him it was as "PA xrw", or "The Criminal", which the Greeks perceived as "Bocchoris".[147]

The great caverns that remained there after the stone was removed from the quarries afforded shelter, at least. One can certainly imagine lepers and other diseased individuals being banished there, as well, especially once the temples were restored to their original purpose. But it availed nothing. Those who followed directly after Akhenaten had an even worse plague to contend with, it seems. Perhaps it was tuberculosis, the very disease that replaced leprosy as the common scourge by the end of the 17th Century CE.[148] *Microbacterium leprae* is a first cousin of the bacterium that causes tuberculosis and may have simply out-competed it because it is a "quicker" pathogen.

While Manetho has the "wise seer" Amenhotep son of Hapu making an appearance, Chaeremon, who tells much

---

[147] Lysimachus, for one, had written that "Bocchoris" had consulted the oracle of Amen regarding the "polluted ones", yet he also claimed the sun was the entity affronted by their presence in Egypt. Evidently the ancient authors had no idea about Akhenaten's aversion to the god, Amen, whose cult image served as the usual oracle of the pharaohs.

[148] Whatever the illness was, it killed the Hittites over a period of at least 20 years.

the same tale of the pharaoh and "the polluted ones", calls the purveyor of bad advice "Phritobautes"[149], instead.

Another interesting statement is the phrase *"Not venturing to make a prophecy himself to the king, he left a full account of it in writing, and then took his own life."* I have little doubt that what was meant by the "full account" was a prediction on the order of "The Potter's Oracle" or a catastrophic composition like the famous "Admonitions of Ipuwer", excerpted below: [150]

"Door[keepers] say: "Let us go and plunder." The pastrycooks [are idle]...The laundryman refuses to carry his load... Bird[catchers] are lined up for battle... [Men of] the Delta marshes carry shields. The brewers [are grown] sad. A man regards his son as his enemy. Hostility [pits one against] the other. "Come and conquer," [one urges a great one] "what was ordained for you in the time of Horus, in the age of the Nine Gods."

---

[149] Which could be translated as "PA-Hry-tp-wDA" , the "Chief of the Storehouse" (Great Governor) or perhaps "PA-Hry-tp-n-pr-HD", the "Chief of the Treasury".

[150] The time-frame of the writing of the "Admonitions" has been in dispute ever since Sir Alan Gardiner's translation of the difficult text. His view was that the "Admontions" was the work of a 12th Dynasty author who was describing the First Intermediate Period. Miriam Lichtheim disagreed, writing that the theory was "contradictory and untenable". The only copy of the "Admonitions" in existence is the much-damaged Papyrus Leiden 344, dated to the 19th Dynasty. Donald Redford asserts that "*a passage (from Ipuwer) was excerpted as early as the 12th Dynasty for inclusion in the "Instruction of Amenhemhat*" but it is obvious that the reverse may have occurred. The fact that the text is written in Middle Egyptian may not be significant in that the author may have intended to pen the "gloom and doom" in an archaizing fashion, perhaps having, himself, had access to similar works from earlier periods.

... A man of character goes in mourning because of what has happened in the land. The [evil-doer] walks [with his head held high]. Foreigners have become people everywhere...[151]

Verily, the face is pale....What the ancestors foretold has happened.

Verily,...The land is full of gangs.   A man goes to plow with his shield   Lo, the meek say [what they please now. And the beggar] is a man of substance.

Verily, the face is pale.   The bowman is ready. Robbery is all around.   There is no man like that of yesterday. Lo, the robber [plunders] everywhere. The servant takes what he finds.

Verily, the Nile is in flood, (but) no one plows for himself, (because) every man says: "We do not know what may happen throughout the land!"   Why really, women are dried up, and none can conceive. Khnum cannot fashion (mortals) because of the state of the land.

Verily, the River is blood. If one drinks of it, one rejects (it) out of humanity and thirsts for water.   Lo, doors, columns, and coffers are burned up, (but) the structure of the palace - life, prosperity, health! – (still) remains firm. Truly, the ship of the South founders.   Towns are ravaged, Upper Egypt has become a wasteland.

Behold, the desert has claimed the land. The nomes are destroyed. Barbarians from outside have come to Egypt. ... There are really no true Egyptians anywhere. Look, gold, lapis lazuli, silver and turquoise, carnelian, amethyst, ibht- stone and ....are strung on the necks of female slaves. Noblewomen roam the land.   Ladies say "We want to eat!"   Behold [the

---

[151] That is to say—those who were of foreign extraction now called themselves Egyptians.

wretched] great ladies, their bodies suffer in rags, their hearts shrink from greeting one another.

Why really, laughter had disappeared, and is [no longer] made. It is wailing that pervades the land, mixed with lamentation... Those who were familiar people are now strangers to whom one shows the way. Lo, everyone's hair [has fallen out from hunger.] One can't distinguish the son of man from a wretch. Lo, [one is numb] from noise. Not [one civil voice] in years of shouting. No[body makes a cheerful remark]. Truly, great and small (say), "I wish I were dead."

Why really, the entire Delta is ruled by the Degai.[152] Lower Egypt puts trust in trodden roads.[153] What is it that one could do? One says, "There are no [gods] anywhere." One says "Woe!" to the Place of the Secrets. Behold, it is in the hands of those who did not know about it, as if they were those who knew all; foreigners are (now) skilled in the work of the Delta....

Lo, citizens are put to the grindstone. Wearers of fine linen are beaten with [sticks]. Those who never saw daylight go out unhindered.[154] Those who were on their husbands' beds, "Let them lie on boards," [one remarks]. If one says "Those boxes of myrrh are too heavy for me", she is loaded down with jars filled with [water]." No longer does she know the palanquin, and the butler is lacking.

---

[152] This enigmatic passage has been variously interpreted—mainly as "*the entire Delta cannot be seen*" (dgi). I think it may have something to do with the passage in the text of the El-'Arish naos, which says of King Geb (Seb): "*Asiatics carried his scepter, called Degai, who live on what the gods abominate*".

[153] People make an exodus?

[154] The "secluded ones", the wives of the nobles, or perhaps the inmates of the king's harem.

Lo, [one eats] grass washed down with water. Birds find neither fruit nor herbs. One takes [garbage] from the mouths of pigs. No face is bright [but drawn with] hunger. Truly, grain is lacking on all sides. One is devoid of clothing, unanointed with oil. Everyone says, "There is nothing."

Lo, the sacred library, its books are stolen. The secrets in it are laid bare. Spells are made worthless through being repeated by (ordinary) folk.

Lo, the writings of the scribes of the land-register have been destroyed. The grain of Egypt is (now) a come-and-get-it.

Behold now, something has been done which never happened for a long time: the king has been robbed by poor men.

Behold, he who was buried as a falcon is [plucked as a goose]. What the pyramid hid has become empty.

Behold now, it has come to a point where the land is despoiled of the kingship by a few men who ignore custom.

Behold now, it has come to a point where (men) rebel against the uraeus, the emblem of Re, which makes the Two Lands peaceful. . Behold, the secret of the land, the place that was off-limits, is laid bare.[155] The Residence (may) be razed within an hour. Egypt has fallen to pouring water.[156] Behold,

---

[155] Meaning the palace. The next phrase indicates a longing for a deliverer. An Egyptian term for "herdsman", which is "mni" must be added to our list of possible words that make up a name of Moses, "Monios".

[156] The phrase "*sti mw*", "pouring water" is a rather mystifying one. It is used in two different texts, for example, in what appears to be completely different contexts. In the "Instructions of Amenemope", there is "*sti mw n wnnfr*", which seems to mean that the son of Amenemope was a "water-pourer of Wennofer", serving Osiris in a priestly capacity. On the other hand, the "Instruction of Amenemhet", has "*He whom I gave my trust*

the (guardian-) serpent is taken from her hole. The secrets of the Egypt's kings are laid bare. ...

If [one would come] that he could bring relief to our hearts, (then) people would say: "He is the herdsman of all men. Evil is not in his heart. Though his herds may be small, still he has spent the day caring for them.".....

If only he had perceived their character from the first generation! Then he would smite down evil; he would stretch forth the arm against it; he would destroy the seed thereof and their inheritance. ... (But) there is no pilot in their hour. Where is he today? Is he then sleeping? Behold, the glory thereof cannot be seen. ...

That which Ipuwer said, when he answered the majesty of the All-Lord: "...It pleases the heart to ignore it. Thou hast done what makes them happy. You have elevated people among them. (But still) they conceal their identities for fear of the morrow.

Once upon a time there was a man who was old and in the presence of his salvation, while his son was (still) a child, without understanding..."[157]

---

used it to plot. Wearers of my fine linen looked at me as if they were needy. Those perfumed with my myrrh poured water while wearing it." Lichtheim notes "Sti mw has generally been interpreted as an act of disrespect or defiance...*The 'pouring water' in* "Admonitions", 7, 5, *suggests a menial task."* Likewise in the "Instructions of Amenemope". I observe that, since "being on the water" of someone (*Hr mw=f*) has the meaning of being a loyalist, "*sti mw* " can have also meant "spilling water", that is to become a betrayer.

[157] The final phrase seems to be a parable that Ipuwer was about to tell the pharaoh—or perhaps it is a story related to the *Admonitions* added by a copier. After the translations of J. A. Wilson, *ANET*, pp. 441-444, and M. Lichtheim, *Ancient Egyptian Literature*, Vol. I, pp. 149-163.

Nothing is known about this Ipuwer except that he had access to the pharaoh. His name is not mentioned in the text, *"The Immortality of Writers"*[158], which lists the great sages and soothsayers of the past:

> *"Is there one here like Hardedef? Is there another like Imhotep? None of our kin is like Neferti or Khety, the foremost among them.. I give you the name of Ptahemdjedhuti and Khakheperseneb. Is there another like Ptahhotep or Kaires? Those sages who foretold the future, what came from their mouth occurred. Their pronouncements are written in books.... Death made their names forgotten, but writings make them remembered."*

On the other hand, there is a wall-relief from a Ramesside-era tomb at Saqqara, which shows figures of famous men from the past. Imhotep, Kaires, Khety and others are represented and there is, in a horizontal line between the figures, mention of an Ipuwer, a Chief Singer. This seems to me to indicate that *someone* by this name was renowned in his own time and that, since "Ipuwer" is a name not commonly written in ancient Egypt, this can have been the same individual. It would also indicate that Ipuwer was a performer, a bard, who perhaps sang of the sorry state of Egypt, to the astonishment of the pharaoh.

One or two primary Egyptian sources from the end of the 19th Dynasty agree, in essence, with what is contained in the "Admonitions". The *Great Harris Papyrus,* a text from the 20th Dynasty, seems to corroborate it all "in a nutshell" in its recounting of the state of Egypt prior to the accession of King Setnakht.[159] A private letter to a Ramesside princess from two of her servants also hints at insurrection:

---

[158] Papyrus Chester Beatty IV (British Museum 10684), attributed to Ramesside times by an unknown author.

[159] The founder of the 20th Dynasty.

"The Singer Pentawere and the Singer Pawekhed) greet [their lady], the Princess Isis-nofret. Salutations! A message to say that I invoke all the gods and goddesses of Pi-Ramesses, 'May you be healthy, [prosperous] and alive! May you enjoy the favor of my god, Ptah. Further—we are alive today, but don't know how we'll be [tomorrow]...May Ptah have us brought (safely) back, so we may see you!...We are extremely concerned about you!"

Even Merneptah's vast palace at Memphis was evidently not immune from the vandals as, when it was excavated by the University of Pennsylvania, signs were discovered that it had been burnt to the ground.

Near the end of the "Admonitions", the statement is *"How does every man kill his brother? The troops we raised for ourselves have become Bowmen bent on destroying! What has come from it is to let the Asiatics know the state of the land..."* The implication here is that civil war has so undermined Egypt that it is more susceptible than ever to invasion from the east and even Egyptian soldiers have defected to the enemy.

Before we go any further, it is advisable to provide a better introduction to the immediate family and relations of King Merneptah—or at least attempt to do so. While we know quite a lot about the wives and children of Ramesses the Great, the same cannot be said for those close to his successor. Merneptah's chief queen was called Isis-nofret, and was possibly his niece, the daughter of his deceased elder brother, Khaemwaset.[160] By her the pharaoh had a daughter, also named Isis-nofret, who is already attested by Year 52 of Ramesses II, the princess about whose safety the

---

[160] Eldest son and one-time heir of Ramesses II. Khaemwaset, an intellectual and man of letters, was interested in the antiquities of his country and is considered the world's first Egyptologist.

singers were concerned. It is presumed that Queen Isis-nofret also gave birth to Merneptah's son and heir, Seti-Merneptah.

The late Khaemwaset[161], who had once been the crown prince of Ramesses II, had a wife named Mehusekhe and a son named User-Mont-Hor. This last, nicknamed "Hori", became an important official. According to the "Setne Cycle", a collection of tales written in the colloquial or Demotic Egyptian language, Khaemwaset also had another son, Si-Osire, an amazing young wizard who simply "vanished"[162] and a foster-brother named "Inaros" who served as a sort of "side-kick" to the immortal and was otherwise known in Demotic literature as a "prince of Heliopolis".

In reality, there was also a relative of Merneptah named Amenmesse, who might have been the son of Ramesses II by his own daughter, Takhat—although this is not at all certain. With the introduction of this prince, matters become much more complex—perhaps hopelessly so—because we now arrive at the point where the archaeological record only supplies enough clues to confuse us.   At any event, Amenmesse was doubtless to figure largely in the events surrounding the Egyptian version of an exodus and there are those who think he was Moses, himself. Chief among these is German Egyptologist, Rolf Krauss.[163]

In the Bible, there are only a few facts given about Moses: He grew up as the adoptive son of pharaoh's daughter, while also having Hebrew parents and siblings. After killing an Egyptian, Moses was forced to flee the country and dwell with Midianites. He married a daughter of

---

[161] The Greeks wrote this name "Chamois", which is close to its pronunciation, the meaning being "Appearing in Thebes". "wst" was the ancient appellation of Thebes, vocalized, the reader will be amazed to learn, rather like "Oz", the lair of the famous Wizard.

[162] Due to the fact that he had really been the re-incarnation of another sorceror.

[163] *Moïse le Pharaon* (France, 2000)

their chief and had sons by her. But he also, at some point, married a Nubian woman, whom Josephus claims he met while acting as the king's Viceroy in her land.

Krauss is of the opinion that Amenmesse is to be equated with one, "Messuy" who was a Viceroy of Nubia for a number of years and had held that office in the time of Ramesses II. True or not, even though the designated heir of the pharaoh, Merneptah, was supposed to be Crown Prince Seti-Merneptah, it is clear from the archaeological evidence and the king-list of Manetho that Amenmesse managed to succeed him! How did this come about?

According to the accounts of Manetho and Chaeremon, "Amenophis" was a king of Egypt who supposedly had to go south for the duration of 13 years where he relied upon the hospitality of the King of Ethiopia, who protected him. The pharaoh's five year-old son was handed over to the custody of a friend, Manetho would have us believe. Chaeremon dramatically differs in that the heir was born at the time of the flight of "Amenophis", the wife of the king stopping in a cave to be delivered of her baby.

There is only one New Kingdom pharaoh of whom Egyptology has concluded that he both lost and reclaimed his throne[164] and *possibly* had a son named Ramesses—and that is Seti II, presumably once known as Prince Seti-Merneptah.

Needless to say, there are many persons today who simply assume that Ramesses the Great was the Pharaoh of the Exodus (with the idea that there was only one). But, curiously, even though the ancient historians, whom I have already discussed in this book, were all familiar with Manetho, considered by them to be an ancient and reliable source[165] of Egyptian history, none of them appear to dwell on the name "Ramesses" when it comes to the Jews leaving

---

[164] Papyrus Rainer, a Demotic document from the last centuries before the Common Era, claims the banishment amounted to only 7 years.

[165] Except by Josephus, who had his reservations about the "polluted" tale.

that land—except perhaps in seeking vengeance against them on behalf of another. Ramesses II, called "Ozymandias" by the Greeks, seems to have been remembered by them for his great deeds as a warrior and a builder—but not particularly for ridding Egypt of a foreign element.

That is why I have concluded that the little prince of the *"Tale of the Polluted Ones"* did not become Usermaare Ramesses II when he grew up. I think he could be none other than Ramesses-Siptah, born to Merneptah in his old age by a concubine named Tiaa, who later changed his name to Merneptah-Siptah.[166] There are some who believe that Siptah was the son and rival of Seti II and there are others who assert he was the son of Amenmesse. But it would seem to me that the arch-foe of Prince Seti-Merneptah was surely a prince named Amenmesse, a very handsome young man, judging by his extant monuments.

Most interestingly, the *Great Harris Papyrus*[167] actually says that there was a time before the advent of King Setnakht, the founder of the 20th Dynasty, when there was no king in Egypt at all.

> *"Thus says King Ramesses III, the son of Setnakht, the great god, to the princes and leaders of the land, to the warriors and to the chariot soldiers, to the Shardana*[168], *and the numerous foreign mercenaries, and to all the inhabitants of the land of Tamera:*[169]

> *Hear ye! I will make you to know my glorious deeds which I performed as king of men. The land of Egypt was abandoned to ruin, every man a law unto himself. There was nobody at the helm. So passed dreary*

---

[166] He also seems to have had two different prenomina.

[167] A lengthy document from the reign of Ramesses IV, extolling the deeds of his late father, Ramesses III.

[168] One of the "Sea-Peoples", probably from Sardinia.

[169] Egypt.

years until other times came. Egypt belonged to mayors of cities. They slew one another whether great or lowly. Other times came on afterward, during years of scarcity. Then it was that Irisu, an Asiatic, raised himself among them as prince and forced the entire land to pay him tribute. As soon as one had gathered something, the other robbed him of it. The gods were treated the same as the common folk. None of the mandatory temple-offerings were made to them.

Then did the gods turn this state of things to prosperity. They restored to the land its even balance, such as its condition properly required. And they established their son, who had come forth from their body, as king of the whole land on their exalted throne. This was King Setnakht-Meryamun. He was like the person of Seth when he is indignant. He organized the whole land. He slew the wicked of heart who were in the land of Tamera. He purified the exalted throne of Egypt, and so he was the ruler of the inhabitants on the throne of the sun-god, Atum, while he raised up their faces. Such as refused to acknowledge anyone else as an equal, he had them walled up."

Clearly, this document corroborates, in concise fashion, the state of affairs described by Manetho and Chaeremon. Egyptologists have refused to believe this, in the past, and have asserted that these passages in the pHarris refer to the Second Intermediate Period—which had occurred hundreds of years previously. This makes little sense. It is most apparent that what Manetho and Chaeremon wrote is true; the king and many of his important people abandoned Egypt to marauding forces, who plundered the land. The government having collapsed, local bigwigs, "the mayors of cities" vied for control of the nomes and blood was shed. "Times of scarcity" seem to mean that a famine caused by civil war was another problem and that the foreigner,

"Irisu"[170], whoever he was, had subdued these local lords and had become the ruling force in Egypt.

It was not until all this had occurred that King Setnakht, a native Egyptian and perhaps a commoner, had managed to muster sufficient might to "purify the throne of Egypt"—that is to say—rid it of the alien influence. Some of the details of how he accomplished this are set forth on his "Elephantine Stela", to be viewed later.

Since we have already read some of the *Admonitions of Ipuwer*", we are acquainted with all the details of a war within Egypt's own borders. Nothing could describe it more vividly. But, of course, the "Admonitions" do not supply any information about what circumstances could bring on such a chaos. Ipuwer only seems to imply that foreign invaders were not responsible for the collapse of Egyptian society; they were merely taking advantage of it.

So let us, in the spirit of the dreadful picture painted by Ipuwer, imagine that, during the summer months of the penultimate regnal year of King Merneptah[171], strange omens had appeared, such as had not been seen "since the time of the gods". Flies pestered the houses in such multitudes that they lined the walls. Ants swarmed so thickly that they could be scooped up a handful at a time from the ground. At night, the croaking of an inordinate number of frogs could be heard in the ditches, creating such a din that people had trouble sleeping.

A fanciful assumption? Perhaps--yet all the signs and portents, reptiles, insects, celestial phenomena[172] and

---

[170] Most likely, "Irisu" is not a name but an avoidance of naming a hated enemy, something seen in another text from the early 20th Dynasty, the "Harem Plot Papyrus", as well. "Irisu" means "one who makes himself" and has been accepted by most Egyptologists as a reference to Chancellor Bey.

[171] Papyrus Sallier I gives Year 10, this being the highest attested regnal year for Merneptah.

[172] The English astrologers had seen a conjunction of Mars and Saturn in November. In former centuries, London—like Egypt--was never completely free of plague, but the outbreaks were usually isolated and contained.

242

virulent smallpox all occurred prior to the Great Plague of London of 1665 CE. Just before the English pestilence, "a new star" was seen to arise with particular brilliance in the horizon at the end of December, lasting a week or two until it was gone. In February fire-balls darted to and fro across the sky for nearly an hour. During March a comet was observed visible two hours after midnight and continuing until daybreak. Astrologers found that a conjunction of the stars, particularly Jupiter and Saturn, presaged war, pestilence and famine. The Egyptians, for their part, called all the planets "stars", although they observed the heavens no less keenly for signs. What they saw at the end of the reign of Merneptah is difficult to know, but a piece of Old Testament pseudographia, *"The Tale of Jannes and Jambres"*, relates that Jannes, a scribe or official attached to the court of the pharaoh in Memphis, witnessed a portent in the form of a setting star or planet, which he interpreted as signaling the downfall of a corrupt generation. Apparently other astral omens were seen as well.[173] A disease began to break out in the land at this time and Jannes, himself, died of it.[174]

With the coming of the Akhet, the indunation, the season of sickness would just have started. That, as has been mentioned, was the time that the pestilences were said to arrive from Ethiopia. The rising of Sirius signaled the start of another astronomical year, but it could prove to be a death star for many.

1665 was different. Nearly 70,000 Londoners succumbed to the disease within a period of a year and other areas of England were stricken, as well. It was the worst visitation of disease since the Black Death of the Middle Ages, at which time, it is estimated, that one-third of England's population was carried off.

[173] Papyri Chester Beatty 3a+[verso] and Vienna B.

[174] Smallpox. In the summer before the Great Plague of London, this sickness had made an exceptionally strong showing.

As an example, in 430 BCE, a man named Thucydides described what is known as the "Plague of Athens". According to the Greek writer,

> *"The disease began, it is said, in Ethiopia beyond Egypt and then descended into Egypt and Lybia and spread over the greater part of the King's territory. Then it suddenly fell upon the city of Athens, and attacked first the inhabitants of Piraeus..."*[175]

It was a most terrible sickness, indeed, resembling the worst influenza, where the victim's very circulatory system became so compromised that some lost their fingers and toes, eyes, and even memory. The 540 CE Plague of Justinian (named after the emperor of Rome) likewise was said to have come from Egypt, spreading to Palestine and then the rest of the world. 10,000 people died each day from what appears to be a bubonic plague, which means that swollen glands or "bubos" in Greek, appeared under the arms and in the area of the groin. Returning again and again, the plague lasted until the year 590. Some maintain it contributed to the collapse of the Roman Empire.

---

[175] Sailors were not unknown to spread disease from one place to another and many plagues began in ports, such as Piraeus.

It is difficult to know how much of the *"Tale of the Polluted Ones"* refers to the 18th Dynasty and how much to the 19th, but it would seem that the disease of the story, itself, is not a true plague of swift-acting deadliness—although the one mentioned in the Book of Exodus fits that criterion.   If a king named Amenhotep had something in common with one or two called Merneptah, it was surely more than simply that their names sounded much alike. Perhaps these kings faced internal strife occurring simultaneously with the visitation of a pestilence.   Yet plague, as has been mentioned, was nothing unusual in Egypt.   What has not been considered, to my knowledge, is that both Amenhotep IV (Akhenaten) and King Merneptah suffered from a disorder called elephantiasis, whether the form known as *lymphatic filariasis* or *elephantiasis graecorum* ("true leprosy").

These two diseases are quite different but both result in terrible disfigurement of the body. In some instances, they could be mistaken for one another. *Lymphatic filiariasis* is present mainly in Africa and results when an infected female mosquito bites an individual, introducing worm larvae, called microfilariae, into the blood. The microfilariae can live for many years in the blood of the host. Often disease symptoms do not appear until years after infection. As the parasites reproduce in the blood vessels, they can restrict circulation and fluids build up in surrounding tissues. Grossly enlarged arms, legs, genitalia, and breasts are the most common signs of the illness.   Sometimes it manifests itself as a kind of erysipelas, such as *phlegmasia dolens* (white leg), hard, swollen red skin or persistent eczema and multiple warts. In such condition it may be confused *with elephantiasis graecorum* .[175]

King Merneptah, himself, surely died in Egypt and was buried in his spacious tomb. (The Greek-era Egyptians had

---

[175] Or the tubercular variety, caused by the *bacillus lepræ*. The ancients could distinguish between none of several afflictions, all being lumped together in the category of "leprosy".

probably confused him, when it came to being exiled, with his son and heir, Seti-Merneptah—or perhaps Akhenaten!) His is the only royal mummy, however, that shows evidence of having been castrated before or shortly after death!

> *"A very curious feature of this mummy is the complete absence of the scrotum, although the penis was left. Midway between the root of the penis and the anus a transverse scar is visible. It represents the place from which the scrotal sac was cut away, but as it is now thickly smeared with balsam it is not possible to say whether it was removed during life or after death. It certainly was done before the process of embalming was completed because the wound is coated with balsam. The fact that there is a wound suggests that Meneptah (sic) was castrated either after death or within a short time of death."* [176]

I would venture to say that the surgery was probably the work of the embalmers, these last perhaps finding it advisable to remove Merneptah's hugely enlarged scrotum, the result of a certain awful form of elephantiasis! [177]   If it was not done in order to deal with such an unsightly deformity in a mummy, then other reasons for depriving a dead man of his scrotal sac do not readily spring to mind. King Akhenaten's elephantiasis, if that is what he had instead of true leprosy, which had attacked one foot, was nothing compared to what a man with a scrotum larger than most pumpkins must suffer.   When Artapanus wrote that "Chenephres" was the first to die of elephantiasis, he perhaps meant that at least one succeeding king of Egypt had succumbed to it, as well.

---

[176] G. Elliot Smith in *The Royal Mummies*, supra, page 9.

[177] Certain men afflicted with this disease have had to push their cumbersome scrotal sacs before them in a wheelbarrow.

That *lymphatic filiariasis* is not spread by human contact or that *elephantiasis graecorum* is not easily transmittable was, of course, unknown to the ancient Egyptians. They did not understand about worms in the blood or microbes.[178] One can comprehend how a pharaoh, himself stricken with one or the other, can have been persuaded that it was just to expel or quarantine persons similarly afflicted as a punishment for having somehow given the loathesome disease to the sovereign or to protect healthy Egyptians from becoming infected. If a pharaoh, in his relative isolation, can have contracted such a thing, then it must have been deemed very contagious, indeed. According to Manetho, even a sage like Amenhotep son of Hapu, later worshipped as a god of healing, advised "Amenophis" it would be best if he "*purged the entire country of lepers and other polluted persons*", including "*some of the learned priests who were afflicted with leprosy*".

Although the advisor of the pharaoh cannot be blamed for his suggestion of making outcasts of the lepers—as all societies have done this to an extent more or less humane— the implication is that the ruler acted on his counsel in a manner so radical and unreasonable as to cause the wise man to commit suicide in either shame or protest.

It is difficult for us, living in modern times, to associate leprosy with a plague or epidemic. We think of the disease occurring, now and then, in faraway, exotic locales where we are never likely to venture. However, there were times and places which saw leprosy occurring quite frequently. Not surprisingly, Egypt was regarded as the place from which leprosy was carried into the Western world. By the Middle Ages, leprosy was well established in Europe, striking even royal families. The Crusades appeared to aggravate the situation and laws were enacted against lepers, forcing them to be segregated from the populace and to announce their approach by means of a bell or wooden clapper, should their

---

[178] Although Artapanus wrote that "a certain winged creature" produces sores that will not heal.

paths cross those of individuals not similarly afflicted. The number of leper-asylums in Europe is estimated at 19,000 by 1200 CE; any sizeable town had one or more nearby. The seventeenth century saw the virtual disappearance of the disease due to the strict legislation and enforcement against lepers. Also, it has been theorized that the catastrophic bubonic plague, the Black Death of 1346, killed off the greater part of the leprous population, in any event.

Leviticus, chapters 13 and 14, are very much concerned with leprosy—and the various diseases that may have resembled it, for the ancients were unable to distinguish among them. So there is no doubt but that the contamination had affected the Hebrews, evidence with which Flavius Josephus apparently did not care to deal. At any rate, he preferred the proto-Jews to be distinguished from the Egyptian lepers, which Manetho had identified. Yet, clearly, these persons were allied, at least in a romance, due to the ostracism they shared in common. That their differences could be reduced to insignificance is very plausible, indeed, in light of their severe lifestyle.

Visitors to Palestine at the turn of the 20th Century CE found life there to be little different than it had been in ancient times. A Dr. A.E. Breen wrote of the lepers he had witnessed trying to eke out an existence:

> "Leprosy, as also scald-head,[179] is often supposed to be caused by the Gecko, 'abu brais'; and leprosy is called 'barass'. Few lepers remain in the villages, but are mostly found around the principle towns in the passages mostly frequented by pilgrims; in Jerusalem at the Jaffa Gate, in Ramleh on the Jerusalem road, and so forth. They are also called 'the poor', simply 'masakin', and the fellahin very readily give them alms of the fruits and wares which they may be carrying to town. Every visitor to Jerusalem has seen the miserable men and women, stretching their fingerless hands and imploring alms in a piteous hissing

---

[179] A disease of the scalp, common among the fellahin and thought to be contagious.

voice, squatting down with their stick and tin pan along the road. They live in separate colonies, but come to town for their living. This hideous disease is not so contagious as was supposed, for the lepers' asylums established in Jerusalem by different missions have carried on their work for more than thirty years now and none of the Sisters or hospital aids have ever become lepers though almost in daily contact and living under one roof. Complete cures, on the other hand, are, so far as I am aware, unknown."[180]

Indeed, to be perceived as "cured" of leprosy would have been deemed miraculous. Therefore, the Biblical Moses was temporarily afflicted with leprosy as a sign of the might of his God.[181] According to Leviticus, clothing and even houses could be contaminated with the "plague" of leprosy:

"This is the law for all manner of plague of leprosy, and for a scall; and for the leprosy of a garment, and for a house, and for a rising, and for a scab, and for a bright spot; to teach when it is unclean, and when it is clean; this is the law of leprosy."[182]

Dreadful though it may be, elephantiasis or leprosy in any form is not the aggressive malady that quickly kills people and even beasts that is the final plague of the Book of Exodus. This was a true, virulent contagion. Polio, to which children are especially susceptible, has been suggested as the thing that took off "the first-born".

In *"The Tale of Jannes and Jambres"*, the first "magician" realizes that he has a "serious tumor" on his body and secludes himself in the "hedra" in an attempt to be rid of it.[183] The "hedra" seems to have been a chamber containing a

---

[180] *A Diary of My Life In the Holy Land* (New York, 1906).

[181] Exodus 4:6

[182] Leviticus 14:54-57

[183] Vienna Fragment B 1-13.

bath in which an Egyptian could immerse himself in a kind of ritual. However the "tumor" leads to the demise of Jannes. Apion the grammarian, to the disgust of Josephus, stated that the Jews, six days after leaving Egypt, developed lumps in the groin "*for disease of the groin in Egypt is called sabbo*". Thus, resting on the seventh day, they called it "Sabbath" after this symptom.

That is nonsense, yet that an Egyptian plague can be associated with a tumor or lump is evidently true.[184]

We have a first-hand account of a European who lived through one of the worst pestilences of Egypt—which was doubtless cholera. An Englishman, Alexandre Kinglake[185], arrived in Cairo ca. 1834. Once there, he discovered that the entire city was fatalistically resigned, going about its normal business although death was everywhere. Out of a population of about 200,000, the plague claimed as many as 1200 persons daily until it was finished. (Half the people of the city of Alexandria were fated to die.) Noisy funerals, complete with "howlers", as he termed them, passed by Kinglake's window all day long. To the foreigner's disbelief, the Moslems celebrated the festival of Khourban Bairam, pitching tents and setting up swings for the children. Everything that was transpiring around them was, evidently, perceived as the will of Allah. Therefore Kinglake, too, determined that the raging pestilence would not alter his habits. The Englishman roamed about feely, even frequenting the bazaars.

Kinglake wrote that the signs of the disease were headache, racing heart and a swelling of the armpit, "*a small lump like a pistol bullet*".[186] He also mentioned that, unlike the ethnic Egyptians, certain Levantines or Europeans who

---

[184] Perhaps the lump was an enlarged lymph gland denoting infection, which can emerge in the groin area or under the arm.

[185] *Eothen: Traces of Travel Brought Home from the East.*

[186] Perhaps the proper Briton refrained from mention of lumps elsewhere on the body.

had resided in the east for some time, were secluding themselves in the belief that the plague could be caught by contact with others.

"*It is part of their belief that metals and hempen rope, and also, I fancy, one or two other substances, will not carry the infection: and they likewise believe that the germ of pestilence lying in an infected substance may be destroyed by submersion in water, or by the action of smoke. They, therefore, guard the doors of their houses with the utmost care against intrusion, and condemn themselves with all members of their family, including European servants, to a strict imprisonment within the walls of their dwelling. Their native attendants are not allowed to enter at all, but they make the necessary purchases of provisions: these are hauled up through one of the windows by means of a rope, and are afterwards soaked in water.*"

Now we begin to understand how quarantine, instead of the act of bloodying the doorpost, may have saved the Hebrew population from being cut down by "the Angel of Death" along with their Egyptian neighbors—against the advance of some plagues, but not cholera.[187] Kinglake, who had decided not to go into seclusion, came down with a fever and throbbing head, not knowing whether it was the plague or not. For a few days, he shut himself away, drank copious amounts of tea and ate nothing, hoping to sweat out whatever had entered his body. This worked and Kinglake quickly recovered. But he had learned his lesson and left Cairo with a sense of relief.

In a curious digression, Alexandre Kinglake described how he had sought out a magician in Cairo "*because I considered that these men were in some sort the descendants of Aaron.*" He sent for an old man who had a reputation in the neighborhood as being "the Chief of the Magicians", who took a boy from the street, needing an innocent for the

---

[187] Cholera, however, seems able to penetrate any quarantine and chooses its victims haphazardly, so perhaps the Egyptians were not wrong to carry on with life despite its presence.

purpose of exercising his powers. "A *mangale (pan of burning charcoal) was brought into my room, and the Magician bending over it, sprinkled upon the fire some substances consisting, I suppose, of spices or sweetly burning woods; for immediately a fragrant smoke arose that curled around the bending form of the Wizard, the while that he pronounced his first incantations. When these were over, the boy was made to sit down, and a common green shade was bound over his brow; then the Wizard took ink, and, still continuing his incantations, wrote certain mysterious figures upon the boy's palm and directed him to rivet his attention to these marks without looking aside for an instant.*"

Alexandre Kinglake then was asked to think of a person of his acquaintance and he recalled a school-fellow at Eton. But the lad declared he had a vision of a female. Not discouraged by this failure of the occult (explained by the magus to be due to some sin in the boy), Kinglake made plans with the old Egyptian to meet him at the Great Pyramid so they could attempt to conjure up the Devil within its passages, but the magician succumbed to the plague before he could keep this appointment.

Chapter Thirteen

In most ancient Egyptian stories, it was considered more or less mandatory to include an element of magic—just as is the case with European fairytales. The Book of Exodus has all the elements of an Egyptian "novel" even though factual components are also present—just as they were in many Egyptian tales.[188] The indispensable factors of the tales are: 1) A hero 2) A pharaoh—sometimes not identified; 3) Magical occurrences—on occasion the hero, himself, performing the feats of magic. Some stories featured a renowned magician, who was not actually the hero of the piece.

It even happened that the hero could do his magic in a time later than he had actually lived, if he had been a real human being. In the "Setne Cycle", examples of Demotic writing from the Late Period,[189] Prince Khaemwaset who died while his father, Ramesses II, was still king, had a son named Si-Osire who apparently predeceased *him* –yet this Si-Osire appeared before the pharaoh, Siamen, of the 21st Dynasty. The reason Si-Osire could manage this is because he had magical powers, making him an immortal like his sire, Khaemwaset, for whom all things were possible because he could read the mysterious writings in the House of Life.

This illustrates that the main way for the author of the Book of Exodus to do away with the problem of just when Moses and Aaron had actually lived was to make them magicians, especially Aaron. Moses, it went without saying, was every bit the equal of the famed Khaemwaset, as he had been educated in the manner of Egyptian princes, which means he could read anything set before him and no doubt had access to those same secret books that Khaemwaset had seen. The latter had been a "*stm*-priest" ("setne" in Demotic)

---

188 Perhaps there really is no such thing as "pure fiction" from ancient Egypt. It may have been an unknown concept.

189 1070-324 BCE.

and Moses, too, would have been assigned some priestly office—before he became a monotheist. One could say that Khaemwaset, the first Egyptologist in all of history due to his interest in the things that were already ancient when he was alive and who was probably a polymath, was a kind of "saint" in the eyes of those who came after him. His kind were reputed to keep their powers after they passed from life and perhaps they even knew how to elude death, itself, being so extraordinarily clever and learned. Who knew but that they could not pop up in another era, if their services were required or if they merely felt like making an appearance. This is how Moses and Aaron could be involved in any and all of the exodoi until the day arrived when a work was composed, the Book of Exodus, which implied that, just as there was only one Moses, there had been only one exodus, as well.

In the "Setne Cycle", the magicians who oppose the heroes are important enough to be named. There is no reason to believe that these were not actual people, as well, maneuvering between one time and another. That Moses and Aaron had opponents, too, is made plain in the Book of Exodus, but the fact that these were never identified therein was evidently seen as a most unsatisfactory lapse. At some point, therefore, a work called *"The Book of Jannes and Jambres"* appeared, not only purporting to fill in this missing information but to elaborate on the sorry fate of those who had the temerity to challenge Moses and, by implication, God, Himself.

The apocryphon of Jannes and Jambres is presumably in reference to Exodus 7:11. There is no mention of them by name there, but Jewish tradition has provided these names for the Egyptian magicians; the Talmud mentions them in Men. 85a. and the New Testament in 2Timothy 3:8-9. Jannes is also identified in one of the Dead Sea Scrolls dated to about 100 BCE: "... *In ancient times, Moses and Aaron arose by the hand of the Prince of Lights and Satan [Belial] in his cunning raised up Jannes [Johana] and his brother when Israel was first delivered.*" Origen, of the 3rd century, mentions a *Book of Jannes and Jambres*. The 7th century

Chronicle of John of Nikiu, an Ethiopic text, includes the remark *"Pharaoh Petissonius, who is Amosis, King of Egypt, reigned with the help of the book of the magicians Jannes and Jambres."*

The Book of Jannes and Jambres survives only in various fragmentary copies. They are Papyrus Chester Beatty XVI (Greek, iv CE); Papyrus Vindobonensis[190] (Greek, iii CE); Papyrus Michigan (Greek, ii-iii CE; British Library Cotton Tiberius B (Latin/Old English, xi CE), which also includes pictorial illumination. A most able scholarly work has been written on these fragments by Albert Pietersma in recent times.[191]

The names of Jannes and Jambres appear in Hebrew, Aramaic, Syriac, Arabic, Greek, and Latin texts and are variously seen as Johana, Joannes, Johannes and as Joambres or Mambres. Palladius, in his 5th century history, wrote that Macarius of Alexandria once visited the garden tomb (kepotaphion) of Jannes and Jambres -- and was accosted by 70 demons who resided there--probably in the form of crows or bats.

Rabbinic traditions maintain that the brothers, along with their father, Balaam, were counselors to Pharaoh and that it was they who advised him to murder the first-born males. Later, they went to Ethiopia and returned a few years after that to become the Biblical magicians of the king, which is, biographically, quite similar to the legend of Moses. Prior to the exodus of the Hebrews, Jannes was sitting with some friends under an apple-tree in his garden, when an earthquake struck, cracking a limb off the tree. This was viewed by Jannes as an ill omen, in addition to the astral ones. Things go downhill for the brothers from there, with the Jewish lore even having them as part of an exodus, this being possible because Jambres conjured up the spirit of Jannes from hell.

---

[190] Vienna.

[191] *The Apocryphon of Jannes & Jambres the Magicians* (Leiden, New York, 1994).

Is it possible these magicians can have been actual people? I don't see why not. Even though Khaemwaset had not been exactly an ordinary man or even an ordinary prince, he had once arisen in the morning, had a shave and a bit of breakfast like everyone else and put on his sandals one foot at a time, never dreaming that one day he would become part of some fantastic stories in which he did not even, in every episode, behave with the proper decorum befitting his great station in life.

It is written that Jannes and Jambres lived in Memphis, which rather eliminates them from having been a part of the courts of Ahmose I and Akhenaten, although not that of a pharaoh named Thutmose—or one named "Chencheres". Two Egyptians with names that resemble "Jannes" are "Ineni", a prominent person at the court of Queen Hatshepsut and a certain "Inana", which seems to have been an attempt to write "Yoanna[192]", a Hebrew name, in Egyptian. This last was a scribe, whose name we see more than once, of the late 19th Dynasty, reign of Merneptah. He either wrote or copied the famous "Tale of the Two Brothers" and was also the one who penned the dispatch informing that the "Bedouin tribes of Edom" were coming in to graze their flocks. Inana worked directly under a man named Qagabu, the Chief Scribe of the Treasury. The actual name that lurks behind the vocalization "Jambres" eludes definition, but it is clear that this brother played a secondary role in the story. Some scholars, like Pietersma, believe that the origin of *The Book of Jannes and Jambres* is a Jewish one and that Jannes, himself, was a Hebrew.

Probably, we will have to agree with the Book of Exodus when it points out in no uncertain terms that quitting Egypt was no easy matter unless the king gave his permission. At least not in the time of the 19th Dynasty. The Bible seems to say that the Hebrews were required to remain for the reason

---

[192] Yoanna means "God-given". In fact "Inana" is written in Egyptian beginning with the sign that denoted "give" or "gift".

indicated by their name. They were the "servers", the "apiru". Even the cup-bearer/butler of King Merneptah was called Ben-Azen, obviously a Semitic name. How much the Egyptian economy of the late 19th Dynasty depended upon these Hebrews as administrators, servants and laborers is quite impossible to say. Kitchen cites a bit of text from the middle part of the reign of Ramesses II when it is noted "*the soldiers and the Apiru who are dragging stone for the great pylon-gateway of ....Ramesses II.*[193] Donald Redford supplies that "*One young Canaanite, Pas-Ba'al, possibly taken prisoner under Thutmose III, became chief draftsman in the Temple of Amen, and six generations later his descendants are still occupying this office.*"[194] We see a chief physician of the House of Life, Ben-Anath, and various scribes and butlers of Canaanite extraction. Certainly, the Book of Exodus does not want us to think that the Israelites were integrated into Egyptian society—despite the claim that one of them had become a prince living in the royal court.

We do know, from the aforementioned communication, written by Inana in Year 8 of the pharaoh, Merneptah, that people were required permission to pass into Egypt in the area of the eastern Delta. The very same could be said of a group who were departing, especially a large number. These would certainly not escape the scrutiny of the fortress personnel at Djaru or other checkpoints. So the Book of Exodus is correct in that respect. If one did not have leave to pass through, one might expect to tangle with the soldiers of the garrison.

An officer of the Delta stationed on the edge of the Wadi Tumilat, Ka-Kam-ur, issued a report, in the time of Seti II, relating his progress in searching for some runaway slaves:

---

[193] Kenneth Kitchen, *Pharaoh Triumphant* (Canada, 1982) page 70.

[194] *Egypt, Canaan, and Israel in Ancient Times*, supra, page 225.

"I was sent forth by the king—life, prosperity, health— in the third month of the third season[195], day 9, at the time of evening, following after these two slaves. Now when I reached the enclosure wall of Tjeku on the third month of the third season, day 10, they told (me) they were saying to the south that they (the slaves) had passed by on the third month of the third season, day 10. Now when I reached the fortress[196], they told me that the groom(?) had come from the desert [saying that] they had passed the walled place north of the Migdol of Seti-Merneptah—life, prosperity, health—beloved like Seth!"

We never learn whether these slaves were caught or why they had bolted. What is interesting is that there may have been certain days, perhaps on the birthday of the chief god of the Delta, Seth, on which anyone could come and go as he pleased. Perhaps this free passage was possible on any of the "five days over the year", the birthdays of the gods. As it happens, those days would have occurred about the time when the Inundation began, just before New Year's Day—but only in a "perfect year" and a number of years thereafter. If a Moses had asked the pharaoh to allow his people to leave during the epagomenal days and the king refused, then that would have been about the time of the phenomena, the "Green Nile" and the "Red Nile"! So the Bible is correct in making the first plague a "river of blood". The author seemingly knew his basic facts. But this concurrence of

---

[195] Season of Shomu, month of Epiphi, day 9. Taking the arbitrary datum of 1212 BCE, it is April 26 by the Julian calendar or April 15 by the Gregorian. If it is already, say, 1193 BCE, then these dates would change to April 21 or April 10. At any rate, the time of the pursuit would probably have been April no matter what the year of Seti II in his six-year reign. One cannot help but comment that this is certainly the season of choice for people leaving Egypt!

[196] Probably Tjaru/Sile.

events was only possible during a limited time in Egyptian history.

It is rather strange that we should have so much more information about what transpired in the time of the war between the Theban princes and the "shepherds" than the later "civil war" at the end of the 19th Dynasty, but that is the case. All we know of the latter troubles is gleaned from a few "cries and whispers" from primary sources and, of course, the brief excerpts from Manetho and Chaeremon.[197]

Communications and inscriptions found at Deir el Medina, the tomb worker's village near the Valley of the Kings, allow some glimpses into this time. From these we learn that the Opet Festival was celebrated there in Merneptah's Year 8 with an abundance of food provided by the king's vizier as a reward for the excellent progress on the king's tomb.[198] The Opet Festival, was a merry and even ribald one, lasting twenty-four days. During this time the god, Amen, was carried from the temple at Karnak to visit his harem in the temple of Southern Opet (Luxor).

From an ostracon, a piece of limestone, we learn that in *"Year One, first month of winter, the scribe Paser came with good news saying: 'Seti II has arisen as ruler'* ". [199]

Many Egyptologists tend to believe that Seti-Merneptah had already become king prior to the usurpation by Amenmesse. Perhaps, due to his father's advanced years, Seti had become a co-regent, as he seems to have begun a tomb with masterfully carved reliefs in the Valley of the Kings. However, before this project could progress very far,

---

[197] The *Admonitions of Ipuwer* can possibly be included, but they are of a genre of prophetic writing of uncertain historic value.

[198] This work had, of course, been ongoing since Merneptah's first regnal year.

[199] The scribe, Paser, was around quite a long time. He is known from year 8 of Merenptah down to year 17 of Ramses III, a duration of appr. 41 years, if we assume Merneptah only reigned for 10 years. (B.G. Davies, *Who was who at Deir el Medina*, p. 102-103).

the cartouches in the tomb were excised and Amenmesse is the one who is blamed. Egyptology has never offered an entirely satisfactory explanation as to where King Seti II disappeared to during the few years of rule that Amenmesse is attributed. Some believe he never left Egypt and reigned in the Delta while Amenmesse had control of the south. Yet for modern scholars to divide the land between these kings, completely ignoring the writings of the ancients, is perhaps not wise. According to the latter, it was not possible for an Egyptian ruler to hold Lower Egypt, as it had been invaded by foreigners yet again. If Manetho and Chaeremon say a king, "Amenophis", fled south, then there must have been a reason for it. Pharaohs were not routinely ousted and the occasions on which they had been assassinated were so rare that Manetho appears to have been moved to point out whenever it happened in the same way that he indicated natural disasters, like terrible earthquakes and floods. Manetho and Chaeremon also maintain the exile returned, and all indications do point to Userkheperure Seti-Merneptah having come back to claim the throne and then eradicating the names of Amenmesse, wherever they occurred, and usurping his monuments. Truly, Seti II was an unlucky, short-lived king. He accomplished very little and never did much work in his own tomb, at all—certainly not six years worth. As has been previously stressed, the state of an Egyptian king's tomb is a good indication of the length of his reign, as one was begun for him practically the moment of his accession. Even if, let us say, civil war had still continued for another six years after he resumed his kingship, progress should have been made beyond the mere corridor that is the first phase of the tomb's construction and the hasty adaptation of the corridor as a burial chamber that is the second. It is really mysterious.

How can we hope to unravel such a Gordian Knot as is presented by the twilight years of the 19th Dynasty? And how can we hope to reconcile all this with the story of the Book of Exodus, which says nothing at all about the internal politics of Egypt and is seemingly only concerned with the plight of the Children of Israel, called "Hebrews" by the

Egyptians? Did the Hebrews actually have reason to want to leave at the end of the 19th dynasty? By then, they had grown very numerous in Egypt once more, but their exact situation, where tolerance is concerned, cannot be ascertained. Yet even minorities within a country love their land, although they may not always love the government or their fellow citizens. Suffice it to say that times were bad, with kings and counter-kings battling for supremacy.

Whether there was a famine/plague cycle in effect after the death of Merneptah—the "times of scarcity" mentioned in the Great Harris Papyrus-- is not documented from that time and we cannot be as certain of an epidemic being present during the civil wars as we are of a plague having occurred during the late 18th Dynasty reigns. Yet civil war, as history tells us, usually brings want and hardship. Besides, signs of a dwindling Nile flood already occurred in the reign of Merneptah. A delta palace that depended upon water from a certain branch of the river had to be abandoned when the source dried up. By the time of Ramesses X, a century later, the south was desiccating and the grain reserves were gone. Without a cushion against low Niles, the people were helpless in case of poor crops. Perhaps the increased aridity caused by the series of lower floods had occasioned an outbreak of *pasteurella pestis*, the bubonic plague that favors dry conditions and is carried by rodents. A story woven around Ramesses XI seems to indicate that mice saved Egypt by gnawing to bits the weapons of the enemy but at the heart of this legend may be that there were a surplus of rodents in Egypt at the time, these being connected, yet not in the correct sense, to the downfall of an invader.

What we do know is that xenophobia and a need to seek out a scape-goat is a phenomenon recorded as a result of other plagues that manifested themselves throughout the history of the unenlightened ages. In addition to blaming the heavens,[200] the Jews and their alien, suspect ways were ignorantly but predictably deemed to be the cause of spreading pestilence in the Middle Ages and they were persecuted in large numbers for this reason.[201] Pogroms, massacres and expulsions occurred all over Europe in time of plague, with the locals routinely murdering or ordering all of the resident Jews, the perennial "other", to leave. The largest Jewish community in Europe during the plague beginning in 1345 CE was in Mainz, Germany, where at least 6,000 Jews were burned in hopes that the mortal sickness might abate. The canton of Basel sequestered all 4500 of its Jewish citizens on an island in the Rhine and burned them to death, after which a law was passed barring Jews from residing in the canton for 200 years. Pope Clement the VI had to issue two papal bulls saying that the Jews were innocent. Nevertheless, these problems caused a migration of Jews from western to eastern Europe, where they were afforded better tolerance and this accounts for the large number of Jews in the east prior to the Holocaust of the Second World War. For the same reason, some of the people of foreign extraction who lived in Egypt during the reign of Akhenaten may have been forced to leave the country.

In the Torah, there is a variation on this theme. Since the pharaoh repeatedly refused to allow the Hebrews passage out of Egypt, their God sent various plagues to persuade him to change his mind, including one that swiftly killed the first-born among the Egyptians. It was almost as if the author of the Book of Exodus was saying "You would blame us for the calamity in any event, so why should we not, in turn, claim that our God brought it upon you to punish you for sinning against us?" By the same token, those who were considered as being responsible for pestilence in the past could also use disease as a threat in the present. In fact, the God of the

---

[200] A group of learned men in Paris, commissioned by the pope, concluded that the plague was a result of a conjunction of Saturn, Jupiter, and Mars in the 40th degree of Aquarius at 1:00 p.m. on March 20, 1345.

[201] The Jews were accused of poisoning the wells.

Hebrews was so omnipotent as to be able to control the plague so that it affected the Egyptians in the order of their birth, meaning, of course, that the most important person in the eyes of the pharaoh and his subjects, the heir to the throne and the future of Egypt, would likely be among the first to perish. There the unwritten threat is that the succession might then be in dispute and the pharaoh, himself, jeopardized by the scheming among the various supporters of the other eligible successors. That a king may have actually lost his life as the result of such a "harem plot" is illustrated by the annals of Ramesses III. Or the entire land could be given over to chaos in a fight over the crown.

The pRainer, the story of the "*Potter's Oracle*", was written in Ptolemaic times, but purports to deal with something that happened a thousand years earlier. In this account, King "Amenophis" encounters a pottery-maker who predicts that the "Girdle-wearers", otherwise known as "the Children of Typhon" (Seth) would take over Egypt, with Egyptian citizens fleeing and the land going to ruin.

> "'Wretched Egypt, you are wronged by terrible iniquities wrought against you.' The sun will be hidden, not wishing to look upon the evil things in Egypt. The land will not accept the sowing of seed. These ... will be scorched by the wind. And the farmer does not sow on account of this, but tribute will be required of him. They are fighting in Egypt because of the lack of sustenance. What they till, another reaps and takes away."

The potter goes on to prophesy that, after the foreigners had seized hold of Egypt for a time, a new native king would appear to drive them out. As it happened, there was an Egyptian word "mss(t)", surviving into Coptic as "mous[a]", that means "girdle" or "tie". One must wonder about its connection to the name "Moses" because we will also recall Chaeremon asserting that the Egyptian name of Moses was "Tisithen", probably the Egyptian "Tstn", meaning "girdle" or

263

"band".   Finally, we see two appellations that really are interchangeable—unlike "Osarseph" and "Moses", as Josephus pointed out.[202]   Some scholars have concluded that the "Girdle-wearers" of the *Potter's Oracle* must be the Greeks, but ties do not necessarily refer only to what goes around a waist.   The ancient Egyptians quite usually depicted their Asiatic foes wearing a "bandlet" about their heads.   These were the true "Children of Seth" in their eyes, those who had become numerous in the Delta at various times in Egyptian history.

And so, very often the factor that makes one man change his mind is the input of another man or woman or group of people and often this "influence" consists of a show of might or insurrection.   And that, precisely, is what I believe the Book of Exodus is hesitant to reveal.   My thought would be that the truth in the form of many interesting but perhaps not very acceptable historical facts could not be told about all the exodoi from Egypt because of the posthumous heroic status of Moses, who had become an indispensable part of any such migration in the minds of all people for all time— although obviously he cannot have been physically present at each and every one.   It may even have been that Moses, to the chagrin of the author of the Biblical account, was much more Egyptian than Hebrew—by choice.

Therefore a "biography" had to be invented for the hero. For example, while the actual Hebrew names of his family members may have been accurate, we are not told just who these people were and what they were doing as *Egyptians*— for having been in Egypt since the time of Jacob, that is exactly what they were.   It would have been unlikely in the extreme that a family could actually remain enslaved for five generations (at least) in ancient Egypt.   There seems to have been a name for Asiatics that was written "dgAi".   Since this term could refer to something "hidden", it is possible that it

---

[202] By the same token, it makes sense to believe Manetho intended that Osarseph really did not change his name at all but became one of the "band" like his new confederates, the Jews.

had an analogy with the Spanish *marano*, an individual who, at the time of the Inquisition, pretended to be a Catholic but was a practicing Jew in secret. Were the "dgAi", by the same token, people who appeared to live as Egyptians in every sense, even worshipping the gods of Egypt, but who nevertheless retained a veiled identity as Children of Israel?

Since the reason Moses came to the attention of an Egyptian princess might reveal too much about the assimilation of Moses' parents, it was better to place him in a reed cradle on the Nile. However, once the adoptee was being raised as a prince, his own assimilation could hardly be circumvented. And that, perhaps, is why the particulars of his life are left rather sketchy in the Book of Exodus—and also why it was preferable to leave the reader with the impression that Moses was entirely absent from Egypt for most of his days, in the manner of Sinuhe, whose famous story may have been very convenient to imitate. In the Jewish legends, it is held that Moses became "king of Ethiopia" at the age of 27[203] and remained in this position of authority for 40 years. When the son of the Ethiopian woman he had married was crowned king, instead, Moses left for Midian at the advanced age of 67. He did not return to Egypt because he feared the pharaoh there.

In the Bible, even though Moses had become an Egyptian among the privileged, he was scarcely allowed to "be" an Egyptian. In the end, it strikes one as odd and a shade too convenient that the leader was not able to enter the Promised Land after forty years of wandering (and presumably writing!) and that even the whereabouts of his place of burial had been forgotten. It was just somewhere "*in the valley in the land of Moab over against Beth-peor; and no man knoweth of his sepulcher unto this day*".[204] Perhaps this is perfectly true—or maybe the reason it was erased from memory is that Moses was buried in Egypt, after all, returning there as

---

[203] Ginzberg, supra, Vol. II, page 286.

[204] Deuteronomy 34:6

another old man of Egyptian literature had done, receiving the boon of pardon from a pharaoh who did not particularly care what had happened in the reign of a predecessor. If the life of a man of 80 could be preserved until he reached 120 by roaming about the harsh wilderness, that surely would have been the greatest miracle of them all.

We will recall Josephus stating that the lawgiver had achieved a level of divinity in the estimation of the Egyptians and he was, of course, first among the great men of the nation of Israel. Usually, the ancient Egyptians only thought a commoner "divine" if he had achieved the status of "sainthood" by benefiting others by dint of his superior intellect and sagacity. Or he might have been a prophet whose oracles proved correct. Why Moses, if all he had done was to lead his fellow Hebrews out of Egypt, was so revered by the Egyptians is not easy to understand. He would have had to be a hero for other reasons, as well, as was previously discussed. Without a tomb/chapel in Egypt, where cult offerings could continue to be made and where inscriptions could be read by passers by, it seems remarkable that Moses would have been remembered in Egypt at all.[205]

Perhaps, if this secrecy regarding Moses and his actual life and deeds had not been considered necessary and proper, more information would have been retained about him and we would know for certain in which era he had actually lived. The Egyptians, who also thought Moses extraordinary, perhaps had some more details to add to the mix, but Josephus, who might have given them to us, was not inclined to believe any of them and so refused to bother.

---

[205] Unlike the tombs of the pharaohs of the New Kingdom, the burial sites of the nobles and officials were not always hidden away deep in the earth. Their tombs consisted of a finished pit beneath a superstructure, often in the shape of a small pyramid, this being the offering chapel. Sometimes the superstructures were magnificent affairs, in the manner of a small villa. Statues of the deceased and his family resided there and sometimes very important persons even had cult statues in the precincts of certain temples in the areas where ordinary people were allowed so that prayers and offerings might be made to their souls.

Ironically, even though the folklore of the Jews seems to indicate that Moses was not a part of Egyptian society since the age of 27 and did not return to his homeland until he was an old man, the truth is that, in ancient Egypt, 27 years was already a life-time and many lived no longer. Most Egyptian men could have expected to be at the height of their careers by this age and so to remove Moses from Egypt for the next 53 years hardly guarantees that he was but a youth when he left, scarcely influenced by Egyptian mores and beliefs.[206]

Although the majority of the ancients thought Moses lived in the time of Ahmose I, it would seem, however, that the Hebrews of the days of King Ahmose did not really require a Moses. True, those who were enslaved may have longed for deliverance from bondage, but how was it to be achieved? The most powerful pharaoh in Egypt at that time was in the Delta and the southern Egyptians, themselves, felt they were under his thumb. But that king was about to be expelled from the land. Somehow, Ahmose, the Theban prince, does not make a very good candidate for the despot who would not let the Hebrews go. His family, judging by the confession of his predecessor, Kamose, on his stela, did not feel themselves to be very powerful. They, also, were waiting for the day of liberation. Of course, to have put this into the Book of Exodus would only have served to distract attention from the plight of the Hebrews, which was certainly real enough all too often throughout the history of Egypt.

The final point that must be made about Moses is that, even if we encountered him in the annals of ancient Egypt, he may be totally unrecognizable for reasons already stated. The assimilation of the leader and his family into Egyptian society may have been complete—but with a secret recollection of their roots. For example, there was a very

---

[206] One cannot help but wonder if the years that Moses was absent from Egypt were not influenced by the "extra" or "lost" years of the 18th Dynasty that the ancients sought to explain in one way or another and to which modern Egyptology gives no credence at all.

important official of the time of Queen Hatshepsut whose total disappearance has puzzled Egyptologists for years. The man, whose name was Senenmut, had two tombs but was buried, as far as we know, in neither of them. Born in the Southern On, or Arment, a traditional birthplace of Moses,[207] this Senenmut's parents and siblings had ordinary Egyptian names. The parents were called Ramose and Hatnofret. Judging from the burial of the father, the family had once been poor but, somehow, Senenmut had become an educated individual. By the time his mother died, it was obvious that the fortunes of Senenmut had increased considerably and he was able to give her a noblewoman's funeral.[208] The mummies of the parents of the great man were once examined by Dr. Douglas Derry, the same man who examined Tutankhamen, but we don't have his notes and even the bodies have been lost.[209]

Senenmut was an architect and had been in the service of Thutmose II and probably his two predecessors. He likely saw military duty in Nubia because in one of his tombs there is a disjointed inscription to that effect. Under Hatshepsut, he became the highest administrator in the realm, known as

---

[207] According to Arthur Weigall. The reference for Senenmut's natal location is J. Tyldesley, *Hatchepsut*, supra, page 180.

[208] It would appear that Hatnofret had been in the service of Queen Ahmose, the mother of Hatshepsut and sister of Amenhotep I. There is also evidence in the form of a stela that Senenmut began his military career under Amenhotep I (Helck). It is interesting to note that, since Amenhotep I had no living son, a male child of one of his sisters, adopted or otherwise, would have been a candidate for the throne. The same Queen Ahmose had a sister named Meryetamen (who married their brother, Amenhotep I) and possibly also others named Mutnofret and Sitamen, their father having been Ahmose I. Hatshepsut's father, Thutmose I, is thought to be of non-royal origin, but it was he who became the heir of Amenhotep I.

[209] It seems odd that the parents of such an important figure in Egyptian history would have been treated so carelessly. After all, the mummies had once been of sufficient interest to be examined by Dr. Derry.

the "Great Steward" and "the Greatest of the Great"[210] and it
has been speculated, without any real basis, that he was the
queen's lover.[211] Certainly, he was the guardian and tutor of
the little princess, Neferure, and is most often shown holding
her on his lap.   In ancient Egypt, the word for such an
individual was "mnyw", perhaps to be translated as "tutor",
but probably having the additional prestige of "guardian" or
"surrogate father". Could this "mnyw" be the source of
"monios", the name by which Moses was known?

Since some of the portraits of Senenmut that have come
down to us show him to have wrinkles and sagging chins, it
is assumed that the official was a middle-aged man.
Actually, since Senenmut was portrayed with the face of
Hatshepsut instead of his own, it is difficult to know his
actual age when he disappeared.[212]   According to the
accepted chronology of ancient Egypt, if a young Senenmut

---

[210] Senenmut had 80 titles in all.

[211] No mention is made in either of Senenmut's tombs of a wife or children.
He is shown with his brother, Amenemhat, however, in his second tomb,
which also has an astronomical ceiling, depicting a calendar, the northern
constellations and the planets Mars, Venus, Jupiter and Saturn.
(Tyldesley)   Two of Senenmut's brothers, Amenemhat and Minhotep, were
priests of Amen. It has been considered that Senenmut was the senior of
Hatshepsut in years as he was sometimes shown as an aging man in
unofficial drawings, considerably wrinkled. In truth, the great man was
portrayed with the lined face of Hatshepsut, herself, after the custom. The
first tomb of Senenmut is at the hill Sheikh Abd el-Qurna (TT71). This
tomb contained 150 ostraca , including sketch plans of the tomb, trial
portraits of its owner, calculations, reports and also parts of literary texts,
among which The Satire of the Trades, The Tale of Sinuhe and the
Instruction of Amenemhat I were represented.

[212] Or the age of the queen, for that matter. If there is any truth to the
rumors from antiquity, her father Thutmose I, (as "Chenephres") may
have ruled jointly with Amenhotep I (as "Palmenothes"), thereby having a
longer actual reign than the appr. 6 years currently assigned him.
Thutmose II, who reigned 13 years thereafter, died in his early 30's. If
Hatshepsut, his half- sister/wife, was roughly his contemporary, that
would indicate that she was about 50 years old when she died 20 years
later. Senenmut can scarcely have been much younger than the queen.

served Amenhotep I and the first two Thutmoses, he cannot have been in the first bloom of youth by the time he vanished. [213] In a rebus that Senenmut created of Hatshepsut's name is contained "Renenutet", the patron goddess of Arment. Indeed, Hatshepsut, herself, may have been afterward recalled as "Thermutis", the benevolent lady who nurtured both Senenmut and Egypt.[214]

Besides Senenmut, the other most powerful official in Egypt was Ineni, who may have been in the position of a rival when it came to being in charge of building projects.[215] Suddenly, no more is heard about Senenmut and his monuments are defaced.[216] For a non-royal person, the official had quite a number of images—23 extant statues. Scholars have taken the position that the *damnatio memoriae* was due to the discovery of a secret—Senenmut was surreptitiously making for himself a second tomb, hidden within the environs of the queen's great funerary temple at Deir el Bahari, called the "Holy of Holies"—presumably in order to have some connection with his mistress in the afterlife. It has been concluded that the architect, who had come so far, had finally exceeded his limit with this presumptuous burial spot.

---

[213] The year of Senenmut's "disappearance" (Egyptologists presume he died) is disputed. Peter Dorman, the author of *The Monuments of Senenmut* (London and New York, 1988) wrote: *"Thus there remain a number of uncertainties regarding the date of Senenmut's death and nothing conclusively prohibits that he lived into the sole reign of Thutmose III."*

[214] The Persians call her "Assieh", which can be a possible vocalization of "Hatshepsut", just as "Sisera" can be "Shepsyre".

[215] According to Tyldesley, other greats of the day were *"Hapuseneb...High Priest of Amen...Chancellor Neshi, leader of the expedition to Punt, the Treasurer Thuthmosis, Useramen the Vizier, Amenhotep the Chief Steward and Inebni, who replaced Seni as Viceroy of Kush."* Is this "Inebni" what is meant by the name "Jambres"?

[216] If Senenmut fell from grace in Year 19 of Hatshepsut/Thutmose III, that year was perhaps 1485 BCE.

No one really knows just what brought about Senenmut's fall from power or if it was Hatshepsut who caused his portraits and name to be mutilated or her successor, Thutmose III.[217] Who can say for certain that the great man did not vanish because he was actually of Hebrew heritage and left on an exodus? And who can swear that Senenmut was not the Moses of the Torah just because he did not have a name like Aper-el, Ben-Azen, Pakhoir (the Asiatic) or even Maya, the nickname for Mose?[218] Thus ends, on this note which some will find rather disconcerting, the list of the possible candidates for the honor of being Moses

Naturally, for the Book of Exodus to mention that Semites had, at one point, been so powerful in the land that they had been able to "hold the scepter of a king" would have been a different story altogether, one that certainly did not fit to the "we were slaves in Egypt" theme. And how could one possibly relate, in a narrative that described the background of the traditional observance of Passover, that the Israelites had once been allied with a leprous Egyptian priest, who was irreverently dubbed another "Moses" because he proved to be an anti-Pharaoh who sided with the Asiatics? Even though leprosy is not left out of the exodus tale of the Pentateuch by any means, Egyptian priests as companions in revolt and the

---

[217]Thutmose III was actually king of Egypt during the entire reign of Hatshepsut. She began as the wife of his father, became the young heir's regent and then crowned herself "pharaoh". However, Thutmose III appears with Hatshepsut in some reliefs, dressed just as she was, crowned and in kingly attire. But he stood behind her, very much a "junior partner". After Hatshepsut's death, her monuments were defaced and broken, as well.

[218] Senenmut's name means "brother of the mother" in Egyptian, the Semitic equivalent being "Akhem". We know of another such name from the Bible and that is popularly spelled "Ahab", meaning "brother of the father". Perhaps it was really actually "Akhem" that Clement of Alexandria ought to have given as the Hebrew name of Moses and not "Yoakim". Why would Senenmut be called "Moses"? The answer to this question would depend upon what sort of a word "Moshe" (Arabic "Moussa") was and what it meant in its language of origin.

exploitation of civil wars with king pitted against his kinsman were, one suspects, a period that was deemed best forgotten. Yet some vestige of it is recalled in Exodus 11: 2-3:

> "Speak now in the ears of the people, and let them ask every man of his neighbor, and every woman of her neighbor, jewels of silver and jewels of gold. And the Lord gave the people favor in the sight of the Egyptians. Moreover the man Moses was very great in the land of Egypt, in the sight of Pharaoh's servants, and in the sight of the people." Also "And the children of Israel did according to the word of Moses; and they asked[85] of the Egyptians jewels of silver, and jewels of gold, and raiment. And the Lord gave the people favor in the sight of the Egyptians, so they let them have what they asked. And they despoiled the Egyptians." **Exodus 12:35**

If Seti II is the same man as Crown Prince Seti-Merneptah, son of King Merneptah, then Amenmesse cannot have become king without a coup d'etat. Indeed, the 20th Dynasty, which came after, did not recognize Amenmesse as a legitimate pharaoh. Because of the short duration of his reign, which was anywhere from two to five years, the crew at Deir el Medina were not able to complete the tomb of Amenmesse—although, to start with, it had been intended to be identical to that of Merneptah.

The manner in which Amenmesse came to be king is surely reflected in the histories of Manetho and Chaeremon. Did he seize power after the son of Merneptah was defeated by the rebels of Egypt and their Canaanite allies or was he actually involved in the rebellion? Probably, we will never know the answer. Yet it was likely the existence of this

---

[85] While the difference between "ask" and "demand" is not so great in all languages, it is rather disingenuously stated in the Book of Exodus that the Egyptians obligingly handed over their gold and silver to the Hebrews because God caused the former to look favorably upon them—something rather out of character for Egyptians.

man, an actual prince of the blood who opposed an "Amenophis", that gave rise to the Jewish legend of Moses being considered a pretender to the throne—instead of a mere civil servant or priest.[219]

Earlier, I had promised to re-visit the subject of "Sethos and Hermaeus". First we must view the description of king "Sethos", as written by Herodotus:

> *"The next king, they said, was a priest of Hephaestus (Ptah), whose name was Sethos. He had no respect or regard for the warrior class of Egyptians, because he thought them useless, and one of the ways he affronted them was by depriving them of their plots of land—each of them having held as a special boon, during the reigns of earlier kings, twelve arouras of land. Some time later, Egypt was invaded by a huge army of Arabians and Assyrians under their king Sennacherib, and the Egyptian warriors refused to do anything about it. In desperation, the priest went into the temple, approached the cult statue, complaining of the danger he was facing. And, in fact, after he had voiced his laments, he fell asleep and dreamed he saw a god standing over him and telling him not to worry. Nothing terrible could happen to him if he went out to confront the Arabian army, because he would send him allies. Sethos took courage from this dream. He enlisted any Egyptians who were prepared to follow him and established his position near Pelusium, because this is where the routes into Egypt are. His army did not consist of members of the warrior class, but only retailers, artisans and traders.[220] The opposing army arrived-- but at night a swarm of field-mice gnawed through their quivers and their bows, and the handles of their shields as well. Upon the next*

---

[219] Even though it states nowhere that Moses actually became a king of Egypt as did Amenmesse.

[220] Since "Sethos" was the High Priest of Ptah, the patron deity of the craftsmen, the "demiurgoi", it stands to reason he would have been supported by them.

day, seeing they were weaponless, all they could do was flee, and their losses were heavy. A stone statue of this king can still be seen today standing in the sanctuary of Hephaestus with a field-mouse in his hand, and on the statue is an inscription which reads 'Let all who look upon me reverence the gods.'"

Herodotus was surely referring to a fine statue of Seti II (any "Sethos" would do by this era), actually usurped from King Amenmesse, where he holds on his lap the small head of a ram[221] that, at a distance, could certainly have passed for a big-eared mouse. But there is more to this apocryphal story of the man known as "the father of history". Quite a lot more.

I ask the reader to recall that Josephus had written:

"For it was in the reign of Tethmosis that they (the Jews) left and, according to Manetho, the succeeding reigns covered a period of 393 years, down to the two brothers, Sethos and Hermaeus..."

Of course, this is absolutely right! And, again, Manetho was not referring to Seti I and Horemheb-- as is universally accepted. Remember, Manetho believed that the Israelites had left in the reign of Thutmose III, as he has seemingly demonstrated by placing Joseph in the time of the Hyksos king, Apophis—instead of in earlier dynasties. Here now Manetho proves **numerically**, in my opinion, just who he thought was the pharaoh involved in one exodus.

If Year 22 of Thutmose III, the time of his first foray into Canaan, was 1482 BCE, then 393 years later puts us directly in the reign of Ramesses XI, who lived in the timeframe of 1098-1070 BCE. Now Herodotus makes it plain that he was informed by the sages of the temples that this "Sethos" or "priest of Hephaestus" was the last pharaoh of

---

[221] The ram figured largely in Ramesside iconography.

Egypt.[222] According to Herodotus, "341 human generations" had passed between the first king of that country and "Sethos".

Of course, we know that nobody named "Sethos" was actually the ultimate native Egyptian king. That ruler happened to be Nectanebo II (360-343 BCE). Still, it may have been that the priests who advised Herodotus felt that the true glory of the pharaohs had died out with the last of the Ramessides, Menmaare Ramesses XI, after him coming the Third Intermediate Period and the weakening of pharaonic might. Why this 11th Ramesses was also called "Sethos" will be immediately apparent to those who remember that the prenomen of the famous warrior-king, Seti the First, was also "Menmaare". This evidently engendered confusion. But Ramesses XI was "Menmaare Setepenptah", this last meaning "Chosen of Ptah", which was in keeping with his role as head of the cult of the god in Memphis---as told to Herodotus, at least.

The remarkable thing about Ramesses XI is that in his time there was civil war with a man named Herihor (yes, that is our Hermaeus)[223], who rose through the ranks until he attained the title of High Priest of Amen and Viceroy of Kush. The end result was that Ramesses XI was reduced to becoming strictly a king of the North, with Herihor reigning supreme in the South. Ramesses outlived Herihor, who seems to have died in 1075 BCE,[224] but after that Egypt was not united again for many years and the Third Intermediate Period lasted from 1069-525 BCE. It would appear that Ramesses XI was not discontent to share power with Herihor and never did reclaim a hold over his entire kingdom. That,

---

[222] The priests of Ptah at Memphis were the primary source of Herodotus when it came to the kings of Egypt.

[223] The main reason that Ramesses was called "Sethos" for the purpose of this legend is due to the ancient mythological contendings of the gods, Horus and Seth, Herihor obviously being connected to the former deity.

[224] He was then replaced in the south by his relative, Piankh.

as it happens, was something that had been done by another, earlier "Sethos" of Egyptian folklore. The problem was, simply too much interesting drama existed surrounding kings either named Seti or who had the prenomen of Menmaare for the Egyptians (much less the foreigners) to keep them all straight. Evidently, the triumph of Seti-Merneptah over his rival(s) had not been forgotten—even though he had been fused into one mythical "Sethos" with the others.

The 20th Dynasty was a period when the pharaohs, in an effort to brighten the diminishing light of Egypt, adopted the throne-names of great kings of former times. We have already become acquainted with the example of Menmaare Ramesses XI. There were several rulers who took the name "Usermaare", which had belonged to Ramesses the Great and Ramesses VI (1141-1133) styled himself "Nebmaare" after the opulent Amenhotep III. During the day of this later Nebmaare there was civil war, again, possibly brother against brother, with the suspicion that Ramesses VI was either reigning concurrently with his sibling, Ramesses V, or had actually usurped his throne. Unrest led to more of the same and relative stability was not known again in the land until the reign of Ramesses IX. In his administration, the Papyrus Abbott was written, detailing what had occurred in the process of an inspection of the royal tombs at Thebes. Because of prolonged civil war and famine, people had taken to robbing these sacred repositories, knowing of the riches they contained. At the end of the day, we don't know very much about what happened during the years this dynasty reigned but I have no doubt that certain details of the "*Tale of the Polluted Ones*" and "*The Potter's Oracle*" hark back to this time, as well.

Josephus had written:

> "*Sethos and Hermaeus, the former of whom, he says, took the name of Aegyptus and the latter that of Danaus. Sethos, after expelling Hermaeus, reigned fifty-nine years*

and his eldest son, Rampses, who succeeded him, sixty-six."

Scholars have long pondered the significance of those two names "Aegyptus" and "Danaus". "Aegyptus", of course, equals Egypt—but this appellation for "Misr" (the true name of Egypt today) is surely derived from "Hut ka Ptah", a name of the great northern city, Memphis. On the other hand, I believe the reason why Ramesses XI was known as "Aegyptus" comes from his earlier title as high priest, which was "wr xrp Hm" (The Great Director of the Hammer) or even "wr xrp PtH" (Great Director of Ptah), pronounced in Egyptian, with its tendancy to drop its "r's", as something like "uh-khop-Ptah". Herihor, down in Thebes, even though a co-ruler, was still known as "Hm nTr tpy n Imn" or "High Priest of Amun". But his designation of "Danaus" probably comes from the term "idnw", instead, which refers to Herihor in his capacity as Viceroy (of Kush) or simply "deputy" or associate king. That Herihor was banished to the Aegean, settling Argos and becoming the founder of the Danaidae tribe is a pure fiction of the classic writers.[225] However, the Greeks stood convinced that "Aegyptus" was also called "Nileus" and that the river was named after him because *"this ruler constructed a very great number of canals at opportune places and in many ways showed himself eager to increase the usefulness of the Nile".* [226] Actually, this was just another misapprehension due to an apparent inability to grasp the difference between the title of Herihor, "idnw"[227] and "itrw", which means "canals". But it is true that the name

---

[225] Although—who knows—this may have been the fate of someone else who had the god, Horus, as an element of his name.

[226] Diodorus Siculus, Book I, 63.

[227] Apparently, even Menmaare Ramesses XI and his "partner" were confused regarding which one was "Aegyptus". Another part of the problem with this whole picture was that Horemheb was also an "idnw", by his own admission in his autobiography on a statue in Turin, Italy. Therefore, Horemheb and Herihor became blended as "Hermaeus".

"Nile" does come from "nA iwrw" or "the waterways"—the various branches and ditches of the Great River.

It is difficult to say who first equated this compromised "Sethos" with Seti I, the father of Ramesses the Great[228], but it may have been Josephus, himself, the very reason being that the latter believed the Jews had left Egypt so long ago that the 393 years that Manetho had specified between the migration and "Sethos also called Ramesses" had to indicate Seti I in his estimation.[229] In fact Seti I lived and reigned 393 years after no exodus and was never known as Ramesses, even though some of the ancients attempted to manipulate the numbers to make sense of what they thought Manetho was trying to say. They padded the reign of Menmaare Seti I outrageously and tinkered with the 18th Dynasty, as well, striving mightily to get 393 years between the exodus of one tradition or another and Seti's rule. Yet, unfortunately, they misunderstood their authority, Manetho, completely.

Nor was it to stop there. The copiers of Manetho also fell afoul of his "Tutimaeus" narrative and the "*Tale of the Polluted Ones*", as we already know, because, being Jews and Christians committed to a belief in the Bible, it was not possible for them to accept the idea of more than one exodus from Egypt. In my opinion, the chance that the Egyptian historian actually called two pharaohs "Misphragmoutosis" (corrupted MnxprraDHtims —Thutmose III) is not very great, nor that he had written that Ahmose was also called Thutmose, as he seems to have specified that one was the "son" of the other.

One must doubt very much that Manetho would have placed "Deucalion's flood" in the reign of the real "Misphragmoutosis", as he would have known, as surely as

---

[228] Who was, in reality, never known as "Aegyptus".

[229] Since Seti seems to have succeeded in 1291 BCE by the accepted chronology, 393 years earlier would have been 1684 BCE, in the foggy Second Intermediate Period. At any rate, Josephus' quotes from Manetho's history are the earliest that have come down to us.

he knew the positions of the stars in the heavens, that this calamity had occurred in the day of Ahmose. There can be no doubt at all that Manetho considered that "Misphragmoutosis" or Menkheperre Thutmose III had ushered the proto-Jews and a "mixed-multitude" out of Egypt and the Bible is perfectly correct when it states that the Temple was built 480 years later.[230] Moreover, Manetho obviously had quantified the years between the start of the era of Ahmose I and that of Thutmose III-- because Africanus and Eusebius indicate he did, giving 69 and 71 years total, respectively.   Their numbers would be very close to the truth[231], which they can only have known via Manetho. The Egyptian also understood that Thutmose III and his son later reversed the entire process and brought thousands of Canaanites back to Egypt where, as it happened, they remained to fulfill their eternal role as scapegoat in times of disaster and pestilence, fleeing or being expelled as circumstances dictated. In fact, it was Manetho, the man of the Delta, who attempted to write the saga of the Jews in Egypt up to his own day-- not the author of the Book of Exodus. Manetho the Egyptian ironically was the one who did not hesitate to point out that the day came when the tables were turned on Egypt—at least for a while.

As a pagan and a priest of an Egyptian god, Manetho labored under no Biblical constraints. One can only lament that no original, uncorrupted copy of his *Aegyptiaca* survives because the suspicion in my mind is (as it was in antiquity) that Manetho really had "achieved the pinnacle of erudition" and was a wonderful source, indeed. As I write this, I feel a pang of sadness for him and how his honor and clarity as an

---

[230] Also "Misphrammoutosis". It is really "mn-xpr-re (Thumosis)", Egyptian /x/ and /S/ being interchangeable, as mentioned before. /n/ is one of the consonants often elided into the next in pronunciation.
"Misphragmoutosis is a naturally-occuring vocalization, the "g" being actually a corruption of a "t" sound which was the eventual fate of Egyptian /D/.

[231] Whatever that may be. Egyptology counts 66 years—1570-1504.

historian has been snatched from him by presumptuous others.

Perhaps not even Manetho could have answered the question "How many contenders were there actually for the throne after Merneptah's passing?" One, I think, may have been entirely overlooked by Egyptology, another "priest of Hephaestus", who possibly became king of Egypt—at least temporarily—as "idnw". User-Mont-Hor, familiarly "Hori", was certainly in the line of succession because his grandfather had been Ramesses II. User-Mont-Hor was not only a "priest of Ptah", he was the High Priest of that god in Memphis. It is certainly possible, if Crown Prince Seti-Merneptah had been exiled, that this cousin of his, Hori, can have attempted to take his place—just one more individual with a name like "Hermaeus" who may have served in a vice-regal capacity.

Then there was the little son "Ramesses", who had become King Siptah. Just who his father was is also not known for certain but there is some evidence he was of Semitic heritage on his mother's side. The most significant information about his reign is that it was entirely under the control of an Asiatic.

The truth is that Siptah was nothing but a hapless puppet. He, as a youngster, was placed upon the throne by a servant of the crown named "Bey", one who had already been around in the day of Merneptah. What other name "Bey" was the hypochoristicon for cannot be known—perhaps it was Ben-Azen, the cupbearer. In other words, a "foreigner" was now the one who told the king of Egypt what to do. Not only were the Asiatics having a "golden age" in Egypt at the end of the 19th Dynasty, they were at the helm.

My scenario of choice would be this one: Troubles brew at the moment that King Merneptah appears to be dying of his malady. The "shepherds" come in droves to graze their flocks during the intercalary days, as usual, but no one allows them in and they grow short of water. They become desperate or enraged—or both. All sorts of undesirables and disenfranchised souls join in the spirit of revolt already being fomented by Prince Amenmesse. They empty the quarries and, joined by any one else who cares to accompany them, go to live at ruined Avaris, forcing people out of the adjacent Per-Ramesses-Mery-amun because it is not safe there anymore. The "polluted ones" form an alliance with the disgruntled "shepherds" and perhaps others from Canaan, who had come for their own reasons.

Chaeremon: *"The exiles on reaching Pelusium fell in with a body of 380,000 persons[232], left there by Amenophis, who had refused them permission to cross the Egyptian frontier. With these the exiles concluded an alliance and marched upon Egypt."*

Perhaps even Amenmesse is part of the coalition and promises this heterogeneous group free run of the Delta if they aid him in defeating Seti-Merneptah. As indicated by Manetho and Chaeremon, when Seti-Merneptah, the general, arrives in the area from Memphis to find out what has become of the fortress at Djaru and its personnel, he sees that matters are beyond his control and turns back, probably with Amenmesse in pursuit.

Whatever the true facts are, since the old king is dying and the succession is disputed, many will try to take advantage of the situation. Seti-Merneptah cannot fight all the trouble-makers because he is too busy battling the forces of Amenmesse. So the outcasts and outsiders seize the opportunity to overrun and plunder Egypt's Delta. Merneptah dies and Seti-Merneptah, his eldest son and head of the army, goes into exile. What Hori does at this time, if anything at all, is impossible to guess.

Why should it not have happened this way? Merneptah, known as "the Binder of Gezer", had said it, himself—the

---

[232] It must be recalled that the weakest element of all these ancient histories is the numbers, most of which are simply too great. Why the people were at Pelusium and why Amenophis went there to meet them is obscure. It must have seemed to the ancients a logical place to fight a battle.

Levant was a "widow on account of Egypt" and brooding widows have been known to seek vengeance. What remained of the Canaanites had not forgotten the terrible destruction—and "Israel" remembered everything better than most. It was, crudely put, "pay-back time".[233]

A Midrash or commentary on the Hebrew Bible describes how some Egyptians came before Alexander the Great, demanding that they should be compensated by the Jews for all the wealth that their forebears had seized from the Land of Egypt a thousand years previous. A certain Gevia ben Psesia defended this claim before the conqueror, pointing out that, as the Israelites had not been paid for all the labor they had performed as slaves of the Egyptians, the score could be tallied as even.

Amid this upheaval, Amenmesse becomes king in Upper Egypt, but his is an uneasy reign. After four years or so, he is through. Seti II returns and rules for perhaps six more years. Bey, his Asiatic administrator, makes Siptah a nominal king. Ramesses-Siptah is, indeed, so young that a woman, Tausret, must become his regent. There is no doubt that she is allied with Bey. Tausret may have been a daughter of King Merneptah. Some believe she was already married to Seti-Merneptah before he was ousted.

Bey had the audacity to commission a tomb for himself in the Valley of the Kings, an unheard of license for a mere commoner—right next to that of Queen Tausret.[234] Siptah received a tomb in the vicinity, as well. Even though Seti II never did have the chance to construct a mortuary temple, Tausret, built herself one next to that of Merneptah. Siptah was allowed to have one, too. Perhaps, since he was crippled with a club-foot or because he had contracted polio, the two

---

[233] Gabriel Barkay cites the Papyrus Anastasi III reference to a fort of Merneptah near Sar-ram (Jerusalem?), ANET p. 258. He also discusses probable Egyptian temple remains that are most likely 19th Dynasty; see Barkay, "A Late Bronze Age Egyptian Temple in Jerusalem?", IEJ 46, 1996, pp. 23-43.

[234] However, there is no indication that these two were ever buried in their tombs.

people in charge of his reign (certainly he did not "rule) felt he would not have very long to live, in any event. But, while he was a child, he served their purposes very admirably.

I am sure that King Siptah would have considered the fact that the Greek historians recalled him as a woman the unkindest cut of all. Because his throne-name, "Akhenre" sounded to them like a Greek feminine name, "Alkandra", poor Siptah was transformed into the wife of "Thuoris", also called "Polybos", a king of Egypt who is seen as the last ruler of Manetho's 19th Dynasty. Of this Polybos, it was said: "...*in whose time Troy was taken, reigned for 7 years*". "Thuoris" is, of course, Tausret, and the "Polybos", which means in Greek "rich in cattle", I believe to be an amalgam of Tausret, Userkheperure Seti-Merneptah and Userkaure Setnakht, all of whose names contain the element "wsr", which in Egyptian has the meaning of "wealthy", as well as "powerful".

At the end of five years, the lad, Siptah, had grown up and was no longer so malleable. Siptah, who had already altered his name from Ramesses-Siptah to "Merneptah-Siptah", evidently gained some support from some important source because it is thought that a certain inscription says that Siptah "killed the Great Enemy Bey" in his Year 5[235], having somehow managed to form a plan of insurrection.

My conjecture would be that Bey, concluding that Siptah was becoming dangerous, arranged to have Tausret made pharaoh in a Hatshepsut-like maneuver. Some believe that Tausret's elevation to this office did not take place until after Siptah's death, but this may not be the case. They can have become rivals at different locations. Hartwig Altenmuller has calculated that Siptah had already died before II Shomu 28 of his 7th regnal year.[236] If one can divide another six years

---

[235] "Year 5, 3 Shomu, day 27. This day the scribe of the Tomb Paser has come to say "Pharaoh, lph, has killed the great enemy Bey". Pierre Grandet, "The Chancellor Bey's Execution" (BIFAO 100 p. 340). Indeed, Year 4 of Siptah is the last we see of Bey in other records.

[236]Altenmuller, Hartwig, *Die verspätete Beisetzung des Siptah*, GM 145 (1995), 29-36.

between Amenmesse and the successor of Siptah, (probably Tausret) that makes 13 years of "false rulers" before Egypt was once again ruled by a lawful king. Tawosret was unlikely to have occupied the throne for seven additional years, but simply counted those during which she was regent for Siptah.

As is told by Manetho and Chaeremon, the son(s) of Merneptah battle the Asiatics. "*Ramesses, who, on reaching manhood, drove the Jews, to the number of about 200,000, into Syria, and brought home his father Amenophis from Ethiopia*".[237] Who was the "Amenophis" that was brought back from Ethiopia? Perhaps, again, this harks back to the 18th Dynasty, with a successor of Akhenaten bringing back the body of the exiled monarch for burial. We do not really know what happened to the heretic in the end, but we have what seems to be Seti II's mummy and that of Siptah. Oddly, these individuals do not appear anything like the other Ramesside kings. Their features resemble those of the Thutmosid pharaohs and they are very short. Perhaps these remains have been mislabeled.

Tausret's own tomb seems to have seen some more work, with the images of Siptah therein being replaced by those of Seti II. Perhaps she was also responsible for replacing the names on the few monuments of Amenmesse with that of her late husband. Probably, she was overthrown by the new Egyptian hero, Setnakht, because part of a hidden treasure belonging to her and her steward, Atumemtaneb, was found at Bubastis, in the Delta, where she had perhaps fled to be among her supporters.

For the first year of his reign Setnakht is engaged in strife, probably with Tausret in the north.[238] When the new pharaoh started to excavate a tomb for himself, as was the

---

[237] Again, Seti-Merneptah seems to have been confused with Merneptah.

[238] The reign of Setnakht started in month 1 of Shomu and lasted two, possibly three years. Next to the Elephantine Stela there exists a second stela from Serabit el-Khadim (Sinai) from year 3. (von Beckerath)

custom, the diggers ran right into the burial chamber of Amenmesse, no one evidently recalling where it was!

Regardless, as soon as King Setnakht saw this tomb of Amenmesse, it would seem he desecrated it so thoroughly that, not only did he remove this king's names from the walls, he scraped off his images as well. Amenmesse, however, does not seem to have ever been buried in the tomb. Also, it may have been Setnakht who replaced some of the images of Amenmesse with the name of the rightful sovereign, Seti II, as the latter had so few of his own.[239] The 20th Dynasty, of which Setnakht was the first, recognized only Seti II as an heir of Merneptah and made this plain in a scene at Medinet Habu. Even Siptah was omitted from the succession, although he was made king through no fault of his own, being a minor at the time, and had probably killed the presumptuous Bey when he grew up. Yet his kingship had presumably occurred contrary to "maat", the legal and proper way of doing things.

The 20th Dynasty began in a rather spectacular way but was not destined to be remembered as being covered in glory. Its second pharaoh, Ramesses III, was summed up by Diodorus Siculus in these terms:

"....he had been not so much a king as an efficient steward. Instead of a fame based upon virtue he left a treasure larger than that of any king before him; for according to tradition he amassed some four hundred thousand talents of silver and gold."

That seems to be correct as the Great Harris Papyrus does indicate that Ramesses III was fabulously wealthy. His successors, down to Ramesses XI, were dismissed by Diodorus in even more dismal prose:

"After Remphis (Ramesses III) died, kings succeeded to the throne for seven generations who were confirmed

---

[239] Even the cartouches of Siptah's burial chamber were first erased and then restored. Just who mutilated them is difficult to imagine. This was certainly a confusing period.

sluggards and devoted only to indulgence and luxury. Consequently, in the priestly records, no costly building of theirs nor any deed worthy of historical record is handed down in connection with them, except in the case of one ruler, Nileus...."[240]

And so, we conclude our Exodus Chronicles with the demise of the 19th Dynasty, about which we, unfortunately, know only too little. Ultimately, Setnakht, the victor, took over the tomb of Tausret and was probably buried therein.[241] But that was at the end. In the beginning, the first act of Setnakht, also a short-lived king, was to rid Egypt of the Asiatics—once again.

From the Elephantine Stela:

> "....*His Majesty—life, prosperity, health—stretched out his arms like his father, Seth, in order to rid Egypt (of those who) violate her. His might encircles (her) with protection, repelling the enemy before him and they withdraw for hear of him in their hearts. They flee like birds in frenzied flight, the Hawk after them. They leave behind silver and gold to the Egyptians because of their helpless retreat to Asia from the strong pursuit of Egypt's finest. The clever ones among them manage to escape no further than their sluggards because the appearance of all the gods and goddesses was a bedazzling sight to them. They hailed His Majesty, these enemies, and the same was done in all lands....*"

It was ca. 1185 BCE and, with the advent of the Trojan Wars, the era of the "Sea Peoples", was about to be launched.

---

[240] This is an exaggeration as Ramesses IV, for one, was known as a prodigious builder, although his reign was cut short by his death.

[241] His mummy has not been identified. There is no sign that Tausret, herself, was ever interred in the tomb, even though the mummy of a female (?), thought to be this queen, was discovered in KV35 in the lid of a coffin belonging to Setnakht.